Penguin Books
Autobiography of My Mother

Meg Stewart was born in Sydney and spent her first five
years living in the city before moving to greener North
Shore suburbia. After graduating in Arts from the
University of New South Wales, she joined Film Australia
as a production assistant. She has since worked as a
freelance documentary film director and a radio writer
and producer. Her film credits include *Last Breakfast in
Paradise,* winner of the fiction section in the Greater
Union Awards presented at the 1982 Sydney Film
Festival. Meg Stewart has also written for the *Sydney
Morning Herald* and the *National Times.*

Meg Stewart

AUTOBIOGRAPHY OF MY MOTHER

PENGUIN BOOKS

Penguin Books Australia Ltd,
487 Maroondah Highway, P.O. Box 257
Ringwood, Victoria, 3134, Australia
Penguin Books Ltd,
Harmondsworth, Middlesex, England
Penguin Books,
40 West 23rd Street, New York, N.Y. 10010, U.S.A.
Penguin Books Canada Limited,
2801 John Street, Markham, Ontario, Canada, L3R 1B4
Penguin Books (N.Z.) Ltd,
182-190 Wairau Road, Auckland 10, New Zealand

First published by Penguin Books Australia, 1985
Reprinted 1986, 1987

Copyright © Meg Stewart, 1985

Typeset in Garamond Light by Leader Composition Pty Ltd
Editorial: Jackie Kent, Kelly Davis
Design: Helen Semmler
Production: Norma Callen
Made and printed in Australia by The Book Printer, Maryborough, Victoria

CIP

Stewart, Meg
Autobiography of my mother.

ISBN 0 14 007589 5.

1. Coen, Margaret, 1913–. 2. Women painters—
Australia—Biography. 3. Water-colourists—
Australia—Biography. I. Title.

759.994

The author and publishers would like to thank the following for help given in producing this book: Peggy Adams, Mick Blunden, Alec Bolton, Janna Bruce, Mike Elton, Jane Glad and Curtis Brown (Aust) Pty Ltd Sydney, E.A. Harvey, Doreen Hubble, Nancy Keesing, Jacqueline Kent, Peter Lindsay, Ron and John McCuaig, Ruth O'Dwyer, Mark Rubbo, the State Library of New South Wales, Douglas Stewart, Rita Young.

For Douglas Stewart, who died on 15 February 1985, without whose encouragement and love this book might not have been written.

1

Patrick Maloney Sends for a Bride

'Margaret Maloney' by an unknown artist

My mother's grandmother Margaret O'Connor was seventeen when she arrived in Australia to marry a man she had never met.

Patrick Maloney was old enough to be her father, almost her grandfather. He had come out to Australia from King's County, Ireland, in 1838. Margaret O'Connor's husband-to-be worked first on the land near Bathurst but ended up at Boorawa.

Boorawa, in hilly sheep country, 250 miles south-west of Sydney, halfway between Young and Yass, was hot and dry in summer, frosty cold in winter. Patrick Maloney settled on the Boorawa River, then moved to a property on Stony Creek. The Stony Creek property prospered and, when he felt established, he wrote to the parish priest in Ireland to find him a wife. The only way he could be sure he wasn't marrying a convict woman, he said, was to bring out a bride from Ireland.

And so in 1844, the young Irish girl Margaret O'Connor and the fifty-year-old Patrick Maloney were married in Yass.

Margaret Maloney quickly fell into domesticity at Boorawa. She got used to the flies, forgot to be frightened of possums thumping on the roof and bandicoots stealing from the kitchen. Kookaburra laughter and magpie calls became familiar birdsong. Wattle yellow, creeping sarsaparilla purple and the blue haze of Patterson's Curse replaced the greenness of Ireland and the brilliant hedges of fuchsias and rhododendrons.

She cooked, sewed, washed, made candles, bore children; they had eleven children in twenty years. Patrick Maloney was

1

seventy-four when his last child Brigid was born. Mary Maloney, their seventh child, was my mother's mother.

Life in New South Wales wasn't much harder for the Maloneys than it would have been back in Ireland, but there was one big difference. At home they would always have been battling poverty; here, if they worked hard, they could live in affluence.

Ireland was still the mother country. As special treats for his wife, Patrick Maloney would order presents from Dublin. Trunks would make their way into the bush filled with new material, dresses, shawls, all sent out from Ireland.

My mother used to tell me how Margaret Maloney hid their money from bushrangers. Country kitchens had great tin dishes full of fat for cooking and Margaret Maloney put their sovereigns at the bottom of this dish then poured fat over the coins. My mother also told me stories about the bushranger, John Gilbert, handed on by her mother.

Before he took up bushranging, John Gilbert used to break in horses for Paddy Maloney. He was eventually shot down by troopers at Binalong, close to the Maloney property. The inscription on his tomb says that, despite his wicked ways, John Gilbert never harmed any women. He certainly never hurt any of the Maloney women. The girls wept when he was killed and one of them obtained his bloodstained shirt as a memento.

I visited my great-aunt Maloney's house at Summer Hill in Sydney just after she died and asked my cousins where the shirt was.

'We don't know,' they replied. 'Mother collected masses of rubbish and we burned it.' To burn John Gilbert's shirt seemed sacrilege to me.

When tall, good-looking, black-haired, black-bearded Michael O'Dwyer asked Patrick Maloney for the hand of his daughter Mary, Patrick Maloney said, 'I like the colour of your name, but I don't like the colour of your coat.' Michael O'Dwyer was a policeman; the memory of John Gilbert's death was still strong with Patrick Maloney.

Michael O'Dwyer was born in 1830 at Drenolief, a place consisting of about half a dozen stone houses – hardly big enough for a village – three or four miles from Sneem in County Kerry. His father was killed, thrown from his horse on his way to

Michael O'Dwyer as a young man

Killarney, when Michael was about eighteen. His mother then married a man called Brennan and they had two more sons.

Brennan, being a fair man, insisted that Michael O'Dwyer, the oldest, should still inherit the farm; farms in Ireland were only big enough for one son. But Michael O'Dwyer renounced his inheritance because he wanted to emigrate, either to Australia or to America, he couldn't decide which.

He joined the Royal Constabulary in Dublin, then arrived in Australia in his mid-twenties. Already a skilled horseman, he was accepted in the New South Wales Royal Mounted Police Force.

Mum used to tell us endless stories about his adventures as a

Left: Mary Maloney and Michael O'Dwyer shortly before they were married
Right: Bessie O'Dwyer aged four

mounted policeman. He was at Lambing Flat during the gold rushes of the 1880s. Strangely clad, pigtailed 'Chinamen', as they called them then, were among the many who flocked to the paddocks near Young to look for gold. The other prospectors regarded the Chinese with suspicion, which turned to resentment and violence. Michael O'Dwyer was with the troopers called in to quell the riots.

He had to take a number of Chinese prisoners from Young to Goulburn. The 'Chinamen' were chained together. They walked while the troopers rode alongside on horseback. As soon as they were out of Young, Michael O'Dwyer ordered the prisoners' chains off so they could walk more easily.

Every Christmas thereafter a parcel mysteriously arrived from China for Michael O'Dwyer. It usually contained jars of ginger, thanks for his kindness from one of the prisoners who had returned.

Like her mother, Margaret Maloney began married life with a much older husband. She was about twenty-two when she married Michael O'Dwyer, who was forty-nine. As a wedding present, Patrick Maloney gave each of his daughters 2,000 guineas. With his wife's dowry, Michael O'Dwyer was able to leave the police force and buy an hotel in Boorawa.

My mother Elizabeth, always called Bessie, was their first child, born in 1878. She was born in a caul, like a beautiful transparent bag, she described it. Her mother had been born in a caul, too, and so was I. My mother told me that sea captains considered such people very fortunate and tried to take the caul to sea with them in a bottle, the superstition being that anyone born in a caul would never drown. This is why I will go anywhere by boat, though I am terrified of planes.

My mother told us, too, about a Negro who called at the hotel looking for work as a cook. My grandmother said that they already had a cook, but she offered him something to eat before he went on his way. He set off after his meal, but hadn't gone far before he returned, begging my grandmother to let him stay just for one day to show them how well he could cook. He turned out to be a marvellous cook, so he remained at the hotel with the O'Dwyers.

My mother and her sister Margaret loved sneaking into the kitchen. The Negro was over six feet tall and wore a white coat and a tall chef's hat. He would pick up my mother, put her on one shoulder, pick up Margaret, put her on the other and dance around the kitchen.

Things were not always so happy for the O'Dwyers at Boorawa. There was a big age gap between my mother's younger sister Margaret and her brothers Frank and Joe. Several babies, including twins, were born in that gap; they all died. The twins went within three days of each other; one on Saturday, the other on Monday. Out of eleven children Mary O'Dwyer bore, only five lived.

The hotel did not make money and eventually the O'Dwyers sold out. Michael O'Dwyer bought a corn and hay store at Darlington in Sydney and the family moved to the city. Mary O'Dwyer put up with their new life for a while, even though she hated it, but then she rebelled. 'I am not going to bring up my children in the slums of Sydney,' she told Michael O'Dwyer. With the last of her wedding money, she bought a property at Murrumburrah. Her husband called it Drenolief in honour of his

Mary Maloney after becoming Grandma O'Dwyer

Grandma and her sisters. Left to right: Lizzie, Linda, Grandma

Irish birthplace. Murrumburrah was a forgotten pocket, only thirty miles from the bustling town of Yass, but far from thriving. Finding gold had always been a dream of Michael O'Dwyer's. He was sure the creek that ran through the property was full of it. With what little money they had left, he bought machinery for working alluvial gold and installed it on the creek. But the creek dried up in a drought; Michael O'Dwyer sat and waited. When the rain came, the creek flooded. The machinery was washed away and with it went his dreams.

He was much older, too, by this time; he was now in his mid-seventies with a young family to support, his youngest daughter Aileen having been born only a few years before. Michael O'Dwyer's prospecting days were over for good.

When I was about five or six, I was sent to Drenolief for a holiday. Michael O'Dwyer was dead by then, but Grandma O'Dwyer was still alive. She was tall, slim and very stern, with beautiful silver-white hair pulled back from her face in a knob at the back of her neck, just as my mother's looked when she was old. Grandma O'Dwyer gave me a little glass tube full of gold dust. It was gold from Drenolief Creek, I firmly believed, and I treasured it.

Being the oldest, my mother was forced to look after the younger O'Dwyer children. She grew very tired of being a nursemaid. She didn't like the bush or the dusty little township of Murrumburrah. As well as looking after the babies, my mother did more than her share of chores such as the washing up; there is always a great deal of that in a large family.

She longed to get away to the bright lights of the city. A milliner was what she wanted to be. If she could go up to Sydney and stay with her aunt Lizzie Flanagan (the one who saved Gilbert's shirt) she could do her apprenticeship.

One day, Grandma O'Dwyer washed her hair. She was sitting out in the sun to dry it while my mother washed up inside. My mother finished the dishes and opened the back door to throw the water into the yard. She didn't notice her mother sitting there and the washing up water drenched Mary O'Dwyer. Bessie got a sound trouncing. It was the last straw. My mother determined to leave home that day and marched down to the railway station to buy a ticket to Sydney. She was fourteen and a half.

The stationmaster at Murrumburrah had a soft spot for her.

Either someone had left a ticket behind, or returned a lost one; all Mum told us was that the ticket didn't cost her very much.

She went home from the station, wrapped a cake of soap and 4½d in a handkerchief and told her sister Margaret she was going, but forbade her to tell their mother.

Margaret walked down to the railway station with her, crying all the way. The train came, my mother got in. Margaret watched it disappearing down the track, getting smaller and smaller until it dwindled to smoke in the blue sky.

Margaret didn't return to the house until it was dark; she didn't want to face their mother.

'Where's Bessie?' Grandma O'Dwyer demanded when she went in.

'She's gone,' Margaret answered.

'Gone where?'

'To Sydney,' Margaret said. And that was that.

Now we come to the Coens.

My father kept a diary on his honeymoon. In it he describes a visit to the stone farmhouse in Ireland in which his father was born and where the Coens had lived for hundreds of years.

May 1902. Got up early, very nice morning indeed, after breakfast hired a car and drove out to Clunemare, about two miles from Tuam.

My uncle was delighted to see us as we were to see him and find him alive. Was shown the old stone farmhouse in which my father was born and where my uncle now lives. The River Clare flows right past the door and there are plenty of salmon trout and other fish to be caught therein.

After dinner we walked over to the Clunemare cemetery and saw the graves of my grandfather and grandmother, also the grave of Mr Patrick Waldron.

We plucked some shamrocks from the graves then walked back to Tuam with my uncle and his wife. On the way we visited several farmhouses of people who knew my father well and they were all delighted to see us and accorded us a hearty welcome. Had some tea, said goodbye and then went to bed.

My mother's comment about this visit back to Tuam was that at all these farmhouses they were offered plenty of Irish whiskey and it was too much for her. But it does show how close were the Coen family ties to Ireland.

Dad's father Michael Coen was born at Clunemare in 1840 and educated at a nearby monastery. This was quite unusual in those days because it hadn't been long since Catholics in Ireland were forbidden any education at all.

Michael Coen as a young man was well educated and restless. Excited by the news of discoveries of gold in Australia when he was about twenty, he decided to emigrate. He wasn't interested in prospecting as such, but Australia held promise of a future that didn't exist in Tuam, or indeed anywhere in Ireland.

His first business venture was a hawker's cart at Dubbo in western New South Wales. The hawker's cart was successful and Michael Coen was soon able to buy a store for himself in Dubbo. He married a woman named Margaret – the first Margaret Coen. They had two sons, then Margaret Coen died giving birth to twins.

Michael Coen despaired. He didn't want to stay in Dubbo after that. Life seemed too sad. But he had his two little sons to think of and hired a governess to look after the boys. Margaret Trainor was a clever woman. Her father had been a teacher who educated his daughter himself. A year after they met, Margaret Trainor and Michael Coen were married.

My father, their first child, was born in Dubbo in 1879. Michael Coen still wanted to start afresh, so with the new baby the Coens moved to Yass, where Michael had bought the Australian Stores.

Being their first son, my father was a great favourite of his parents. They called him 'little King'. His real name was Michael Joseph, but all his life he was known as 'King'.

The Coens had three more sons and six daughters. The second youngest, a little girl called Annie, died of diphtheria when she was five. With Michael Coen's two sons from his first marriage, it made eleven children who were being raised in the pisé house next to the store. A huge room above the store was turned into a dormitory for the boys.

Michael Coen did very well. He was able to send money back to his parents in Ireland so that they could buy some land. He also brought out a number of his sisters and cousins from Ireland, including Tom Waldron, 'the strongest man in the world'.

The Australian Stores, Yass
Opposite: Grandpa Coen and his family. Back row left to right: Timothy and John
Alphonsus (Margaret Trainor's sons), Grandpa, King. Front row left to right: Joe,
Grandma, Evangelista (in Grandma's lap), Frank, Barney

Tom Waldron was one of our most famous family legends. The newspapers of the day were full of his prodigious feats of strength. When he joined the police force, louts used to shape up to him in pubs. Because he had such a soft Irish voice, they never guessed he was so strong.

'Come with me, my pretty boys,' he used to say. Next thing, Tom Waldron would emerge from the hotel with a lout under each arm and another between his teeth.

When he was sent in to clean up a notorious grog joint in Melbourne, he threw out ten men, one after another. The eleventh man had a bulldog that attacked the giant Irishman. Tom Waldron picked up the bulldog by the tail, twirled it round his head, then hurled it through the air. The bulldog landed on a roof several houses away. Such was the legend of Tom Waldron.

Michael Coen took a keen interest in civic affairs. He became an alderman almost as soon as he arrived in Yass and was three times Lord Mayor. Yass was off the train line and Michael Coen

was responsible for the tramway that linked the town to the main line. He was also instrumental in getting gas to Yass. The local paper described how as Lord Mayor he performed the ceremony of driving the last rivet into the gas holder. 'The spectators numbered upward of three hundred, and considerable interest in the proceedings was manifest.' Seeing 'M. Coen' written on all the gas lamps in Yass greatly excited us as children.

To celebrate the opening of the gasworks, he gave a grand ball which was attended by His Excellency the Governor, the Earl of Jersey. There was a miraculous display with dozens of fairy lights and globes lit with the new gas. 'More like a fairy bower' the press enthused over the decorations in the town hall. There was dancing till dawn and a sumptuous supper provided by Mr T. J. Sheeky. Only one guest complained to the local paper that he missed out on his share of the wine jelly at supper.

The day after the ball, over five hundred schoolchildren accompanied by the Yass town band marched to the showground to attend a picnic, again organised by Michael Coen. According to my mother, people said that Michael Coen had a genial, generous nature like a homespun shawl.

Michael Coen made money, enough to buy two more sheep stations, but in 1896, when he was only fifty-six, he died suddenly. Kathleen, his youngest daughter, was only three weeks old.

Michael Coen was much mourned, his obituaries were glowing. His bequests included a trust fund at the Yass hospital so any derelicts admitted would not be entirely destitute when they took to the road again. Grandma Coen, now forty-six, stalwartly took over his business.

The Stores ran smoothly under Grandma's iron hand. The profits from them, together with the money Michael Coen had left to the family in his will, ensured that there was no financial hardship for the Coens.

My father went to school at St Patrick's College, Goulburn, and like his brother Joe, he later attended the Jesuit college St Ignatius (Riverview) in Sydney. The younger boys, Frank and Barney, went to the Yass school run by the nuns until they were twelve, then to Riverview.

The Coen boys were bright. The elder son of Michael's first

Left: My youngest aunt Kathleen
Right: Grandma, widowed, takes over

wife became a Passionist priest, the other an orchestral conductor in America. Of the second Margaret Coen's sons, Joe and Barney became doctors and Frank a solicitor. Being the oldest, my father was destined to inherit the business.

My father's great passion was for the theatre. He loved play acting and reciting at concerts. I think he met my mother at one of these concerts in Yass, or perhaps at a dance. Mum loved dancing.

My mother was twenty-three when she married; Dad was twenty-two. Mum never talked about those years between the time she came to Sydney at the age of fourteen and when she married Dad. She told us that she arrived safely at the Flanagans' after her train journey and did her apprenticeship as a milliner in Sydney. After she finished, she worked in stores in country towns such as Mudgee and Forbes. A milliner was very important in a country drapery store at that time because women wore such elaborate hats; all pleated lace and tulle, decorated with everything under the sun – handmade flowers, feathers, little artificial birds. Mum was very good with hats. She could take a handful of flowers and ribbons, twist them around and arrange them in no time.

Eventually she answered an advertisement for a milliner in a shop called Woodhills in Yass, a big general store on the corner of Rossi and Cooma Streets. So my mother came to work in Yass. She boarded with a woman who rented her a room just up the road from the Coens' shop in Rossi Street.

The main meal of the day was lunch. Soon after she had taken this room, Mum came home one lunch time and there was nothing to eat on the table. Mum was hungry after working in the store all morning. She found her landlady out the back of the house, doing the washing in a big old-fashioned boiler.

'I suppose you want your lunch,' the woman said.

Yes, she was hungry, Mum replied.

Left: Dad, King Coen, who loved theatricals of any kind
Right: Bessie O'Dwyer at seventeen

'A couple of eggs will do you.' The woman picked up two eggs and threw them in with the dirty washing.

'Oh no, they won't,' Mum retorted. She went into her room, packed her bag, walked into town and rented a room at one of the hotels – a daring thing to do then.

'The belle of the south,' Mum said they used to call her in Yass. With her waist-length black hair, piercing blue eyes and tiny waist she had a good many admirers, but her heart was set on marrying King Coen.

My mother and father were both very Irish, but as different as could be. The Coens were red-haired, freckled, musical, amiable, fond of playing cards. The O'Dwyers were much more austere; black-haired, blue-eyed, distinguished-looking. My mother called them 'Spanish Irish'. Grandfather O'Dwyer looks wonderfully handsome in his photograph, but Grandfather Coen was foursquare and sturdy.

Friction between my mother and her mother-in-law, Grandmother Coen, started straight away. Grandma disapproved of Mum. Whether it was because Mum was a little older than Dad I don't know – she might have been jealous of Mum stealing her Little King away from her, or she might have thought that a milliner, a store employee, wasn't good enough for her son. Maybe she thought Mum was too pretty; perhaps because Grandpa Coen had died so young, she was frightened of losing another man from her life or from her business.

Anyway, she didn't come to the wedding, which was held on 2 February 1902 at the Flanagans' house in Sydney's Summer Hill. I don't think Mum's own mother was present either, but Mum and Dad had a carriage drawn by four white horses, decorated with bells and ribbons. Mum felt very grand.

Their honeymoon began in Melbourne, where they spent a few days before taking a boat to England and Dad began to write his diary. He found Melbourne an altogether more agreeable city than Sydney. The streets were much wider, he wrote, and the trams all that could be desired, though the fares were excessive.

The Melbourne visit seems to have been a whirl of activity. They dined out in style. At Her Majesty's Theatre they saw the famous actress Grace Palotta, whom Dad described as charming. They went twice to another show, *The Runaway Girl*, which they enjoyed even more, on shopping expeditions, and on a horse-drawn tram ride to the Zoological Gardens. They attended the races at Caulfield on two occasions, and Dad backed a few winners; their wedding photos were inspected at Johnson O'Shannessy and finally they collected £400 worth of circular notes (the equivalent of traveller's cheques) from Thomas Cook and Sons and prepared to depart for the honeymoon proper.

On Tuesday 25 March 1902, they travelled by train to Port Melbourne and boarded the *Arcadia* for the treat of their lives, or so they thought.

Dad was dreadfully ill throughout the voyage. He couldn't go on a ferry without being seasick. 'Never spent such a night in my life, sat on my cabin trunk the livelong night,' he wrote about their first night out of Melbourne. 'I couldn't have cared if they had thrown me overboard,' he wrote a little later. He was constantly feeling squeamish, miserable or very sick – 'feeding the fishes again' – as he put it.

'Who is the longest man in the world?' was the joke going around the ship.

'King Coen, because he retched all the way from Melbourne to London,' was the answer.

But suddenly Dad cheered up when he discovered that seasickness was greatly helped by a bottle of champagne before or instead of breakfast. The Coens were always partial to champagne. While he didn't have any sort of reputation as a drinking man, Dad's father Grandfather Coen enjoyed it greatly. The champagne remedy was repeated at lunch time and again in the evening. Dad was able to join the gentlemen's meetings in the smoking room which organised the shipboard games and amusements, to take part in deck sports and concerts and to win a euchre tournament (ten out of eleven) for which he received a cut-glass inkwell as a prize.

The boat stopped at Colombo. They watched the natives diving in the harbour and joined the other passengers in buying native trinkets which had to be brought up the ship's side on a rope. They went ashore and thoroughly enjoyed themselves taking

Opposite: Mum and Dad in Melbourne before leaving on their honeymoon

rickshaw rides, admiring the Oriental architecture, savouring the food and being entertained by a display of Ceylonese juggling, including what Dad called the 'famous mango tree trick', though he failed to say what it was.

Colombo, Aden, Suez, Port Said, the Red Sea, Italy, Sicily, the Mediterranean, Marseilles, Gibraltar, the English Channel. Still with intermittent seasickness, despite the champagne cure, Dad and Mum arrived in England. How my mother felt during the voyage is not recorded. By the time they reached London, she was pregnant, so her journey might not have been so comfortable either.

Dad's diary is remarkable for its failure to mention Mum. Dad carefully noted every play and concert they attended in London but there was nothing about his bride, her feelings, or what he thought of her. He did acknowledge the birth of their son, my brother King, at Appledore in Kent, in November 1902.

In London, Dad indulged his love of theatre to the full; the diary is filled with names such as Caruso and Melba. Mum loved their visits to the music hall. She always sang us songs she had learned from the shows they saw on their honeymoon.

They travelled through Ireland, visiting Clunemare, Sneem where the O'Dwyers came from, then Scotland, before settling down at Appledore to wait for the birth. In 1903, when King was only a baby, they returned to Australia.

To escape from Grandma Coen, Dad bought a small business of his own, a general store in Nowra on the New South Wales south coast. My sister Molly and my other brother Jack were born in Nowra.

One day Molly and Jack rushed excited into the store, begging Mum to come and look at the big yellow dog in the yard. The dog was a lion that had escaped from the circus. Jack and I have always had a terrible weakness for circuses.

Dad was no businessman. The dairy farmers round Nowra were suffering because there had been no rain. Dad sent a bill out only once; if people didn't pay he let it go. The farmers couldn't pay their bills because of the drought and Dad was going broke. The drought broke, the farmers still didn't or couldn't pay their bills; that was the end of Dad's business in Nowra.

He wrote to Grandma Coen saying he would have to come to

*My brother Jack, who loved the circus
even more than I did*

Yass and work in the store, and in about 1907 he and Mum moved back to Yass. My mother wasn't happy. She didn't like Yass or Grandma Coen. She thought my father ought to have stayed out on his own instead of going back to his mother.

Grandma bought them a house in Rossi Street, Yass. The house was large, my mother found it too hard to look after. She thought the open drains in the back yard were unsanitary. Mum was miserable. Even though she had bought the house, Grandma wasn't any fonder of Mum. In fact, Grandma openly ignored her and refused to speak to her. For her part, Mum thought Grandma was taking advantage of Dad's working in the family business not to pay him a proper salary.

Grandma's hostility scandalised Father Alphonsus, Dad's half-brother who visited Yass for a holiday. Father Alphonsus took Mum aside and told her Grandma had no right to treat her like this. He also had a word to the parish priest. Next time pious Grandma went off to confession, the parish priest delivered her quite a lecture about being uncharitable. If Mrs Coen wasn't nicer to her daughter-in-law, he warned, there would be no absolution for her.

Soon after, while Jack and Molly were playing outside, a strange young woman appeared, looking very friendly.

'Come here, little boy, little girl, come and talk to me,' she said. Grandma had sent Dad's young sister Molly to act as peacemaker. It was the first time Molly and Jack had met her. Relations between Mum and Grandma became fractionally more cordial after that, at least in public.

Mum was expecting another baby at this stage, she miscarried. Then quickly she became pregnant again.

2

The Angels on Palm Sunday Morning

Margaret on Grandma's cedar chest

I firmly believed that the angels dropped me over the wrought-iron lace balcony as they flew past on Palm Sunday morning.

I was born in the Rossi Street house Grandma had bought for my parents. It had been the old Berstein Stores; Grandma had converted them into a private residence. The house was two-storeyed, the front door opened onto the street, the upstairs balcony overhung the street by about twenty feet. We slept on this verandah in summer; in winter we roller-skated along it.

The house was called Kenmare after the Bay of Kenmare in Ireland, but someone had scratched out the 'a' and changed it into an 'o' so it read 'Kenmore', which was the name of the lunatic asylum in Goulburn. As long as we lived in the house, the 'o' remained. The house had ten rooms, which was one of the things my mother had against it. Even though she had a servant to help her, it was still too much work for her. The rooms were enormous.

The playroom-cum-sewing room was huge; I suppose it had been a storeroom originally. We could do anything in that room – draw on the walls or scribble over them; my mother never went near it. We kept our toys in the playroom and on wet days we didn't move from there.

A mission was being held up at the church and lengthy sermons went on. My mother heard strange sounds coming from the playroom. We used to lock ourselves in so she had to look through the keyhole. Jack had draped an eiderdown over his shoulders. He had the cat up on a chair and was giving it a wonderful sermon, like the mission bishop at church, all about the mortal sins cats commit.

Through the gaps between the floorboards in the sewing room, we could look at the swallows building nests on the rafters below; we could see the baby swallows when they were born and watch their mothers feeding them.

Over the wrought-iron lace balcony, we had a grandstand view of the town's funeral processions. We loved the hearse, adorned with black plumes and trappings. Rossi Street led up what was called Cemetery Hill. The horse and plumes would be followed by a line of buggies, followed in turn by men on horseback.

Doctor English, our family doctor in Yass, ordered my mother to take long walks; she complained of being tired and lacking energy, of not enjoying life. The walks were not the right treatment, for they left her more exhausted than ever, but I loved them. Every afternoon, my mother and I set off. Our walks took the same route as the funeral processions. Rossi Street soon turned into a steep hill with quaint little cottages. Their front gardens were crammed with flowers. The hollyhocks planted along the fences were ten feet high; creamy yellow, red and mauve flowers and much taller than I. Bluebells grew everywhere beside the road; bluebells and creeping pink flowers, tiny pink convolvulus which I called pink bluebells, much to my mother's amusement.

At the top of Cemetery Hill, the road turned right and meandered past paddock after paddock until it reached the cemetery. Usually we walked to the first paddock. I would break away from my mother's hand, squeeze under the fence and go racing across the stubble of grass and through the blue and white flag lilies with their wild smell. I would pick a bunch of lilies from the paddock to take home. The next day, we would hold a fete. The flag lilies and anything else I had picked over the fences on the way home I put in jamjars. (I always took any flower I could over a fence; I still do.)

I made mud pies for my stall, too. They were almost good enough to eat, decorated with whiting we kept for cleaning the hearth. All morning I stood hopefully by the stall waiting for customers, flicking away the flies with a gum leaf twig.

The stall was out the back of the house near the yellow pisé wall that ran round it. A gate in the wall led to an orchard and by the gate was an old fig tree. The pisé wall was wide enough to run along, and the fig tree could be climbed from the wall. During summer we stuffed ourselves with the purply figs, waiting until they were so ripe they were ready to burst before we pushed them into our greedy mouths.

A Jersey cow lived in the orchard. Dad used to milk it and Mum left the milk in big basins on the stove overnight. In the mornings she peeled off cream half an inch thick. We put it on our porridge with brown sugar. We also ate bread and jam with a slice of cream.

The orchard had a side fence that was also the back yard of a man who had an open-air picture show. In the evenings we used to go down there, climb the fence, balance precariously and watch the distant flickering screen. We saw crazy Keystone comedies, Ben Turpin looking cross-eyed, Mabel Normand simpering coyly. Then someone would fall off the fence and we would be sent home to bed.

Opposite our house was the court house and behind it the police station. The court house had a porticoed front like a sandstone Parthenon. Whenever I looked at the court house, I thought of Cuckoo Singh.

Cuckoo Singh was an Indian hawker who had lost his mind. I always thought he was called 'Cuckoo' after the bird. Only later I realised where his name came from. Cuckoo Singh had a breakdown and was locked in the gaol, which had cells surrounded by a high stone wall. We were sleeping out on the balcony and lay awake all night, listening to Cuckoo Singh screaming.

The next day he was taken off to the asylum, Kenmore, at Goulburn. On the way, they said, he tore up the floor of the wagon with his teeth.

Cuckoo Singh haunted our nightmares. If we wanted to frighten other children, we told them the story of Cuckoo Singh.

There were other terrors in those early days, such as the greenhide. This was a weapon wielded on the boys by my father, whom I recall as an impressive figure with a gingery moustache.

One day the greenhide vanished. Somehow I knew it was at the bottom of the water tank and that my brother King had put it there. The boys won. The greenhide was not replaced.

Dad loved concerts, theatricals, receptions, dinners, entertainment of every description. There was tremendous shouting from the sewing room whenever he was preparing for a concert. 'Once more unto the breach, dear friends, once more', his voice boomed out.

Dad never stayed around the house much. If he wasn't off to a theatrical event in later years he was up at the Soldiers' Club. The children . . . well, we were very nice, but that was all the notice he took of us. Nevertheless we worshipped him.

One exciting time he won the prize at a fancy dress ball by going as a cabbage. He had spent the day before sewing cabbage leaves onto an old suit. Then he wanted to take me to a Red Cross conscription rally to play the part of a dead Belgian child, but Mum wouldn't permit it. My mother regarded Dad's eagerness to join in other people's parties with little sympathy. She said Dad would do anything for anybody except his own family.

Mum had been very fond of Dad when they were married, but they had different temperaments and she had grown tired of his easygoing joviality and impracticality.

'Your father is a fool,' she would snap, but we loved him because he made us laugh, like the time he took us to see a Charlie Chaplin film at Williams's Picture Show.

A fat aunt who was visiting Grandma came with us. Dad was not a small man either. As we were sitting there, in a row of canvas deck chairs and laughing at Chaplin walking bowlegged in baggy trousers, suddenly Dad's deck chair collapsed.

'Get me out of this!' he shouted. But we were already too weak from laughing to help him up. Then our aunt's chair gave way. We thought we would die of laughter.

Dad was not a practical man. When the Jersey cow was blown, he summoned the boys and they lit a bonfire in the back yard. Dad heated the poker Mum brought him; the boys were to hold the cow while Dad tried to pierce her side with the red-hot poker.

The cow broke loose.

'Hold her, hold her!' Dad's commands were too late; the cow was already out of the orchard and up the lane. Dad's agitation at the cow escaping was nothing to his frenzy when he picked up the poker, which he had dropped in the excitement, by the red-hot end.

'Your father is a fool,' sighed Mum in exasperation.

The tank sprang a leak. Dad's method of fixing it was to nail a piece of tin over the hole.

'Your father is a fool,' became a household refrain.

Dad remained amiable. He retaliated only once. He had come back from some country excursion with a very young white cockatoo. My mother was left the job of feeding it, and it squawked day and night.

Mrs English, the doctor's wife, paid us a visit and Mum told her a tale of woe about the bird. Mrs English liked white cockatoos and told Mum she would be happy to look after even a very young, noisy one.

My mother gave her the cockatoo, telling her not to say where the bird had come from. Mum's plan was to tell my father that it had escaped and flown away.

The cockatoo was in a box. Mrs English left the house and immediately went down to Coen's store to buy a cage for it. By some mischance, my father served her. She explained what she needed and as she departed with the cage, the awful truth dawned on Dad. He came home straight after work and confronted Mum.

'Did you give my cockatoo to Mrs English?' he demanded.

Argument and recrimination lasted for hours, but my mother didn't ask for the cockatoo back. My father never brought another bird into the house, either.

My best friend Gladys lived two doors up. Because my brothers King and Jack and my sister Molly were older than I was, I didn't play with their friends much. Gladys and I shared a passion for cats. We dressed them up in dolls' clothes and dragged them around the yard in a boot box attached to a piece of string.

Gladys came to the door in tears one day when my mother was out, and told me her mother was dead. An angel had come in the night and had taken her mother to heaven, she said.

She asked me to her house and we crept into her mother's bedroom. It was very quiet. In the middle of the room was a long, polished wooden box. We looked into it and saw Gladys' mother lying whitefaced and perfectly still. Beside her was a tiny waxen baby, no bigger than a doll.

I was shocked. The day before, Gladys' mother had been alive. She had given Gladys and me a piece of cake each. I thought the dead baby was the angel who had come to take her away. I couldn't understand why the angel was dead too.

We stood by the coffin crying until someone led us outside. Gladys, still crying, came home with me. I took Gladys into my parents' bedroom where my mother kept two pretty rings in a little silver box on her dressing table.

'Never mind, Gladys,' I said. 'You can have these if you stop crying.'

Gladys accepted the rings. The sparkling stones stopped her tears and she took them home with her. Later, a woman came to the door to ask my mother if the rings were hers. I was in trouble because I had given away my mother's engagement ring.

The funny little steam train that we used to call 'the tram' was quite a feature of Yass. It ran from Yass to Yass Junction, crossing the Yass River by the railway bridge. The boys in Yass, including my brothers, used to walk halfway across the railway bridge, then hang upside down by the sleepers as the tram went past. Gladys and I listened enviously to their stories of this feat. We wanted to be as daring as the boys.

The tram tracks through town ran along a road parallel to the main street. There were accidents wherever the tram crossed the road. People in buggies were killed, then in cars. We were always being told how dangerous it was to play around the tram tracks.

Gladys and I heard the boys saying that, if you put pennies on the tram line, the tram would pass over them and make them twice the size. We decided to try for ourselves. Either we were too slow running away from the line or we didn't run far enough, because the tram stopped where we had put our pennies.

The tram driver got out and chased us. Gladys and I ran for our lives. The tram driver kept shouting that he would tell our parents we had been playing on the tram tracks. Fortunately Rossi Street was just around the corner from the tramline. Gladys and I breathed a deep sigh of relief when were safely home. We vowed never to go near the tramline again.

Brothers could be a torment. I came into the playroom one day and found sawdust scattered over the floor. King and a friend had been operating on my favourite doll. They had cut her down the middle to take out her appendix. No attempt had been made to stitch the patient up after the operation and I fled in tears with my ravaged doll.

I remember very little about my curly-haired sister Molly, except that I envied her curls. By the time I became aware of her, she and King had won scholarships to boarding school. They were whisked away to Goulburn for the next five years.

King had gingery, sandy hair and freckles; Jack was very red-haired with freckles. My own black hair was fine and straight with coppery highlights, different from my mother's and Molly's blue-black hair. I also had freckles, which I hated, but, like Mum, Molly didn't have a freckle on her face.

On a holiday in Sydney, Dad's brother Barney took the boys out fishing in a rowing boat at Coogee. They sat in the boat with their feet up as they dangled their lines over the side. Since they were all so gingery and white-skinned, Barney included, the soles of their feet were badly sunburned.

The boys and Barney retired early to bed to ease their stinging feet. My uncle Frank had left his fox terrier Spot at the house. Spot chose this evening to bite Grandma's sister Auntie Lizzie on the nose, which caused considerable commotion.

Mum had clear skin so she looked the exact opposite of the gingery, fair-skinned Coens. She used to pay us threepence a week to brush her long, black hair, being a firm believer in the value of one hundred strokes a day. Brushing hair for a long time can be tiring and boring. I once brought the brush up the wrong way and tangled her hair. Mum spent hours unravelling the knots I made; I was not in favour.

The boys decided they wanted a tent. Mum was out at a Red Cross meeting so they raided her wardrobe. Her lace wedding dress with the boned sides and waist that she so treasured was hung over a pole in the orchard and the full skirt and train were staked to the ground. The boys were in trouble that night.

The circus came to town. That was an unforgettable event. For months the posters had been pinned up in shop windows and stuck on street lamps. 'Wirth's Circus' was written across them with an orange-and-white-striped tiger's face and, much smaller, a tiny ballerina riding on a white horse.

Elephants led the parade down Cooma Street when the circus finally arrived, pulling a wagon with a 'wild beast' inside.

We loved the animal smell of the sawdust as we sat around the ring at night; the lions and tigers, the elephants, the clowns, all were magical to us. It was the first circus I saw, and I became a circus fan for life.

On the second night of the circus, Jack disappeared. He was found asleep under the benches, in the process of running away with the circus. Jack had run away before; as a very small boy he had taken all his clothes off, put on a hat of Mum's, then, with his legs astride Dad's sword like a hobby horse, had set off down the street to visit Grandma. He had a wonderful time until he was captured and brought home.

An old lady who lived alone by the river wandered into our walled back yard. Once in, she was unable to find her way out. She thought she was in the walled yard of the gaol. 'Let me out, oh God, let me out!' she shrieked. There was a bottle on the bench beside her. We were terrified and enchanted.

I remember my fourth birthday party. My mother had decorated my high chair by twisting ivy leaves around it; she put flowers among the leaves and made a wreath for my head.

For a birthday present I was given a little gypsy's caravan. Steps led up to a covered wagon made of shiny, silvery stuff. I put threepence in the wagon, which was a money box. It was my favourite thing. Somehow I lost it. I don't know what happened, and for a long time I felt that a part of life was missing. I searched high and low for the gypsy caravan.

Another uncomfortable childhood image that remains with me is lying under a bed feeling ill after having eaten a box of chocolate Laxettes.

A joy of my childhood was driving out to buy ripe Black Margaret cherries from the orchard. My mother would pick up cherries on a stem and drape them over my ears for earrings.

'Look at yourself in the mirror and admire the view,' she used to say.

Tommy our pony bolted the day we went to the orchard for a sugar bag of apples. I thought my mother was very brave as she stood up straight, fiercely holding onto the reins.

'Hang on tight, don't stand up,' she told Jack and me. Jack leapt out but I clung on, crouched down in the rattling sulky. At last a man came running alongside and Tommy was subdued.

Tommy hated to be driven out of town. Going to the park to collect pine cones, we had to force him to put one foot in front of the other, but when the buggy was loaded up, he would trot home spryly.

In winter, the fire was piled high with pine cones. We would sit as close as possible staring at the pictures in the flames. My mother would bring in her sewing basket with cotton reels threaded on the handles for the kittens to play with. The old mother cat gazed steadily into the fire, occasionally swishing her tail to and fro for the kittens' amusement.

The greatest treat was to be bathed in the front of the fire in the shallow tin dish that took kettle after kettle to fill. Afterwards my mother would wrap me in a large towel and, bathed and warm, I would fall asleep in her arms.

Then there was Grandma. An awesome and mysterious figure, reputed to be made of money and not amused by life, she went into black the instant my grandfather died and stayed in her widow's weeds for the next fifty years. Her only concession to vanity was a rich brown wig that she called a 'transformation'.

Grandma lived with her daughters. The eldest, Evangelista, had already entered the convent, the next two, Trix and Ina, were preparing to go into the convent and gentle Molly who played the piano secretly wished to become a nun. Kathleen, my youngest aunt, was still at school. There was also a curly-haired general servant named Annie who looked after Grandma and 'the girls' as my aunts were called.

Grandma lived next door to the store in Cooma Street. Her low, single-storeyed home with pisé walls a foot thick was known as The House. Several times I lived with Grandma and my aunts at The House.

Most people were frightened of Grandma. She could be very stern, and her manner to us was always gruff, perhaps because of the hostility between her and Mum. But I got on well with Grandma, despite such episodes as my lapse with the chocolates.

The dining room at The House had a long cedar sideboard with three compartments. One held sherry, whisky and stout or porter,

Left to right: Jack, Trix, Molly, Kathleen and her dog

as Grandma called it. Grandma drank porter every day. (I, too, was given porter because I had such a pale face. A little porter at night was supposed to improve the colour.) The second compartment held condiments, pepper and salt for the table. The third was reserved for special things such as chocolates.

Lent was kept very seriously at Grandma's. Someone had given 'the girls' a box of chocolates but the chocolates were put aside until Easter.

I must have been about three at the time; it was during one of my stays at The House. In my wanderings I discovered the box of chocolates stored in the cedar sideboard. The temptation was too great, I knew they weren't to be eaten, but I couldn't help it. I didn't let myself look at them, just put my hand in, lifted the lid and felt. My finger closed on a chocolate. Having a very sweet tooth, I had to eat it. More and more often I went back to the sideboard until I couldn't feel any more chocolates.

Easter Sunday came. We were seated round the long dining

room table and Ina asked, 'Shall we open the chocolates now, Mama?' They always called Grandma 'Mama'.

'Yes,' said Grandma.

Ina went to the sideboard, brought out the strangely light chocolate box and opened it. Not one chocolate was left.

I left the table and fled down the back yard as far and as fast as I could. My flight established my guilt beyond doubt, but I have no recollection what punishment I received, if any.

I went to school when I was four because it was so close. The back fence of the orchard at Rossi Street was also the back fence of the school. To get to the kindergarten, I only had to squeeze through a hole in the palings.

Sister Loreto ran the school. She used to cane the boys and called them 'sir'. I used to be glad I was a girl when she said, 'Stand out here, sir', and a trembling small boy held out his hand to be caned.

Glass-fronted cupboards ran round the sides of Sister Loreto's classroom and in them she kept a collection of tiny dolls in costume, all under lock and key. I longed to be able to open the glass doors to play with these dolls, especially the gypsy doll. Three or four inches tall and dressed in vermilion and yellow with long, black hair that came down on either side, the gypsy doll sat in a wooden swing about eight inches high.

Although she was ferocious to pupils like me, Sister Loreto was devoted to the Aboriginal children who came to school. She used to go out every weekend to the so-called 'blacks' camp' outside Yass and wash the heads of the women and children. If she didn't, the other children complained they got nits from the heads of the Aboriginal children.

The bigger part of the school was ruled by Sister Dominic. Sister Dominic had a great sense of humour; she was always smiling. I loved Sister Dom, as I called her and named the two clay dogs someone had given me Dom and Nic after her.

A school concert came up. Another nun, Sister Michael, taught me my piece for it. Sister Michael was very stern with fierce black eyebrows that met in the middle. She frightened me.

'Lickings' was the title of my recitation, a tale of children being beaten for wrongdoing. By the time of the concert, I was word perfect.

My turn on stage arrived. Dead silence. I tried to start. No sound came out of my mouth. I could see Sister Michael's face with the black line of eyebrow, making desperate signs at me from the wings to get on with it, but I couldn't.

I just stood there until I burst into tears, then Sister Michael dragged me off by the scruff of the neck. She scolded me so much I was afraid to go to school next day. However, Sister Dominic greeted me, smiling as usual and saying I wasn't to mind about forgetting my recitation.

Green pepper trees, the kind seen everywhere in country towns, grew in the school yard where we played rounders and did a lot of skipping. The pepper trees had pretty pink seeds with a curious smell. They grew around the school and down Meehan Street to the Catholic church.

I was always breaking bones. First, I broke my wrist. My father used to come home from the store between one and two for dinner, as lunch was called. I came home from school for the meal, too. Running back to school after saying goodbye to my father, I tripped and fell on a drain in the back yard. A sharp pain shot through my wrist. A nursemaid who helped my mother picked me up and bustled me into the dark sewing room. 'Keep quiet,' she said. 'Your mother is lying down. Don't let her hear you crying.'

She left me and I sobbed until just before tea time when my mother came in and put my arm in a sling.

After tea Mum took me down to the chemist, but the chemist was shut. At last, in response to my mother's frantic banging, he very crossly opened the door.

'Take her to the doctor,' he said.

Down the street we went to the doctor's. The doctor pronounced the arm broken, pushed the bone into place and bound it up. It hurt for a long time afterwards and when the splints came off, it looked quite crooked.

On special feast days we went to Mass at the church before school. On the way to school after Mass one day, I fell over. I had broken my collar bone, although I didn't know what was wrong. I had cried all morning, but nobody had thought of sending for a doctor until I went home for lunch.

The place names around Yass constantly intrigued me as a

child. Dog Trap Road, Bogalong, the Julians' property, Wee Jasper (named after a dwarf?), Burrinjuck. I loved the sounds and the strangeness of them.

The railway at Burrinjuck Dam had only eighteen inches between the tracks. The tiny carriage, just wide enough to hold my mother and me, looked like fairyland. The jewel-bright wildflowers covering the hills around the dam made it especially magical. Except for bluebells, wildflowers didn't grow around Yass much because the land had been so thoroughly cleared.

The heat in Yass was ferocious, very dry, often over one hundred degrees. Winters were cold with frosts and fogs. The sun wouldn't come through until half past eleven or twelve and disappeared again by half past three.

Rolling plains surrounded Yass, bleached blond in summer, bright green after rain. The plains were the home of merino stud sheep, with the most sought-after fleece in the world. They were also great for mushrooming. In autumn we wandered for miles until our baskets were filled with velvety, pinky-black mushrooms.

Living in a country town gives you the feeling of a complete world on its own. We had the various religions, professions, commercial enterprises, and cultural activities of the outside

The bridge at Yass

world. Yass had a musical society, a library and, of course, the School of Arts, all existing in a small familiar space. Living in Yass felt very safe.

Coming into town from the southern end, we crossed the big, rattly bridge spanning the sluggish Yass River, then we were in Cooma Street, the wide main street that ran right through town and out the other side to the plains. (Cooma Street is spelt 'Comur' now, but then it was always 'Cooma', like the town.)

Iron lace decorated most of the buildings. They were painted white with black, wrought-iron verandahs just like our house in Rossi Street. Steep hills rose on either side of town: Cemetery Hill was one of these hills but both our house and Grandma's were on the flat.

The flat part of town flooded regularly, the Yass River coming as far as Cooma Street in floods. One year we saw muddy water tipped with waves at the bottom of Rossi Street. My brothers and their friend Lenny Cusack built a boat.

The boat was a wooden box, across the bottom of which they nailed planks for reinforcement. The boys set sail down Rossi Street. Water rushed in where they had hammered in the nails and they had to be rescued immediately.

The Catholic church was on the flat in Meehan Street, next to the Convent of Mercy. The Church of England was on the hill opposite Cemetery Hill. It was a handsome building with pine trees planted in front and a few old gravestones in the garden. There were also Wesleyan and Methodist churches.

Yass had a surfeit of both churches and hotels. The Australia was next door to Grandma's store. A few doors up was the Commercial. The Royal was on the opposite side of Cooma Street and there were another two hotels near the bridge, with one more by the court house. The court house, with its white pillars, was the town's most splendid edifice. The court house had apparently been intended for Young, a much bigger town than Yass, but the plans went astray and it was built at Yass.

An argument in planning, too, caused Yass to be bypassed when the train line was put through, which was why Grandpa Coen had the tramline installed.

Taking the steam tram out to Yass Junction was always an

adventure. Little Billy Macnally, who was no more than five feet tall, would be sitting in his cart at the station like a leprechaun. If you were coming to meet someone at the train by buggy or car, Billy would bring the luggage into town with his cart. His pony was a rogue.

Billy lived with his mother opposite the Catholic church. One night Billy's pony got out and went across the road. He was a clever pony, as well as wicked. He opened the presbytery gate and ate the priest's garden. Everyone in town knew about that when it happened. Billy was one of their favourite characters.

The park in North Yass was full of pine trees. We used to gather fallen pine cones and eat the sweet nuts out of them.

Down by the river was a garden belonging to John, the 'Chinaman'. John supplied fresh vegetables for the town, bringing them around in a cart. When one of our cats had kittens, Mum did a deal with him.

'Do you want a cat, John?' Mum asked innocently.

John was delighted; he loved cats. Mum handed him a basket, inside which she had packed the cat and her kittens.

John came back the next day, ecstatic. On the way home, he told us, the cat had had kittens. He had six cats now, instead of the one he thought he had. John was overwhelmed with happiness. In gratitude he brought a giant watermelon up to Rossi Street.

The pitiful collection of tin shanties where the Aborigines lived was down on the river, too. The Yass Aborigines, who were very tall and fine-featured, used to work around town. My grandmother had a gardener named Caesar, a very tall old man who tended her persimmon trees.

Mrs Nelson, another Aboriginal, was in demand by everyone to do washing. I remember my grandmother talking about Mrs Nelson's kitchen. 'It is only a tin shanty,' Grandma used to say, 'but Mrs Nelson has it so nice. She has a beautiful lace cloth over the table, she makes you a cup of tea and cooks you a cake as good as anyone's in town.'

The queen of the blacks was called Julia. She often appeared at our kitchen door dressed in an amazing array of cast-off finery from the whites; a brightly patterned silk coat, a hat bedecked with artificial roses, a feather boa.

Julia was immensely old, upright, regal and very black, though a rumour persisted round the town that her father had been a white man of God, a minister.

A great fuss was made when Julia paid us a visit. Afternoon tea would be served in the kitchen with one of the best cups and a slice of cake. Then for a silver coin – sixpence for children, a shilling for adults – Julia would tell fortunes. She told the most exciting fortunes, full of romantic promise and exotic places: 'A tall, dark, handsome stranger will come, you will visit faraway lands.'

A couple of shy Aboriginal children sometimes accompanied Julia. She would proudly introduce them as her daughter's child or her son's son and ask if we had any old clothing for them. Julia must have had many grandchildren, because the same child rarely came with her twice.

Three miles out of town the river ran through a gorge, at the end of which it took a bend. This was called Hatton's Corner and fossils were found there, seashells millions of years old. An artist who did pastel sketches was a familiar town character who haunted Hatton's Corner.

Miles Franklin lived nearby at Brindabella. They used to talk about her and about her book *My Brilliant Career* a great deal when I was young, because Brindabella is so close to Yass.

I loved books. I could read before I was five. I liked books I could weep over; I pored over *The Little Mermaid*, the saddest story in Hans Christian Andersen. But *Thumbelina* was my favourite and I longed to find a tiny friend for myself.

The boys had the *Boys' Own Paper*, and my sister had copies of the *Girls' Own Annual*. We also had the works of Australian balladists such as 'Banjo' Paterson in our bookshelf, as well as a good selection of Dickens. I read *David Copperfield* and *Oliver Twist*. I agonised over poor Oliver; the illustrations of the fierce Fagin in the condemned cell were the most terrible things in the world to me.

My father never read to us, but he recited, rehearsing for his theatricals. My mother sang us songs like, 'I Wonder Who's Kissing Her Now?', 'I'm the Girl from Gay Paree', and 'I Don't Want to Play in Your Yard'; music hall songs she had learned on their honeymoon.

A rhyme was dinned into us at night about a little boy who wouldn't say his prayers.

Once there was a little boy who wouldn't say his prayers,
And when he went to bed at night away upstairs,
His father heard him holler, his mother heard him call,
And when they went to look for him, he wasn't there at all
And the bogey man will get you too if you don't watch out!

It worked. I was never brave enough not to say my prayers at night. Every hour through the night, the town clock chimed and could be heard everywhere. I never minded the clock chiming; I thought it was rather nice.

Suddenly things changed. My father was crying, sobbing out loud over and over again. 'He's dead – Frank my brother's been killed!' Frank was the golden boy of the Coen family. He had a promising career as a barrister and was just about to enter politics when he enlisted. The war had begun.

Mum was pale and sad. Dad was soon dressed in khaki, the ends of his moustache waxed and pointed. He was to vanish out of my life for nearly seven years. Life was never the same in Rossi Street.

My father was in the permanent army; he failed to be passed for overseas service because of an eyesight problem and some heart trouble. He was stationed at Holdsworthy near Sydney, guarding Germans in a concentration camp. Dad took charge of entertainment at the camp and organising theatricals. There was plenty of time for rehearsals, scenery painting and making costumes. Dad probably enjoyed himself thoroughly, producing the programmes with the prisoners.

My mother was left alone in Yass with four children and Grandma, whom she still didn't like any better. Our big, empty playroom was full of women sitting at wheels, spinning raw fleece into skeins while others knitted up socks with the wool.

At Grandma's, beautiful fruit cakes were sewn into hessian bags, to be sent to the boys at the front.

We prayed every night that the war in Germany would stop; that God would stop the war and look after the little children in

France and Belgium. We had heard terrible stories about what happened to children in the war.

Christmas came. One gift each was all we had; no one could afford toys with a war going on. But even if there were no toys, there were still plenty of flowers. Mary Roach from Normanhurst asked me over to pick violets. Mary Roach was a novelist who had written a book called *Roses* under the name of Molly Braun. Normanhurst was a huge, rambling house at the end of town, with endless violet beds.

'Pick as many as you like and pick a bunch for me,' she said.

A whole afternoon with nothing to do except pick violets! I was in heaven.

Later, Mrs Grace, a round, comfortable-looking woman, said she would take me to play with her daughter Kathy, to stay with them out in the bush.

Ten miles in a buggy seemed to take forever. 'Are we nearly there?' I kept asking. 'Is this it?'

'Not yet; soon,' I was told again and again. At last we turned into a gateway and drove up to the house. Kathy, who had rosy cheeks and long brown plaits, came running out to meet me.

'Come and eat walnuts,' she said.

I followed her to a shed. We climbed a steep ladder into a loft where there were bags and bags of fresh walnuts.

'Eat as many as you like,' Kathy smiled at me and I smiled back. We ate until we could eat no more.

Kathy and I were to sleep together in a room at the end of a long verandah. It felt strange and unfamiliar. When Mrs Grace took the candle away, I missed my mother in the darkness. A terrible moaning and groaning started up.

'Kathy, wake up! It's the ghost of Cuckoo Singh!' Perhaps he had escaped from the asylum and followed me. Frantically I shook the peacefully sleeping Kathy.

'Don't be silly,' she said. 'It's only the dingoes.' Kathy went back to sleep immediately but it was ages before I could close my eyes.

Next day, dingoes and Cuckoo Singh forgotten, I cheered up and fed a pet lamb from a bottle. Then a sheep was going to be killed, Kathy told me; obediently I trailed along after her. There was the poor sheep. A man held back its head with one hand, while his other held a knife at its throat.

I started to run home. The Graces picked me up in the buggy and took me back into town. I was very glad to be back inside the pisé walls of the house at Rossi Street and never went out to the Graces' again.

My mother was determined to leave Yass and get back to Sydney. Apart from the problem of Grandma, she hated the Yass climate and suffered from the snobbery of the town. The Catholics felt the the Protestants, particularly the Anglicans, looked down on them. Equally strong, though it didn't affect my mother, was the social discrimination between the various Protestant groups. The Wesleyans and Methodists were at the bottom of the ladder.

For the Catholics with whom my mother could have socialised, card playing was the favourite activity, but my mother wouldn't play cards so she didn't fit in. No one in her family played cards; Mum said her father had made her promise never to do so.

The other snobbery was about people 'in trade', as the shopkeepers were called. Graziers, doctors and lawyers headed the desirable list in Yass. People who worked in the bank were just acceptable and shop owners certainly less so.

My mother did have two women friends in Yass. Neither was a Catholic and both were very independent women. They were Mary Yeo, an historian (called Pol Yeo by her friends), and Kit English, the doctor's daughter who studied insects. A species of blowfly she discovered was named after her.

My mother enjoyed the company of both these women, I think, because she would have liked a freer, more adventurous life herself. I always remember her talking about the importance of the Married Women's Property Act. This was the Act that stopped a husband automatically taking any monies belonging to his wife. The injustice of her own mother having to hand over her wedding present money to Michael O'Dwyer, who spent it so rapidly, remained strongly in her mind.

All this time, too, my mother was sick. The malaise of which she complained to Doctor English was a stomach tumour that remained undiagnosed until late 1918. Finally Mum went up to

Sydney for an operation at Lewisham hospital. After this she became well again. But ill health added to her dissatisfaction with life in Yass.

The war was almost over, but Dad was still away with the army at Holdsworthy. Mum couldn't stand being alone in the big house by herself any more. Molly and King were at boarding school, Jack and I were the only company she had. She wanted to be near my father. So, without consulting anyone, she decided to leave Yass forever. She never came back to live there.

Mum took Jack to Sydney with her. I was left with Grandma. For the next few years I remained in the pisé house next to the store with the short, formidable figure in black and a collection of female relatives.

3

A House
Full of Women

Grandma

Grandma had a cockatoo that said, 'A piece of toast, please.'
Cocky had tea and toast for breakfast every morning, which won
me immediately.

The House was full of women. There was Grandma, who
thought she was Queen Victoria; her stumpy figure really did
look like Victoria's. Her daughters, Trix Ina and Evangelista had
gone off to the convent, but Molly and Kathleen, who had just left
school, were still at The House and so were Grandma's two
sisters Linda (Belinda) and Lizzie. There was also Annie who did
all the work.

The aunts, as Linda and Lizzie were known, were short and not
very good-looking. They were the most close-mouthed and
secretive couple. Linda was a retired schoolmistress; with her
knowing eye and beaky nose she reminded me of a cockatoo.
Lizzie had lived with Grandma as her housekeeper since the
death of my grandfather.

Molly was about to enter the convent. She was older than Trix,
who was already a nun, and had wanted to enter for a long time,
but wasn't brave enough to tell Grandma. Grandma was growing
a bit upset about all her daughters becoming nuns. Molly had
beautiful long brown hair, so long she could sit on it. I thought it
was terrible that it would soon be cut off in the convent.

Molly loved music and playing the piano. She used to sing to
me:

Listen to the watermill all the livelong day
How the grinding of the wheel wears the day away,
The mill will never grind with waters that have passed . . .

It was so sad. I cried and cried.

'Margaret,' Molly used to chide, 'I won't play for you any more because it makes you cry.'

'But I like crying,' I assured her.

On the day she left, Molly gave me a gold medal she had won for her music. It had an Irish harp on one side and an Irish wolfhound on the other.

In Molly's bedroom was a portrait of a saintly lady, her hands joined in prayer, smiling sweetly against a stained glass window, an arum lily, the symbol of purity, growing up beside her. I asked permission to copy this painting and the request was granted. I made a careful copy in pencil which was much admired by Grandma and the aunts. They even framed it.

'You're quite the little artist,' they said.

I was convinced that this was what I wanted to be, an artist. I also copied or tried to copy a framed drawing of the nursery rhyme, 'Hickory Dickory Dock', with the mouse running up the clock.

Grandma, Linda and Lizzie all wore wigs. Nobody told me they were wigs, but you would have had to be blind not to spot that their hair wasn't their own. I don't know if they were bald or just had very fine hair; the three of them were redhaired, and redheads sometimes do go bald early. Grandma had a surprisingly youthful face and her wig was a rich red. She never wore a white 'transformation'. At ninety-three her hair was still as brilliant as ever. Perhaps because she ran a business, Grandma was determined not to show her age. Auntie Lizzie had a little white through her wig, but Linda kept hers deep red until she was eighty.

Before she went away to boarding school, my sister Molly had a terrible fight with a girl at the Yass school.

'Your grandmother wears a wig,' the girl sang out in the playground.

Molly was stung. She didn't even know what a wig was (they

were always called 'transformations' in front of us), but she knew
she had been insulted.

'She doesn't wear a wig,' Molly said. 'She does *not* wear a wig!'
'Oh, yes, she does! Everybody knows that,' the girl retorted.
They were so secretive, these Victorians; I never saw a wig
hanging up. They wore quite fetching mobcaps to bed, caps with
lace edging and ribbon threaded through.

Grandma used to get up at half past five, summer and winter.
She would go down to the icy outside bathroom wearing a towel
draped over her head, hanging to her shoulders like a sheik's
headdress, to have what I can only presume was a cold bath.

Curious though I was, I couldn't manage to catch her with the
wig off. I used to cross-question Annie about it, but she would
only go off into peals of silent laughter at the mention of
Grandma's wig.

The aunts disliked each other. There was great jealousy about
rival plots in the garden. Lizzie grew chrysanthemums but Linda
fancied delicate plants that wouldn't flower in the Yass climate.
She had a passion for tiny rockery plants called geums. If Linda
appeared in the garden while Lizzie was watering her chrysanthemums, the hose was accidentally on purpose turned on Linda and
a shrill series of short screams ensued.

Linda picked on Lizzie. Linda picked on everyone. She was
perpetually the reproving schoolmarm. Among other things, she
didn't care for the cats that hung about under three large tanks
behind the kitchen.

At the back of the store were bins of chaff and cattle feed. The
grain was kept in a shed where I loved playing, climbing over hay
piled twenty feet high.

Mice were a problem because they chewed through the bags of
chaff to make their nests so Harry Smith, who was in charge of this
side of the business, used to encourage stray cats. They came
round the back of the house, where Annie surreptitiously fed
them with scraps sneaked from the fowls' tin.

I loved cats. I begged Annie to give me a saucer of milk for
them. 'Don't let Linda catch you,' Annie warned me. But Linda
saw me pouring the milk into an old saucer. Linda spoke very pre-
cisely, as if she were still addressing a class of school children.

'Margaret, you are not allowed to feed the cats or give them milk. Your grandmother does not want to encourage cats,' she said. 'We have to eat off that saucer.'

'We'll never eat off this one,' I retorted.

I picked up the saucer and threw it against the brick wall at the side of the house, where it smashed instantly. It's a wonder I didn't throw it at Auntie Linda, I was so angry.

Annie's anxious face was peeking out the kitchen window. She was delighted but didn't dare show it.

'Your grandmother shall hear of this,' Linda stormed off. Linda never liked me and I never liked Linda. I never heard anything from Grandma about the smashed saucer.

Grandma's brother Luke Trainor, who was general manager of the store, also lived at The House. There were always visitors such as Uncle Barney or Dad's other brother Joe, or various

Christmas holidays at The House. Back row left to right: Uncle Luke, Pauline, Kathleen, Lizzie. Front row: Linda, Grandma

relatives of Grandma's. Like Mum, Uncle Luke's wife Kit couldn't
stand Yass, or more likely Grandma, and lived in Sydney. Pauline,
their daughter, who was devoted to her father, often came to stay
at The House. Pauline and I would rush into each other's arms
when she arrived; half an hour later we would have to be forcibly
separated because we were fighting so violently.

Pauline had long, pale golden hair and glasses. She was
supposed to be very religious and she did eventually become a
nun.

Pauline came up with a new idea for self-denial. 'If you have a
piece of cake or some lollies,' she said, 'you should plant it in the
garden for the angels to eat.' This apparently kept them going.
We fed the angels for a couple of days. The important thing was
not to look back, Pauline told me, because angels didn't like to be
seen.

I had just dutifully buried a piece of my cake under the Isabella
grapevine down the back yard and gone off when something
inspired me to return. I found the angel halfway through my
cake; it was Pauline. In the course of the fight that followed, I
knocked her glasses off, so I was the one who ended up in
trouble.

Pauline and I adored the shop, and spent a lot of time in there
on Sunday afternoons. The door from The House to the shop was
left open and we would disappear into the grocery department.
We liked the biscuit section best. We knew we weren't allowed to
eat them, but we couldn't resist the lure of their sweetness. We
opened the different tins. Arnott's iced vo-vos were our
favourites; we crept in, filled our pockets with biscuits, then
sneaked out again.

One Sunday, Pauline felt daring. Having seen a tin of iced vo-
vos on the top shelf, she climbed up a ladder to reach them. She
was stretching out her hand to the tin when she dislodged the
whole shelf. Tin after tin came down on her as she fell off the ladder in fright.

Uncle Luke was in the office catching up on some work and
heard the clatter. He read us a lecture about stealing biscuits,
then let us go. But it was the end of our Sunday afternoon
expeditions into the shop.

Much later, I spent weekends in Sydney with Pauline and her

mother at Waverley. Auntie Kit was full of complaints. She said Pauline was in the habit of bringing home old men whom she found in the street for a cup of tea. She would discover Pauline in the kitchen giving tea and biscuits to any old derelict because he reminded her of her father, who was still living in the country.

The last time I stayed a weekend with Pauline at Waverley, I woke up on the Saturday morning to find her opening all the drawers of a big cedar chest of drawers. I asked her what she was doing.

'I pray every night that God will give me a baby brother or sister.' She was looking for a baby brother or sister in the chest of drawers.

Pauline became a nurse, then a nursing sister and eventually a nun. She ended up working in an old men's home, where she was very much beloved by the elderly patients. They undoubtedly all reminded her of Daddy.

Mrs Reid, a friend of Annie's, gave me a kitten for a present. I was overjoyed, but I wasn't game enough to take it without asking Grandma first. My throat went dry as I tried to stammer out my request.

'Yes,' came the gruff reply. Grandma had said yes! I could keep the kitten. And what a patient kitten it turned out to be. I dressed it in doll's clothes; its bed was a wooden box with minute sheets and blankets. I took the kitten to school to show Sister Dominic, who usually endured any sort of nonsense from me. Sister Dominic took one look at the kitten dressed in a doll's nightshirt and exploded.

'Take that cat home immediately,' she ordered. Crestfallen, I obeyed.

I discovered I loved mice as well as cats. At the bottom of an old concrete tub, so deep I had to climb into it, I found a shivering, drenched mouse. I rescued it and installed it in a house, a box lined with cotton wool with a few holes for it to breathe through. The mouse soon recovered and its fur grew glossy. I thought I had a pet mouse for life, but three days later it gnawed its way out of the box and escaped. I was disgusted.

The box came from a thrilling room at the shop that held all kinds of delightful boxes; boxes for shirts and corsets, boxes filled with the empty spools from silk ribbons. Any sort of box you wanted could be found in that room. I was allowed free run of the box room, so I had a constant supply of beautiful boxes.

Grandma's shop, an old-fashioned country store, sold anything and everything. It had a millinery department with a milliner to make up women's hats, a men's department with men's clothes, a boots and shoes department, and a drapery department, as well as the fully stocked grocery section.

The room above the shop that had been turned into a dormitory for the Coen boys when they were growing up was now full of disused stock; another place I liked investigating.

Pauline and I loved playing games among Harry West's bags of wheat and chaff in the shed at the back of the store. He was always yelling at us to get down, because he was frightened the bags might fall on us. The bags had a lovely smell of wheat.

There were still plenty of mice in the store, despite Harry's stray cats. This mice plague led to another mouse story (not as pleasant as the previous one).

I had been reading about making garments out of skin and I decided to make something out of mouse skins. I asked Harry to save me some mice. Harry gave me a few dead ones, which I proceeded to skin with some sort of sharp instrument – an awful job. I pinned the skins to a piece of wood, intending to cure them and make myself a pair of nice mouse-skin gloves.

About halfway through the third mouse, I suddenly felt sick; I couldn't go on with the skinning. I showed Annie the hapless victims and she was alarmed in case I caught some disease from handling mice. In the end she laughed and told me to bury the lot of them. I gave the mice a proper funeral. The mangled bodies were placed in the inevitable box from the box room lined with cotton wool, which I took down to the garden. I made a grave with flowers on it and said a few prayers over the box before I covered it with earth.

The grain shed also housed the phaeton, a horse-drawn carriage with seats facing each other. I felt very rich and proud, going for rides in the family phaeton.

My first sight of Canberra was from the phaeton. Grandma took a party of us – the aunts, Annie and me – to see how the new city was growing. The forty-odd-mile drive took us most of the morning. Canberra wasn't much; a few suburbs had been named;

but even so, it was easy to get lost. We seemed to spend hours driving round Canberra in circles.

The House was fascinating. A narrow verandah with iron lace faced onto the street; the front door was just inside this verandah. Our friends could come into the house at any hour, for the front door was never locked, except when Annie placed the key inside at about twelve o'clock each night. The rest of the time, the key was in the door.

Through the front door was the hall, eight to ten feet wide, with a cedar hallstand. Grandma's house was full of cedar furniture. The hallstand held walking sticks, Grandma's ebony cane and men's hats. These were mainly made of felt, though occasionally Dad or Uncle Luke wore a straw hat.

The drawing room was off to the right of the hall. Past the drawing room door was a long cedar sofa covered with stiff, black horsehair. If visitors arrived at The House, instead of showing them into the drawing room, Annie would ask them to sit on the sofa while she fetched whomever they wanted to see. The hall was a kind of waiting room.

Dad's brother, Frank Coen, had been a champion rower for St John's College at the University of Sydney, and his oars were hung up along the hall. Perched on top of the oars was a little doll, a mascot, ten inches high, dressed in a tartan skirt. It maddened me that I couldn't have this doll, but Frank's name was sacred and I knew there was no way I would ever be able to have it.

The walls were painted white and there was linoleum covered with mats on the floor. Carpet wasn't laid through the house until much later.

The drawing room was used constantly. Afternoon tea was served there, carried in by Annie on a tray from the kitchen. Cards were played there every night after the family rosary had been said. The room was full of different-sized chairs, large grandfather chairs for the men, smaller grandmother chairs for the women and assorted other armchairs. Over the fireplace was a print by Elisabeth Vigée-Le Brun which I adored, a self-portrait of the artist with her small daughter.

Auntie Molly's piano was in one corner of the drawing room

and the other held a large rosewood cabinet, Frank's special present to his mother before he went off to war – a wind-up gramophone. This miraculous invention delighted everyone. Records of Caruso, Melba, the Irish tenor John McCormack and Italian singer Galli-Curci would be played over and over. 'Lo, Hear the Gentle Lark' sang their favourite, Galli-Curci, her high voice soaring like a bird. I entertained Annie for hours in the kitchen with my own rendition of 'Lo, Hear the Gentle Lark'.

On the other side of the hall was Grandma's bedroom. It had a dressing table with a bracket on either side to hold candles at night and a marble-topped washstand with a jug and basin on it. The bed was heavy with white linen. The bedspread was beautifully embroidered with white thread and the two pillow cases had 'M' on one and 'C' on the other: her husband Michael Coen's initials. Grandma did the embroidery herself.

Her children were born in this bed and Grandpa Coen died in it. Gentle Auntie Molly was so upset when her father died that she couldn't bear to walk past the bedroom and had to go out by the back of the house.

The next room to the left down the hall was the dining room. A portrait of Napoleon hung at one end and at the other was an oval-shaped, life-sized photograph of Father John Alphonsus, Dad's stepbrother, the Passionist priest. John Alphonsus had a reputation for speaking powerful sermons. Dressed in the black robes of the Passionists with the Sacred Heart attached, even his photograph was intimidating enough. The dining room was dominated by the portraits of these men.

The cedar sideboard in the dining room was the one from which I stole the Lent chocolates. It had a design of oak leaves and acorns carved across the back.

Three meals a day were served in the dining room. The dining room table had so many leaves it could easily sit sixteen and there never seemed to be fewer than twelve at the table. When everyone was assembled, Annie would be summoned from the kitchen by the sound of a gong. If Annie didn't hear the gong, Auntie Linda wildly rang a little brass bell until Annie appeared with the food.

The tablecloth and serviettes were of white Irish linen, the serviettes kept in rings with our numbers on them, one, two,

three, round the table, like a school. One of my jobs was to help
set the table for Annie before each meal. I had to get the salt and
pepper shakers out of the cedar sideboard, then put them back
again when the meal was over. They could never be left out
between meals. The dinner service was white French china. I
remember Grandma sitting at the head of the table carving a roast
on a large plate with a saucer on the side into which the gravy ran.
I loved the gravy from roast beef and Grandma always gave me a
spoonful as she was carving.

A vessel for making soda water stood on the window ledge in
the dining room; because the pisé walls were so thick, the
window ledges were very wide. The soda siphon consisted of two
circular-shaped vessels on top of each other with metallic criss-
crossing; it produced a week's supply of soda water at a time.
Annie used to make delicious lemon squash from real lemons.
The squash went at the bottom of the glass and then it was filled
up with soda water from the siphon.

Auntie Lizzie made wine from the mulberries on the trees out
the back. The mulberry wine was alcoholic with quite a kick to it
but, in keeping with the rest of her secretiveness, Lizzie wouldn't
say how she made it.

Leading off the dining room to the left was Kathleen's
bedroom which she shared with Molly until Molly entered the
convent. This was the room with the painting of the lady and the
lily which I had copied. I slept in Kath's room sometimes.
Kathleen divided the double bed into two with pillows down the
middle. I was not on any account to roll over the pillows onto
Kathleen's side of the bed.

Mostly, however, I slept in one of the two bedrooms off the
drawing room. These bedrooms could be entered from the
drawing room or from the hall and they opened onto the back
verandah that ran along two sides of the house. The shop made
up the third side of the house and a second dining room the
fourth side, so a courtyard was formed. A narrow staircase led
from the courtyard up to the storeroom.

The kitchen was down the end of the verandah. It had wooden
cupboards along the wall – the top half of the cupboards had
sliding glass doors – a large wooden table on which Annie
prepared the food and which she scrubbed down spotless every

The wisteria vine at The House

night with sand soap, and another table next to the black fuel stove.

Washing up was enormous and never-ending. Annie's hands were always red. She washed and we children helped by drying. First she had to fill the tin basin with cold water to rinse the dishes, then they were washed in water heated on the stove and put to drain on the wooden sink before we dried them.

Every spring, the courtyard was filled with a warm, sweet smell and a mass of mauve flowers. An old wisteria vine that must have been forty feet long grew up a pole and twined the length of the verandah under the eaves. Snapdragons, columbines and other annuals grew in the garden beds.

A swing had been put in the courtyard when my father and his sisters and brothers were children. It was shaped like a boat and two children could climb and sit facing each other as they swung; an infinite delight.

The courtyard had wooden seats with wrought-iron ends and a white, marble-topped round table on a wrought-iron base. There was also a cage full of native finches and canaries. Linda bred canaries. She would put the birds and their nest into cages that she hung up high, near the roof. I had to climb onto a chair to see the canaries sitting on a hatch of eggs.

On special occasions, afternoon tea was served in the garden. Often Grandma was too busy in the shop to attend, so one of the aunts would preside. Tea was poured from a tall silver pot with another little one under it to keep hot water in.

An amazing orange tree grew in the courtyard. It was amazing because no one ever grew orange trees in Yass; they never survived the winter. My grandfather had sunk a well in the courtyard as a water supply for the house and to have extra water on hand if the shop caught fire. After he died, Grandma decided to fill the well in, being worried that young children would fall into it. One of my uncles planted an orange pip in the soil where the well had been. The courtyard was protected, no frosts reached it and so the orange tree grew.

On full moon summer nights I used to sit out in the courtyard reading. The stars and the moon were bright in the country anyway, but moonlight seemed to specially congregate in the protected square of the courtyard. I would read a whole book by moonlight some nights.

A long passageway led from the courtyard through to the laundries and past the mangle where I once caught my hand, a painful experience, and on past the big bathroom with the oversized tub to the outside toilet. Chamber pots were kept under the beds during the night. In the morning Annie had to empty them all into the slop bucket, then lug the bucket down to the outside toilet; the passageway ended in the back yard that ran down to a creek.

All summer long, the back yard was full of pungent-smelling yellow broom and the gnarled, black-stemmed Isabella grape-vine, its fresh green leaves twining everywhere, was covered with smallish black grapes that had a blue bloom on them. Whenever I smell yellow broom, I think of Isabella grapes.

A persimmon tree grew in the back yard. The luscious orange fruits squirted over my face when I bit into them and licked up the stray orange drops from my chin with my tongue.

In the courtyard of The House. Left to right: Lizzie, Kathleen (on pony), Frank, Evangelista, Grandma (at table), Joe, Molly, Linda (seated), Ina, Cocky, Trix (seated), Uncle Luke, Barney

Uncle Luke and Aunt Lizzie in the courtyard of The House after a rare snowfall

I loved climbing the mulberry tree when the mulberries were ripe; somehow the fruit managed to stain not just my teeth, but my arms, my legs and even my clothes. The mulberry tree·was also good for feeding silkworms, fat white grubs I kept in a box, waiting patiently until they turned into cocoons that could be spun into real silk.

In the netted fowl run lived a turkey gobbler, a ferocious bird that fascinated and terrified me at the same time. I would edge up to watch the turkey spread its wings like a peacock, then flee from the awful, gobbling noise that suddenly issued from its swelling throat, with the flaps of red, coarse skin hanging off, as if its neck was inside out. Besides, if I lingered too long, the turkey would peck.

At the bottom of the back yard, on the other side of the fence, lived a woman and her brother. The woman was not quite right in the head, everyone said. Her days were spent endlessly raking up leaves. She wasn't gardening; there was no garden, their yard was a wilderness. If I sneaked along the fence I could hear her talking to herself. Sometimes she had a scythe and was cutting the grass. One day I crept as close as I could to hear what she was saying. As she swung furiously at the grass, she was singing to herself, 'Old mother Coen and her college-bred brats.'

*

The food was one of the things I liked best about The House. I thought it was much better at Grandma's than at home. Annie did a lot of the cooking, but on special occasions Grandma either supervised or cooked herself.

There was always a huge soup tureen on the stove, which held broth made with everything. The beef soup was particularly good. It was made from shins of beef, which the butcher saved specially for Grandma.

Auntie Lizzie made French pastry; it was the only thing she ever cooked. I used to beg her for the recipe, but it was another of Lizzie's secrets. I think it came out of the *Goulburn Cookery Book*. After the pastry was made it was placed in the safe on the verandah to cool; there was never a refrigerator in The House. Then it was taken out, rolled, folded up, put back in the safe again before being shaped into small and large tartlets or cheese straws with cayenne pepper sprinkled on them. Lizzie's pastries were delicious.

At Christmas time, Grandma made cakes and puddings which she sent to members of the family. The mixture was stirred in the tin baths used for washing children. Grandma made her puddings twelve at a time. The baker put them in his oven for her after the bread was done, as the bakery was only a few doors down the street.

Grandma also made trifle at Christmas, New Year, Easter and any other celebrations. I haven't tasted trifle like it since. The sponge cake was kept until it reached the right degree of staleness, then soaked overnight in sherry. Next morning, a layer of apricot jam was spread over it. A thick, creamy custard made with eggs and a peach leaf for flavour was cooked in a double boiler; when it had cooled the custard was poured over the cake.

Brilliant red and green jelly for the top of the trifle was prepared next. I had the job of peeling the Jordan almonds. They had been allowed to stand in hot water first, so the skins came off easily. Whipped cream covered the custard and the jelly was placed in a pattern over the top of that. The almonds, cut in half lengthways, were put all over the whipped cream and jelly.

Pauline was staying with us one Christmas. When Annie went to bring in the trifle for dessert, commotion came from the kitchen. Someone, Annie said, had eaten the jelly off the top of the trifle. I can't remember if Pauline confessed voluntarily or if Annie forced it out of her, but a lengthy scene with copious tears followed in the kitchen after dinner.

Grandma worked in the store every day except Sunday. She loved holding court there, sitting up in the dress materials department with her crocheting. Grandma's crocheting was never out of her hands.

Linda did tatting, making little lace edgings to go around handkerchiefs and collars. Lizzie didn't sew. She preferred tending her chrysanthemums.

Lizzie liked arranging flowers. Everywhere in the house, particularly on the sideboard dressers, Lizzie filled vases with little mixed bunches of flowers. I would have liked to help her, but she insisted on arranging the flowers herself, taking half the day to do it. That was Lizzie's contribution to the housework.

I feel I ought to pay special tribute to Annie. She worked very hard for very little money, loved my grandmother and the family and thought The House was her home.

Annie's mother died when she was little. Her father kept the two boys but put Annie and her two sisters in an orphanage run by nuns. Although he married again, he left his daughters there. Grandma, who always knew all the nuns, got Annie from this convent.

Annie and I were fast friends before I came to live at Grandma's. When I broke my wrist, she came to see me with a threepenny bag of halfpenny lollies. It contained a jelly mouse dipped in chocolate and covered in hundreds and thousands, a crocodile made of tough pale lemon marshmallow, a liquorice stick. Annie loved sweets as much as I did. It was the beginning of a great bond between us. Together we sneaked lumps of sugar, almonds and fancy biscuits. Annie would save me the cake dish after she made the cake for afternoon tea. When I came to live at The House I adopted Annie, in a way. I had no idea I was going to live with my grandmother for so long. I never stopped missing my mother and loved getting her letters, but Annie became my new, everlasting friend.

I particularly missed my mother at night in my small, den-like room. As soon as I was in bed and Annie took the candle away, the nightmares began. Strange faces appeared and wouldn't stay still; the eyes grew bigger and rolled in their sockets, lips swelled back from the teeth, enveloping the whole face and noses grew longer and longer. I would scream out and Annie would come and comfort me.

I spent a great deal of time with Annie in the kitchen. She sang as she did the dishes and I used to dry up for her. Annie had a large repertoire of sad songs.

Put your head on my shoulder, Daddy, and turn my face to the west,
It's just the hour the sun goes down, the hour that mother loved best.

I wept through this song about the widowed father and his child; I relished the pathos of every line.

'Just for the sake of society baby was left all alone,' another of Annie's songs began. Baby played with matches while the careless parents danced the night away at a ball and house and baby were burnt to a cinder.

Annie had jet-black, woolly hair of which she was very proud. The mass of tight curls was her crowning glory; if you pulled one out it snapped back into place.

Annie's real name was Hannah Harriet Allman. We used to tease her by calling her 'Annah, 'Arriet Hallman, at which she laughed as much as we did. A favourite joke was to ask Annie what her name was. 'Allman,' she would say. 'All man and no woman,' and would go into peals of laughter.

Annie cared for anyone who was sick in The House. When I had whooping cough and I coughed all night, I was banished from the rest of the house to sleep by Annie's side. She stayed up looking after me and giving me medicine.

Annie was seventeen when she came to work for Grandma; she would have been in her early twenties when I first knew her. She did a tremendous amount, I don't know how she got through it all. She was a maid of all work, or, rather, a slave. Linda and Lizzie were meant to help her, which meant that they flicked a feather duster around and arranged flowers. Annie did the real work.

Every morning at six, she got up and lit the old black fuel stove in the kitchen. She put the big black kettles on to boil so she could make morning tea and she filled the fountain, the large drum with the small tap in front that kept hot water on the stove during the day. She took a cup of tea in to my grandmother before carrying a tray of cups and saucers round to the various other residents of The House. She didn't just make a cup of tea; with it were very thin slices of bread and butter.

Then she cooked breakfast, which also had to be carried on trays from the kitchen along the verandah to the dining room. After breakfast the table had to be cleared and the washing up done.

The bedrooms were next. Annie emptied the chamber pots into a bucket and filled the china water jugs that stood on the marble-topped stands.

The rest of her day consisted of dusting and sweeping, bringing in the wood, cooking dinner in the middle of the day, washing up, running messages, making a cake for afternoon tea, going to the butcher's, getting tea, washing up again. Visitors helped with the washing up and children ran messages for her.

Every night, she scrubbed the wooden tables in the kitchen, once a week she whitewashed the hearth. Once a week, too, she did the ironing with flat irons kept on the stove.

When she had washed up after tea, Annie went down the street to visit friends, but was back at The House by ten to make supper. Then she read or sewed until past midnight. She boasted that she never went to bed one day and got up the next like other people; she always went to bed on the same day as she got up.

Annie referred to Grandma, the aunts or the rest of the family as 'them'. She and I spent a deal of our time in the kitchen criticising 'them'.

We also gossiped about the town. Annie knew every piece of news or snippet of scandal around. She finished off every story with the injunction, 'But don't tell *them*'.

Despite the criticism, Annie was devoted to the family and in awe of most of 'them'. She was particularly devoted to my grandmother and Kathleen; Kathleen used to say Annie had replaced their own little sister, Annie, who died of diphtheria. Annie didn't like the aunts so much, because they tried to put her down.

Annie had odd tastes in food. 'I haven't eaten a vegetable in my life,' she used to say proudly. 'Only tomatoes.' This was true; she didn't eat green vegetables, but she loved fruit of any kind. She ate no meat except chicken off the breast. Annie's diet for nearly eighty years consisted of bread and butter, tea, cake and lollies, mainly chocolate. She was very healthy. Only once did she spend a day in bed, after she had been to the dentist to have all her teeth out. The next day she was up and back at work.

Dad's brother, Uncle Barney, a doctor, sometimes lived at The House. Barney had been lecturing in medicine at Sydney University and demonstrating anatomy to the students until a widowed lady became enamoured of him and pursued him voraciously, even going to his lectures. Eventually he gave in and their engagement was announced.

His impending marriage, however, was too much for Barney; he had a nervous breakdown which left him mildly dotty, though not objectionable in any way. He spent a lot of time with the Aborigines at 'the blacks' camp' where he was very popular. He sat around talking to the Aborigines all day, wrote out prescriptions for any pills they needed. He was always an excellent diagnostician.

Barney proposed to Annie while he was recovering from his breakdown. He rushed into her bedroom and asked her to marry him, but Annie refused.

'We're not in the same station, Doctor Coen,' she said.

Barney was also fond of gardening; he had a vegetable garden at the back of The House. We had a favourite family story about the time my mother visited Barney and found him in his garden, fanning the lettuces to keep them cool.

As soon as I arrived at The House, Barney grabbed me and took me right down the back yard past the grapevine.

'What does two and two make?' Barney stared earnestly into my face. Barney had asked everyone in town this question.

'Four,' I answered, as they all did.

'Wrong,' said Barney, 'you've forgotten the Blessed Virgin. Two and two and the Blessed Virgin makes five.' No one ever gave Barney the answer he wanted.

Barney dragged Paddy Maguire out of Mass to ask him if he could see the Blessed Virgin in a bush at the back of the church. Paddy Maguire drank too much and he stuttered.

'You might see her, B-B-B-Barney,' Paddy stuttered, 'b-b-b-but I never will.'

When the priest said Mass, Barney would get up and join him at the altar so they said Mass together. Barney's antics became too much for Yass and he was sent down to a hospital in Sydney where he eventually recovered.

However, although he was quite well again, Barney didn't wish to leave the hospital. He stayed on and spent the rest of his life caring for patients at the asylum.

Religion entered very much into life at The House. The rosary was said every evening and grace before and after meals. The nuns were always in and out of the house because the convent was so near. Grandma went to Mass every morning at six, winter and summer, until old age prevented her.

Sundays meant Mass in the morning and Benediction in the evening. Like the convent, the church was only a short distance from The House. Everyone dressed up for Mass. Going to church was the social event of the week, not just for the Catholics, either. Yass was full of people setting out for church on Sunday mornings.

We filled a whole pew beside Grandma, majestic in her best Sunday black dress embroidered with jet beads.

The first thing I remember about Mass was the tinkling of the bell at the consecration.

'Dinner's ready,' I announced.

They also handed round a silver plate filled with coins. I had to part with my copper penny and grabbed up a handful of silver coins in return.

Sunday dinner was the meal of the week at Grandma's, roast fowl and boiling bacon followed by trifle. After a meal like that, particularly in the summer heat, there wasn't much to do except sleep. The uncles and aunts, lulled by the drone of blowflies buzzing against the windows, dozed in the deep drawing room chairs or retired to their bedrooms. In winter they nodded off in front of the drawing room fire. After helping Annie with the dishes, if I wasn't stealing biscuits with Pauline I would pore over the pictures in one of the big books kept on the circular drawing room table. A compendium of art masterpieces of the world was the best. I never tired of looking at Millet's 'First Sermon', Watts' 'Hope, the Blind Girl' or the rounded figures of Rubens and many others.

Benediction was at seven. I liked Benediction, especially the smell of the incense and the music.

The family rosary was recited every night after tea. Grandma wouldn't let anyone out of the house until it had been said. When my father came out of the army and was living at The House, he was forever trying to escape up to the Soldiers' Club without saying the rosary.

'King,' Grandma would say, 'We're going to say the rosary now.'

Everyone had to join in; Annie was called from the kitchen. They knelt down in the drawing room and buried their heads in the chairs. When I was little I disgraced myself by climbing onto the hump of Grandma's back while the rosary was in progress.

Grandma never mentioned Grandfather. Perhaps it was such a shock to her that he had died so young, but she never alluded to him in any way except at rosary.

Grandma said an extra prayer before and after the rosary itself. In these prayers she referred to someone as 'your servant Michael'; this was my grandfather. I had a vision of God up in heaven being waited on by Michael Coen, who had the job of servant.

The Mercy nuns at Yass and the priests all fussed over Grandma because of her daughters being in the convent. Priests often visited The House for a meal, or dropped in for a game of cards after tea. The Sacred Heart being a closed order, Trix and Evangelista were not allowed out, but Ina and Molly in the Convent of Mercy used to come back to Yass every school holidays and stay with the nuns in the Yass convent. Most of their days were spent with us at The House, which added to the permeating religious atmosphere.

The girls enjoyed teaching in convent schools; Grandma herself had been a teacher. By entering the convent, Grandma's daughters were able to lead full and relatively independent lives. The alternative of spinsterhood in a country town might not have been nearly so interesting.

Ina became head of an orphanage at Goulburn, Trix and Evangelista became Reverend Mothers in the Sacred Heart order. As for Molly, music was the only thing that mattered to her and as long she had music, Molly was happy.

I doubt if they had much time to question their vocations, though Trix did slip up once when my mother was visiting her. 'Wouldn't it be dreadful, Bessie,' Trix whispered, 'if it was all a have?' Then she blessed herself and scuttled into the chapel.

I was so impressed by this religiousness that I decided I was going to be a saint. I asked Annie to wake me every morning in time for six o'clock Mass. When she did I usually abused her, told her she was cruel for waking me and went back to sleep. In summer I managed to make Mass about once a month but in winter it was pitch dark at six o'clock and I gave up being a saint.

The religious atmosphere of The House, once accepted, seemed quite natural. It was just the way things were.

A lame Aboriginal named Benji used to walk to Mass from the blacks' camp on the other side of town. He walked five miles in the cold and dark every day in winter. He never dared to come up the front of the church but knelt at the very back, only limping up to the altar to receive Holy Communion and then retreating to the farthest back pew again afterwards.

The church held a mission with a stall that sold holy cards, rosary beads and plaster statues. Mrs Mitchell, a friend of Grandma's who was staying at The House, gave me a 10s note and told me to buy her some rosary beads that cost between 6s and 8s. I asked at the stall if they had any rosary beads for 3d. They had some cheap ones for children; obviously not the beads Mrs Mitchell had in mind. I bought them and pocketed the change, which she had said I could keep. Annie laughed and laughed when I told her the story. She didn't know whether to make me take them back and buy Mrs Mitchell some proper beads.

No, I insisted. Mrs Mitchell hadn't said anything. She seemed to like her new beads. I think she was too stunned to complain.

Another time the Red Cross was raising funds and a woman came in from the country with a beautifully dressed rag doll to be raffled. I was supposed to do the raffling. I got on well with the big staff at Coen's, so I was asked to take the tickets around the store and sell them. The doll had a pretty face and soft, curly

brown hair. Somehow, I thought, I must win the raffle. I had to
have this doll.

The tickets were 3d each. I dutifully gave out the little bits of
numbered paper and asked everyone to write names and
addresses on the other halves. I don't remember anything more.

I was asked for the tickets, I didn't have them. I was asked for
the money, I didn't have it either. I was asked for the doll, I vanished with the doll.

I crept back into the drawing room as Grandma was saying, 'I'll
write you a cheque,' and reaching into her pocket. Grandma
always had a very capacious pocket in her voluminous black
outfits. She drew out a fountain pen and cheque book. The
cheque was for tickets and doll. The doll was mine.

Sex was never discussed but, despite the secrecy at Grandma's,
I found out the facts of life quite young. After school, a girl whose
parents owned an hotel sat a group of us in a buggy out the back
of the hotel and proceeded to tell us 'what grown-ups do'. I was
astonished. Could this be going on behind the bedroom doors at
The House? It didn't seem possible. The answer, I decided, was
clear. Catholics didn't do it, only Protestants.

From then on, I rather despised adults for their secret life and
being hypocritical enough to hide such things from children.

Scornfully I told Pauline what grown-ups did. Pauline told her
father, Uncle Luke, who told Dad and Dad told Mum. It took
Mum forty years to mention the episode to me. I tried to get out
of Mum what the others had told her I said, but Mum's memory
only produced a garbled version that made no sense.

A little red-haired boy at the Yass school was always offering to
show us girls something special, on condition we showed him
something in return. None of the girls ever accepted, but he was
perpetually eager to oblige.

Annie, who had come straight from a Catholic convent into
Grandma's employ at The House, was in total ignorance of the
facts of life for some time. Her discovery of sex also brought a
degree of disillusionment.

Annie loved the Royal family. She had coloured photos and
calendar portraits cut from women's magazines stuck up around
the kitchen.

I was staying at Yass for the holidays when I was about sixteen.

Yet another mission was on at church. Annie and I were in the kitchen after Mass, joking about the severity of the sermon.

'The priest shouldn't have so much to say,' Annie grumbled. 'After all, he came into the world just like everyone. His parents did it, same as everybody's else's.' She laughed.

'Everybody does it, don't they?' she quizzed me, suddenly serious.

'Yes,' I answered her, 'everybody.' By this time I was fully aware of the sad truth that Catholics were as much into sex as the rest of the world. Annie laughed again.

'Even the King and Queen,' she went on. Annie glanced up at the picture on the kitchen wall and sighed sadly.

'Mind you, I never thought the same of them,' she added.

There was no swearing or loose talk at The House, but cards were played. Card playing was a real ritual. At about eight o'clock every night after the rosary, the game began. Grandma and the aunts played solo, poker, five hundred and bridge; much later contract bridge came in. Annie and her friends played euchre and gin rummy and moved on to poker but not bridge.

Annie used to become very wrought up when she played cards. She played for almost nothing, but couldn't bear the thought of losing even her sixpenny stakes.

I lived with Grandma for nearly a year, which was why I became so familiar with The House and its inhabitants, and so fond of them. Grandma wanted to keep me altogether, but eventually, about 1919, Mum sent for me. I always loved the country and hated the city and I continued to come back to Yass for my holidays.

Every school holidays Mum would take me into Central and put me in the ladies' compartment of the train to Yass. Every train had a compartment for women only. Mum would tell the guard and anyone else in the carriage to look after me, and off I set with a packed lunch to eat on the way.

Annie used to make the most marvellous lunch boxes for me to take back on the train: little sandwiches, cut up into quarters and tiny iced cakes. Annie's packed lunches were always a consolation, I felt, for coming back to the city.

Kath, the only one of Grandma's daughters who didn't become

a nun, would have liked to enter the convent, but the others said it was her duty to stay home and look after her mother. Despite her hankering for the religious life, Kath enjoyed not being in the convent, too. She loved playing cards, placing the odd bet on the horses and motoring.

One Christmas holiday when I was ten and getting ready to go back to school, Kath asked me, 'Can you keep a secret?'

'Yes,' I answered eagerly.

'Well,' she went on, 'it's a great secret and you mustn't tell anyone.'

'No.' I was overcome with curiosity. 'I promise.'

'Well,' she said, 'Mama is going to buy me a motor car. When you come back for your next holidays, I'll be able to take you for picnics in the bush in it.'

'A car!' I couldn't believe it. A car was really something.

I didn't breathe a word to anyone all term. Filled with anticipation, I arrived for my next holiday at Yass. There was the car: an early, open Dodge with side flaps that had to be fastened down when the roof came off.

Sitting up very straight behind the wheel in kid driving gloves, her hat securely fastened with a hat pin, Kath motored us about the countryside. We also visited various properties round Yass and went for picnics.

Kathleen's secret outside The House

Picnics lasted all day. We started off very early in the morning, Kath, me, the aunts, Grandma and any stray cousins or odd uncles who were staying at The House.

There were always fights between Lizzie and Linda as to who was to sit in the front seat with Kath. Usually Lizzie beat Linda by going out an hour early and settling herself down in the front seat. Once she was installed, nothing could move her. Kathleen would get quite annoyed.

'Next time, auntie,' she would say, 'you must let Linda sit in the front.' But it was impossible to win with Lizzie. Next time, she would still be in position before anyone else, ignoring all pleas to change places.

At the picnic site, a white tablecloth would be spread out on the ground, then the food was produced: cold chicken, mixed sandwiches, cakes. The people at The House were good providers; or rather, Annie provided well for them.

We often went to Mount Bowning. It was the highest spot in the area, rising abruptly out of the plains; you could see for miles from the top. It was eight miles out of Yass, a shortish trip in the car, but much, much longer in the phaeton or the buggy. It used to be our favourite picnic spot, until one expedition was marred by an unfortunate incident.

Uncle Luke was with us this time, but as lunch was being laid out, he disappeared. He had been seized by some trouble with his bowels and forced to commune at length with nature. But, being well bred, he didn't want to admit to his indisposition in the company of ladies, nor to have the results discovered in any after-lunch wanderings.

'Don't go up behind the rocks,' he pronounced solemnly upon his return.

'Why not, Uncle Luke?' we asked innocently.

'Why not?' Uncle Luke looked disconcerted for a moment, then hit upon a handy subterfuge. 'There's a dead Chinaman up there, that's why not,' he said.

We were flabbergasted; a dead Chinaman! The picnic was hastily packed up. We never felt the same about picnics at Mount Bowning after that.

Driving around the countryside was especially pretty in October and November with the lilac out. Mrs Magennis had over

Isobel McDonagh

a hundred lilac bushes growing on her property, the colours ranging from palest mauve to dark, smoky amethyst. Peonies of every colour and type also flourished, and big opium poppies grew wild in some gardens.

Kathleen's best friend at school was Isobel McDonagh; she and Kathleen stayed close after they left school. Isobel often used to come and stay with Kathleen at Yass. She was beautiful and charming with a great sense of humour, and her career as an actress was about to begin under the stage name of Marie Lorraine. Although she was quite grown up, I loved being with Isobel. She enjoyed fun and games so much that she was like a child herself.

Isobel was the oldest of seven children, five girls and two boys. The three oldest girls were always mad about the movies and were already planning to make their own feature film in which Isobel would star. Paulette, the second oldest, would write and direct, while Phyllis, the third, was to be art director. Kath lent Isobel a lovely sequinned evening dress she bought in Paris to wear in one of their films.

But at this time in Yass, World War I had just finished and an air force hero was passing through town. He fell very much in love with Isobel. With her vivacious teasing manner, Isobel didn't take him too seriously, but the air force hero was invited up to

The House for tea and to play cards afterwards with her and Kathleen.

Before he arrived, Isobel took me down to the laundry at the back of the house. She showed me how to cut up a cake of Sunlight soap into little squares and together we rolled the little cubes of soap in flour to look like icing sugar. Kathleen was renowned for her home-made sweets and at cards that night a dish of Kathleen's home-made marshmallows appeared – Isobel's and my efforts from the afternoon.

The air force hero was invited to try one of Kathleen's special sweets and accepted eagerly. His smile of anticipation turned to horror as he bit into the soap. The air force hero jumped back from the table to spit out a mouthful of suds. He did *not* appreciate our joke, and that was the end of that romance.

The Irish landowner families around Yass were also fond of practical jokes. A large family of boys particularly loved them. Anyone who sat down to dinner at that property was likely to have a packet of firecrackers explode under the chair. The English jackeroos who regularly turned up to work there were frequently the butts of their humour. The boys filled the bed of one young Englishman with yabbies and when he leaped out of bed yelling, they told him they were only Australian fleas and that he shouldn't be so soft.

John, the second eldest of these Irish boys, was in love with Kathleen. Kathleen had great personality, but she was very religious and John was far too terrified to approach her. He was said to have offered a reward of £5 to anyone who would kiss Kath Coen, probably thinking that, if someone else could manage to kiss her, it might make things easier for him. But no one did, and his love remained unrequited.

John was terribly nervous about almost everything. He stuttered badly too, but he was dying for an adventure of some sort. Their father made the boys work for almost nothing; he never paid them a proper wage, though occasionally he handed out some pocket money. John saved his up until he had enough to

Isobel McDonagh in a still from a film, wearing the sequinned dress from Paris belonging to Kathleen

take a trip to Goulburn. On a Saturday afternoon, he set out on his adventure. He got himself into the train at Binalong and sat up in the carriage, waiting for life to begin.

It began a lot sooner than he had bargained for. At Yass, the next stop, about twenty miles from Binalong, his father stormed into the carriage and proceeded to publicly berate his son for spending his money in such a manner.

John's nerves were so affected by this attack that even as an old man, whenever he came down to Sydney (he never owned a car), he had to hide in the lavatory until the train passed well out of Yass.

The old father died eventually. The sons, including John, were left various properties. John had not only failed to win Kathleen but stayed a bachelor all his days. He was, however, determined to build himself a beautiful house with his inheritance. He came up to Anthony Horderns in Sydney to buy the furniture for his new residence. He was most impressed by a splendid long dining table and searched Hordern's until he found a handsome set of chairs, ordering twelve to go with the table.

John gave a grand dinner party to celebrate the completion of his new home. To his guests' amusement and his own embarrassment, the guests discovered he had purchased twelve commode chairs to go with his splendid dining table, unaware of their true use. Upon reflection John decided they were eminently practical. He refused to part with them and the commode chairs had pride of place in his new home.

Grandma knew all the Irish sheep station people from Yass to Binalong, as far out as Wee Jasper.

They came into town on Saturday mornings, and left the children with Grandma while they did their shopping – the children often waited at The House on the black horsehair sofa until late afternoon. When Grandfather Coen started the store, he served afternoon tea on Saturdays for all his customers in the courtyard of The House, with tea for the women and free rum for the men. No wonder his business did so well.

After he died, Saturday afternoon entertaining didn't continue on such a grand scale, but the Irish Catholics still arrived at Grandma's for afternoon tea. Annie made cakes and sandwiches and while the men went about their business the women took tea with Grandma, Kath and the aunts in the drawing room.

About five o'clock, the gentlemen, with their sandy red hair and gingery moustaches, would arrive. In those days, men on the land lived for their sheep and could hardly bear to be away from them. They would be persuaded to have a cup of tea before they headed for home, their big, moustached faces looming over the delicate china cups. Then they would round up the women and children and depart.

On Saturday night, the town was very much alive. The shops stayed open and Cooma Street was full of people. The flow of people stretched almost as far as the bridge over the Yass River and right out on the other side of town. The Salvation Army band played on a street corner, usually the one by the Hotel Royal.

I was puzzled by two women who were always part of Saturday night. They were tall and thin with white faces, bright red cheeks and lips. Although everybody wore some powder and rouge, their faces had a hectic look and their clothes, even to me, were curiously theatrical.

Annie told me they were 'ladies of the town', the town whores, a mother and daughter who lived together in a house on the hill.

Every time I came to Yass for the holidays, before I went back to Sydney, Grandma let me choose a piece of dress material from the shop for a frock. It was always exciting. I remember one Christmas seeing a piece of blue silk with rosebuds embossed on it. I coveted this particular piece of material all holidays. When the time came to choose some material, I knew already what my selection was, though I was nervous about asking for it.

'Well,' Grandma said, 'you have chosen the best piece of silk in the shop, but I suppose I must give it to you.'

So she did. I took the couple of yards home in great delight and Mum made me a frock.

I always enjoyed my stays at The House. I liked the continuity of life there; everything seemed to stay in place, to go on forever. It nearly did, too, because everybody lived to a very old age.

Linda died first in 1942. She had been a teacher at a bush school near Jerilderie in the Kelly country and when she was an old lady, just before she died, I tried to get out of her if she had ever known Ned Kelly. A dreamy look came over her face and she went into a sort of trance and talked about a big man on a big black horse. She almost had me believing she knew Ned Kelly.

Grandma died in her bed at The House in 1943. During the year before she died, Annie slept on the long sofa in the hall outside Grandma's bedroom in case she needed tending in the night. Lizzie died a year after Grandma in 1944.

The shop was sold in 1946 to Meaghers of Temora, a country firm with stores in Temora and Cootamundra. It was later resold to Fosseys, who pulled down the old store and built a new shop.

When the others died, Kath bought herself a bungalow in Meehan Street, next door but one to the Catholic church. She settled in with an assortment of furniture and treasures from The House, and what wouldn't fit she stored in her garage. Annie went to live with Kath. They became totally dependent on each other as the years went by. Molly and Ina, 'the girls', still came back to Yass every year for Christmas with Kath. Ina died in 1968.

In 1973, when she was eighty, Annie died. Kath just faded away after that, and died about three years later. Molly lived on, busily composing music at a home for retired nuns at Young. She died in 1983 aged ninety-three, the last of the women from The House.

4

A Grotesque Sense of Humour

Godmother Trix, Mother Coen

I lasted two days at the first school I went to in the city. When I came up to Sydney, Dad was still in the army, and Mum had installed herself, Jack, and now me, in a boarding house at Coogee called Villa Taormina. I was sent off to a big convent on the hill at Randwick.

During a game of chasings on the second day, I jumped out of a window. Coming from a country school where I was adored and pretty much allowed to do what I liked, I thought nothing of jumping through the window. But at this new city school, one jump and the sky fell in on me. I was seized by a strange nun, taken to the front entrance, told to ring Reverend Mother's bell. When she appeared I was to tell her what I had done. To ring Reverend Mother's bell, I had to pull a rope cord three times. The nun vanished and I was left alone in the hall with my conscience. I was paralysed with apprehension. There was no way I could bring myself to pull Reverend Mother's bell.

I stayed in the hall for what seemed like hours, though probably it was only twenty minutes. Another nun came by and asked me what I was doing there. I blurted out my tale of wrongdoing. 'I'll ring Reverend Mother's bell for you,' she announced briskly, which she promptly did, then disappeared, leaving me to my fate.

How long it took Reverend Mother to arrive I'll never know. I was out the door in a flash, running as fast as I could down the long drive. I ran all the way down the hill, down Coogee Bay Road, down another street. I didn't stop running until I was safely back with my mother at the Villa Taormina.

I told my mother what had happened and said I was never going back to school.

'That's all right,' she answered, and I didn't go back to the convent on the hill.

We moved out of the Villa Taormina into a flat at Coogee, high on the cliffs, overlooking Thompsons Bay. My mother was busy organising men to shift our belongings from the boarding house and sent Jack and me ahead with strict instructions how to find the new flat.

Jack's head was always in the clouds, or rather he had grand dreams. We walked up the hill as instructed, but instead of turning right at the top, we turned to the left. There, perched on the headland, was a magnificent mansion with sweeping gardens and a flight of steps leading up to a huge front door.

Jack was impressed. This was our new home, he insisted. Bravely we went into the grounds, up the flight of steps to the front door and Jack pulled at the knocker. Nobody came, he pulled again. This time after a pause, a maid in uniform answered the door. Jack explained that we had come to live there. The maid looked first confused then alarmed. She fetched a higher authority to deal with us. Jack again explained that we had come to live.

In fact, it was not our new home, we found out. The mansion belonged to the Wirth family of Wirth's Circus and they had a private zoo in the grounds. This was a double blow to Jack. He was bitterly disappointed, not only missing out on a mansion but a circus as well.

Our new abode was much less grand. I can clearly remember a sudden summer southerly storm battering our tiny house on the clifftops. Big waves came right up the cliffs and a piece of cliff broke away under the sea's onslaught. Down on the beach, the surf surged in as far as the Coogee Bay hotel and the tramlines were covered with sand.

I went to school at Clovelly. I had to make an enormous journey up and over a sandhill each day. I stayed at that school until we moved to Neutral Bay, where we lived in a boarding house near the water. The garden ran down to the harbour to a lit-tle sandy beach with translucent silver and rose-coloured shells along the tide mark.

Where the sand ended and the soil began I discovered a quantity of white clay. When the water was squeezed out of the clay, it could be moulded in the hands like dough. I made little baskets, cups and saucers, but chairs and tables were my speciality. I left them out in the sun until they were baked hard and furnished a doll's house with them.

Ferries were as enchanting then as they are now. 'Fairy boats' we used to call them. On hot summer nights we would board a ferry and go backwards and forwards across the harbour. The lights on the water at night, the excitement of being out late, meant that 'fairy boats' were really special.

A large gangling youth known as Beetles lived at the boarding house. He was about sixteen; they called him Beetles because he collected beetles. I was fascinated by his collection. Neatly impaled on pins in a white cardboard box were Christmas beetles of shining green and gold, beetles with elegantly long feelers. He had a marvellous collection; small beetles, large beetles, some sombre, others brilliantly coloured, butterflies that flashed like jewels. My favourite was a vivid, turquoise blue beetle with black spots.

Beetles commissioned me to bring him any beetles I found in the garden. I was so impressed by his collection that I started a small one on the side myself.

Then we moved to a large old house in Botany Street, Randwick. The house had been converted into airy flats with good marble fireplaces and the garden was easily big enough to play in. Opposite the house was a Moreton Bay fig tree, a few hundred yards down the street were sandhills and a paddock filled with boronia and other wildflowers.

I was nine, and Mum told me I was to go to a boarding school called Kincoppal, run by French nuns.

At school in Yass, Sister Loreto had insisted we be friends with the half dozen or so Aboriginal children who attended, but it was hard. They were shy and stood in a little group by themselves. I managed, at last, to make friends with one, a girl, Alice Bolger.

Alice and I were inseparable and I used to sneak biscuits and sweets from the store for her. When I left Yass, I was sad to say goodbye to her.

My first day at Kincoppal, it was raining. Mum and I caught the tram from Randwick to Taylor Square. We had intended to walk all the way to Kincoppal in Elizabeth Bay, but the rain grew heavier. It seemed much further than we thought and Mum worried I would be late on my first day.

Getting wetter and wetter, we stood at the top of William Street, wondering what to do. Another woman with a small girl was standing nearby.

'Are you going to Kincoppal?' she asked my mother.

'Yes,' my mother answered.

'There's a cab coming,' (a horse-drawn cab it was in those days) 'let's share it,' the other woman suggested. She added, 'My name is Mrs Bolger and this is my daughter Alice.'

Another Alice Bolger! I couldn't believe it. I felt immediately cheered. Perhaps going to this new school in the city wouldn't be so bad after all. The four of us got into the cab, Alice and I sitting on our mother's knees, and arrived at Kincoppal together.

Kincoppal was altogether different to any other school I had been to. It was terribly strict, but from the moment I stepped out of the cab on that rainy morning I loved it.

The school was very small, only about thirty pupils including us boarders. My aunt Kathleen from Yass had been a foundation pupil and Trix, my aunt who had entered the Sacred Heart order, was teaching there. Trix was my godmother. It was Trix who had persuaded my mother to send me to Kincoppal.

The nuns wore black habits with a white frill round the face like a pie frill. With a few exceptions like Trix and gentle, charming, big-boned Mother Percy-Dove, a Cambridge graduate who taught us English, all the nuns were French. Reverend Mother and the Mistress-General were the highest-ranking, two most-to-be-feared nuns. A summons to see Reverend Mother meant serious trouble. Every time you passed either of these nuns you had to curtsy, a slow graceful curtsy, down to the count of four, and another four beats coming up.

While they were so strict at Kincoppal, they also gave us great treats. Reverend Mother's feast day was always special. The first one took place about six weeks after I arrived. I was woken at six o'clock by three girls in fancy costumes playing musical instruments. One girl who played a violin wore a man's bell topper and swallow-tailed jacket. The second girl with a beribboned tambourine was dressed like a gypsy with a scarf tied around her head. A third had a feather boa twined about her and played a little flute. I was enchanted.

We presented Reverend Mother with what was called a 'spiritual bouquet'. Instead of flowers, it was made up of all the prayers and rosaries being offered up for Reverend Mother on her feast day. The front page of the long list was decorated by Mother Supplisson. Mother Supplisson was a tiny, rosy-cheeked French nun who taught us French and liked drawing dwarves. The spiritual bouquet was adorned with quaint little bearded men in high hats busy about their fairy affairs, scurrying around with pot plants, climbing up ladders onto window sills. There was nothing religious about them, not the slightest trace of a halo or flutter of angel's wings.

During the day, we had a picnic down on the rocks by the harbour. At night after tea I was introduced to the terrifying game of *loup*. One girl was chosen as *loup*, French for 'wolf'. She ran and hid in the garden. The rest, about twenty of us boarders, huddled together from the wolf. At our head, a girl was the shepherd guarding the flock. Another girl with her arms spread out was the dog protecting the rear.

'*Loup, loup*, where are you?' the shepherd would call out. The wolf answered with a long-drawn-out, blood-curdling howl and we shivered with fright. The shepherd had to try and catch the wolf and the wolf tried to capture one of the sheep. If the wolf snatched a sheep, that sheep became the next wolf. Creeping silently round the totally dark garden was deliciously spine-tingling, waiting for the ear-piercing screams of the sheep when the wolf did pounce was unbearable suspense. *Loup* was the most exciting game I ever played. Apparently the people who lived next door in the grand old mansion Toftmonks were so alarmed by the sounds of screaming girls in the night they sent someone in to find out what was happening at the convent.

Kincoppal was tucked away at the end of Elizabeth Bay Road in a leafy cul-de-sac behind Kings Cross and overlooking the harbour. Kincoppal House had belonged to the Hughes family,

whose two daughters Maria and Susan had become Sacred Heart nuns. When Dr John Hughes died, he left Kincoppal House and the grounds, almost a whole hillside, to the Sacré Coeur order.

'Kincoppal' was written across the wrought-iron gate between the big stone pillars at the entrance to the school. *Kincoppal* is an Irish word meaning 'horse's head'; it referred to a craggy sandstone formation that jutted out of the harbour at the bottom of the grounds.

A short, circular drive dotted with pink and white camellias swung up to Kincoppal House and round so it was possible to drive in and out without turning. In front of the house were garden beds of thickly clustered rich blue, gold and purple pansies tended by a whiskered old gardener named Mortice. The nuns lived in Kincoppal House, the school itself was in another building further down the hill.

Kincoppal House was two-storeyed and made of sandstone. It had a heavy brass-knockered front door set back in a tiled verandah that ran the width of the house. The front door opened into a wide, high-ceilinged hallway. The chequered pattern on the verandah tiles outside changed to a star-shaped design in the hall. On both sides of the hall were two rooms, known as the parlours, which had wooden- shuttered French doors leading onto the verandah. A cedar staircase led up to the second storey, where the nuns slept. The upstairs windows were also wooden-shuttered.

Pupils were never allowed in the nuns' house but one Christmas holidays when the Kincoppal nuns went over to the Rose Bay convent for a retreat, Trix asked Mum to come and look after the house for the nuns. So for three weeks, Mum, Molly, the boys and I actually lived in Kincoppal House.

At the end of our stay, Molly and King asked a few friends over and put some dance records on the gramophone. Someone complained to the nuns about it afterwards, saying it wasn't proper to hear dance music coming out of the convent. Trix was angry and scolded my mother for allowing the party. Mum, in

All the pupils of Kincoppal. Margaret Coen is in the second row, second from the left

turn, was indignant at Trix's disapproval. Trix shouldn't take it so seriously, Mum said. The children were only having fun.

. The school building was tall and narrow with about six storeys. We stepped straight from the nuns' house into the school chapel. Every morning we went to Mass in the chapel at half past seven.

After Mass we had breakfast in the refectory under the chapel, built on another level of the hill as it dropped down to the water. Because so many of the nuns were French, if we spoke at all we had to speak in French at breakfast. Conversation as such was not allowed at any meal. One girl sat behind a rostrum at the end of the refectory during the evening meal and read aloud. The school had an inexhaustible supply of novels to do with the torturing of English priests at the time of Henry VIII and Elizabeth I, the rack being their favourite torture instrument. They made grim reading and grim listening.

Above the chapel were a study and three big classrooms, and next floor up was the long dormitory, where we slept. There was another dormitory on the top floor which wasn't used much; we could see right out across the harbour to the Heads from there.

A long balcony ran the length of our dormitory. If we sneaked out on this in the evening we heard the lions roaring for their din-ner across the harbour at the zoo. We could also hear the bells of St Marks chiming on the other side of Rushcutters Bay Park at Darling Point. Darling Point was an empty hillside except for the spire of St Mark breaking the skyline and a few houses among the gum trees.

Down some steps from the refectory was a huge recreation gym area. On wet days we amused ourselves in here. Trix played the piano for us. We danced the polka round the room to tunes like 'Ta Ra Ra Boom De Ay'.

The playroom opened onto a lawn with basketball and tennis courts. When I arrived at Kincoppal, I was fascinated to see girls with hoops, wooden balls and mallets, playing croquet on the lawn. How quaint and ladylike! I had thought croquet only existed in *Alice in Wonderland*.

The playing fields at Kincoppal were like a giant paddock, with a view stretching from Garden Island round the harbour to Rushcutters Bay. At the far edge of the paddock were two grassy inclines. They were too steep for mowing, so the grass stayed green and lush. In summer they were covered with long-stemmed orange and black ixia flowers, sometimes even rare, pale green ones. On Mondays after we had eaten our lunch and before we went back into class, an Italian organ grinder used to appear on these slopes. He placed a battered hat in front of him so that we could drop our pennies in and played the organ for us. Every Monday he churned out the same tune, 'Killarney'. Very occasionally, he treated us to 'Santa Lucia', but not often.

A gate at the slopes opened onto a winding path through bush. The path wound down cliffs twenty to thirty feet high to the harbour. The path was bumpy with twisted, twining, licheny roots of Moreton Bay fig trees and odd flame-coloured fallen flowers from the coral trees round the chooks' yard. The bush on the cliffs was full of wildflowers, native rosemary, lime-green banksias, pinky-mauve grevilleas, flat starry white flowers, native fuchsia and red honeysuckle from which we pulled the centres to suck the sweetness. Tongue orchids clung to the rocks. Over the years a freshwater spring seeping into the sandstone ledge at the bottom of the cliffs had hollowed out a natural rock pool like a bird bath.

A harbour swimming pool was fenced in for us and beside it was a bath house. Long-legged, black water birds perched on the white lattice roof. Seagulls and other water birds frequented all the grounds at Kincoppal, as well as pigeons and doves. The cooing of doves was a familiar background sound about the school. In summer we swam before early morning Mass. We had to get up at six and, wearing neck-to-knee swimming dresses (far too decorous to be called costumes), we walked silently in single file down to the pool. We were never allowed to talk when walking. It was a real privilege to go swimming. Anybody who misbehaved instantly lost her swimming privilege.

One feast day, a launch picked us up at the swimming pool and took us to a deserted island in the harbour for a picnic. Treats like this were what made Kincoppal so special and why I loved being there.

After I had been about a year at the school, there was a crisis. Mum liked living in Sydney and thought that when Dad came out of the army, he would stay in the city with her. But he didn't. Dad went back to help Grandma with the business in Yass. Mum refused to have anything more to do with Yass and she remained in Sydney by herself. Kincoppal was too expensive, Mum decided now, and told Trix that I would have to go back to the school at Randwick from which I had exited so ignominiously. 'No, don't do that,' Trix said. 'I want to educate her here.' Like all the Coen girls, Trix had private means; Grandfather Coen had provided for them in his will. That's how I stayed at Kincoppal – because Trix paid the fees. I was lucky.

I was a weekly boarder. At the start it was lonely, I did miss my mother and longed for the weekends when I could see her again but I came to accept it. For a while I cultivated the strategem of discovering I had forgotten something vital when I arrived at school on Monday mornings so I had to be immediately sent back to Randwick. However, this didn't work for long. My Monday morning trips home were abruptly curtailed.

Being a boarder and spending most holidays at Yass, I rarely saw my sister Molly and my brother King, who were away at country boarding schools. Jack went to the Marist Brothers, Darlinghurst and I saw him on weekends but when Molly and King turned up at the flat for their holidays, I was setting off for Grandma's. I felt more like an only child growing up than part of a big family.

The dormitory at Kincoppal was divided into cubicles, ten cubicles on each side of the room. Each cubicle was partitioned off like a little room on its own with a white curtain hung across the front instead of a door. It was furnished with a bed and a bed-side chest for belongings. The mattress was of hard horsehair but I became so used to it I couldn't sleep on anything softer. In the end cubicle, next to the showers, a nun slept. There were rumours that in the early days the girls at Kincoppal wore shower dresses to shield them from the sight of their own bodies, but I never knew if this was true or not.

When I began at Kincoppal, we didn't have to wear uniforms. Paula McDonagh, the youngest of Kath's friend Isobel's sisters, used to appear in a long romantic Kate Greenaway dress with a frill around the hem and little shoes like ballet slippers that did up at the ankle. The rest of use were much more plainly attired in ordinary everyday dresses that reached only a few inches below the knee. We cast envious looks at Paula, but then the nuns announced we had to wear a uniform. Our new blue and gold uniform consisted of a navy skirt, a high-necked, round-collared fuji silk shirt, a blue and gold tie, a panama hat with blue and gold band and a navy blazer.

Even the youngest girls had to wear stockings. Stockings were the bane of our lives. We were not permitted to pull them up in public, that was a strict rule. Our stockings were held up with garters, which seemed to be always slipping and our stocking wrinkling. Not being allowed to hitch them up was agony. We never sat with our legs crossed, either; that was another rule.

Up to the age of fourteen, if a girl behaved herself she wore a green sash across her uniform. From fourteen to seventeen, the best-behaved girls wore blue sashes. I managed to earn my green ribbon all right, but the blue one eluded me.

We were also forbidden to dawdle on the way to school or be seen wearing a school uniform in a shop. I used to catch the tram in from Randwick to Taylor Square every Monday morning, a threepenny fare, then walk over to Elizabeth Bay. Not far, really; it just seemed a long way in the rain that first morning. The old gaol at Darlinghurst interested me most on my walk, I used to search for bricks with convict marks.

On the corner of Macleay Street and Darlinghurst Road was an Italian fruit shop that sold cream-centred caramels. To buy sixpence worth meant risking expulsion, but who could resist those caramels with a creamy stripe down the middle?

Many years later, the poet Kenneth Slessor told me he, too, as a young man living in Elizabeth Bay, was addicted to the same caramels from this shop.

Anyone who spoke in the dormitory was almost automatically expelled. Two McDonagh girls were at school with me, little Paula and Anita who was closer to my age. The McDonaghs led a charmed life at Kincoppal, they were as naughty as anything and got away with it. Dr McDonagh and his wife both died young and the three older girls were bringing up these two younger ones. They all lived together in a big old house at Drummoyne. Anita kept us enthralled for hours with accounts of her sisters' film-making endeavours. Her own antics were equally extraordinary to us.

The dormitory was in darkness one night when suddenly we

heard the twinkling sound of a music box. Everyone was instantly alert, straining to make out where the sound was coming from, but not moving at all, lest movement betray or imply guilt.

The lights went on. Next we heard footsteps, and a nun's habit swished up the dormitory.

'Anita!' came the shocked exclamation.

Anita had been playing the music box. She explained to the stern-faced nun that at home she always had to play the music box before she could go to sleep. Tears just rolled down her face and she was forgiven. Only a McDonagh could have done it.

Mortice, the gardener, lived in the basement under the playroom. He kept his tools there and ate his lunch in its shadowy recesses. Anita loved teasing Mortice. She put on a funny old floppy hat and skipped about outside the door mimicking him and singing out rude names as he stoically chewed away at his lunch.

Anita suffered her own punishment, though. She hated insects of any sort, she was scared of them. One day we put a cicada down her back. Anita ran screaming in circles until she got it out, or the cicada fell out, while the rest of us laughed mercilessly. Anita did not forgive us or forget about the cicada for a long time.

The cicadas were deafening in the summer at Kincoppal, at their loudest round exam time, just when we were trying our hardest. We couldn't think for the incessant drumming.

Kincoppal wasn't keen on competitive sport. A tennis coach came in and we had a few tennis tournaments with other schools, but that was about it. Any girl who did achieve something in sport was entitled to a special pocket on her blazer. I won my pocket for basketball. Basketball was my forte; I used to wish they would send out a basketball team, but only the tennis team went round playing other schools. I liked tennis but I had weak wrists, probably from my early breaks. At thirteen I was tall and thin, about five feet seven, still very white-faced. Mum used to feed me up on malt and Robaline, but I didn't put on any weight until I was in my thirties. Because I was so tall, I could just reach up and drop the ball in the basketball net. I could defend well, too.

The men from Bjelke-Petersen's gym in town used to give us physical culture lessons. They taught at all the private schools in Sydney. 'The Emu' and 'O'Grady Says' were my favourite physical culture exercises. 'The Emu' was a high-kicking step walk and 'O'Grady Says' was a game in which we had to follow the leader in a series of quick-changing movements.

I deeply envied a little girl called Honey who lived in our flats at Randwick. I thought Honey was marvellous because she could do handstands over and over on the front lawn. I was always trying to emulate her and failing miserably. Being so tall and thin, I was quite the wrong shape for somersaults. Honey also danced in Christmas pantomimes. Her mother used to do her hair in golden curls so stiff you could put your finger through them. Later Honey virtually supported her whole family through the Depression with her dancing.

But back in her handspring days, Honey was at our place one Sunday morning. We were in the kitchen play-acting and practising feats of physical fitness. Honey was jumping on and off the table in the middle of the room. Somehow her golden curls caught in the long, sticky paper streamers that hung from the light bulb to catch flies. Flies that alighted on these papers stuck there. Flies and all were now tangled in Honey's hair.

'My mother will kill me, my mother will kill me!' she kept screaming. We finally freed the curls but it was a traumatic morning. When I last heard of her, Honey was a dancer at the Tivoli.

I was not very interested in schoolwork. I tolerated geography because of the map drawing and carefully coloured and intricately shaded detailed maps of the world. I liked geometry, too, because of the drawing, although I was no good at solving anything mathematical. But that was about the end of it.

I hadn't forgotten about being an artist.

The Italian artist Dattilo-Rubbo swept into Kincoppal every Friday to teach art. Darkly handsome, his brown eyes flashing, and sporting a black goatee beard, a long scarf flung carelessly round his neck, he always wore a dark green Borsalino hat pulled low to one side. Here was an art master who looked every inch an art master. I was truly impressed.

But art lessons were an extra, a luxury my mother couldn't afford. I yearned desperately for drawing lessons with the dashing Signor Rubbo. I covered my notebooks, my textbooks, everything I could with drawings. I drew all the time.

Antonio Dattilo-Rubbo

The Mistress-General was a Belgian nun called Mother Harmignie. When she smiled it was like the sun suddenly coming out on a grey day. But she seemed more than usually severe and grave on the day she called me into the study. I went in trembling, wondering what I had done wrong.

'Sit down, Margaret,' the conversation began. I sat.

'You wish to draw and make pictures more than anything else?' she went on.

'Yes,' I whispered, worried, remembering the books I had drawn on.

'I have arranged for you to have art lessons with Signor Rubbo,' she continued.

I burst into tears and could not look at her. Mother Harmignie was appalled, firstly by such a display of emotion in public and secondly because she had expected me to be happy about the lessons. Eventually I stuttered out that I was overjoyed and that I was crying because I was so happy.

I couldn't get over the shock of it. I think Mother Harmignie paid for my lessons out of her own pocket.

So once a week for seven years, I had art lessons with Signor Dattilo-Rubbo. I lived for Friday afternoons; art classes were the only lessons I enjoyed and the hour and a half went too quickly. After art lessons we could go home for the weekend, which made me look forward to them even more.

We did still lifes in pencil and charcoal. Sometimes we did designs, but mostly charcoal drawings.

Dattilo-Rubbo held proper art classes in his city studio as well as teaching us girls. He was not a man to waste words of praise on any student, least of all on schoolgirls. He would come along with a feather duster. Without a word he would make one swipe and wipe a charcoal drawing, the whole drawing, off the paper pinned to the board in front of you. Devastating. But now nothing could alter my conviction that I was going to be an artist.

'Sits badly and constantly fiddles,' began one of my infamous school reports. By 'fiddles', they meant 'scribbles'; a reference to my habit of decorating and drawing over my belongings. Being thin and tall, I found it hard to sit up straight, especially on refectory seats with no backs at all. We were supposed to sit up straight at all times. When I won a junior prize for physical culture, the Mistress of Studies wouldn't let me have it because I sat so badly in class.

I was also in trouble during religious instruction, not because I couldn't do the lessons but because I kept falling asleep. Dinner was at twelve thirty and we played outside from one to one thirty, then came inside for religious instruction. Without fail I fell asleep. Maybe this had something to do with being close to the water or maybe it was a natural consequence of eating the main meal in the middle of the day.

My desk was another problem. It probably was untidy for not only did I decorate my books but I collected anything and everything: beetles, moths, lizards, alive and dead and one in a jar of methylated spirits. Much of my collection was housed in my desk.

One year we had a fancy dress parade for Reverend Mother's

feast day. I made a costume by sewing the contents of my collection to my frock and went as 'my desk'. I don't think the Mistress-General approved, but the girls gave 'my desk' first prize. Mother Woodlock, who was then the Mistress-General, had to present the prize, which she did with barely concealed disdain. Years later at an old girls' reunion she had the grace to laugh about it, but she wasn't laughing at the time.

I collected things at home, too. At Randwick I had a collection of Hairy Moll caterpillars. They were the decorative, not the stinging kind of caterpillar and I could handle them easily. I divided a strip of the side garden into areas of grass about a foot square, put pegs in the ground and ran cotton around the pegs like fencing to make stockades, in which the caterpillars could live.

I had about twelve of them. The trouble was they used to wander off. I spent a lot of time looking for and recapturing caterpillars. A few liked being in the stockade, however; they were quite happy to stay put, eating grass.

They were very feminine-looking, and I named them all after actresses. Louise Lovely was especially pretty, with long grey hair (I called it fur) and red and blue spots. Mabel Normand and Lillian Gish were another pair. Because I was boarding, I saw them only at weekends. A pity, I felt, as I was very fond of them.

Margaret and her mother

It's fortunate, I guess, that the caterpillar collection didn't end up in my desk too.

Strange pets have always appealed to me, like my tortoise who was so small I had to cut up his worms for him, which wasn't very pleasant. He lived in my bedroom at Randwick. He used to get into the toe of my slipper at night to keep warm, and in the morning I would see him climbing out of the slipper and making his way across the room with a funny lopsided walk.

There was one other person at school who loved animals: the German countess. She was an old nun, too old to teach. She spent her days wandering around the grounds and in and out of the classrooms. She used to collect all the dead flies off the windowsills.

One winter, to our delight, the Countess was spied tenderly placing the dead flies on the stove. She was trying to warm them back to life – our own St Francis.

At about the time I won the fancy dress competition, I was very taken with those schoolgirls' stories in which they had midnight feasts. I was filled with a burning ambition to have my own midnight feast, but there was little chance of this at Kincoppal. Dormitory discipline was stringently kept.

I had a great friend at school called Eugenia Devlin. Genie was tall and blond, very bright and independent. We put on a play, *The Pied Piper of Hamelin*, and Genie was the piper in a wonderful pied costume which I admired. Genie was also an avid reader. We both loved Dickens, unusual for schoolgirls. We liked the more schoolgirlish novels of Mary Grant Bruce, too; the country settings appealed to me. Together we pored over any novel with a school setting. Genie's bright blue eyes lit up wickedly as we read aloud every detail of midnight feasts. We decided to have our own nocturnal banquet.

The feast was planned for a Monday night. Genie was to bring the lollies, I was to bring the cakes. At Kings Cross on the way to school, I bought six assorted cakes in fancy shapes with different coloured icings.

When we arrived at school on Monday mornings, the beds were already made up. We just unpacked our suitcases, put our nightdresses and clean things away in the chest of drawers, then went downstairs. I unmade my bed, put the cakes in flatly under the sheets and blankets and carefully made the bed up on top of them.

After tea that night, I was told that the Mistress-General, Mother Woodlock, wanted to see me in her office. On the desk in front of her she had a plate of the heavy yellow cake, made with lard, that was served at school tea.

She looked at me across the plate of cake. 'Don't you get enough to eat here?' she began.

I didn't know what she meant. It hadn't dawned on me that they could have found my cakes, because I had hidden them so well, I thought.

'So you have to provide yourself with cake to eat in the night, do you?'

My heart sank. I had never reckoned on the nuns re-checking the beds in the mornings after the girls had put their things away. Mother Woodlock wanted to know who else was involved. They obviously hadn't discovered Genie's sweets. She kept on asking, but I wouldn't say. I just stood there, crying.

Mother Woodlock realised that her questioning wasn't achieving much. She pointed to the two slices of cake on the plate.

'You have to eat this for supper every night because you don't get enough to eat at tea time,' she said.

I took one bite. The cake stuck in my throat and I couldn't get it down; I was choking with tears as well. Mother Woodlock sat there implacably as I slowly forced down mouthful after mouthful. About two-thirds was all I could eat.

'Why did you do this?' Mother Woodlock pressed again.

I didn't answer. Mother Woodlock was an American. She must have known what a midnight feast was. I stared down at the remaining cake. She was still trying to find out who else was involved but I wasn't going to talk so, with a last wry lift of her eyebrows, she released me.

Desperate to warn Genie, I shot off. I had to tell her to get rid of the sweets, but I couldn't let them see me doing it. Somehow I managed to convey the vital message.

I ate two slices of that wretched cake every night for the rest of the week. By the end of the week, I was able to get it down quite quickly, although I always found the first mouthful hideous.

Besides Genie and Alice Bolger whom I had met on the first

day, my other good friend at school was Amber Hackett, who also lived at Randwick. Small, blonde and dainty Amber arrived at school on Monday mornings in a chauffeur-driven white Rolls Royce. Her father was a wealthy bookmaker. Amber had a brother named Noel and, when I didn't go to Yass, the three of us spent the holidays together at Randwick. As I became more friendly with Amber, I was also driven home on Friday afternoons in the back of the Rolls. Very posh.

One Friday afternoon Amber's mother picked us both up and took us into town to go shopping at David Jones. In those days we didn't have modern methods of disposable sanitary protection. We had to use strips of ordinary towel, which we took home at the end of the week to wash out. The chauffeur went off on some business of his own while we were shopping and when we came back we discovered that Amber's beautiful leather overnight bag had disappeared from the car. Someone had stolen it.

Mrs Hackett, Amber and I couldn't stop laughing, because the thief was in for a surprise. The expensive little suitcase contained nothing but soiled towels.

I remember three English sisters at school, with clear blue eyes, blonde hair and the fairest, palest skin imaginable. They were not allowed to expose their skins to the sun and never appeared outside without gloves and hats lined with red veiling that hung down over their faces. For their entire time at school they were veiled like this, by their mother's special request. Their skins stayed flawless.

The Eton crop caused a sensation when it appeared at Kincoppal. This was the time of Colleen Moore in the Hollywood film *Flaming Youth*. Colleen Moore was tall and sparkling. She danced the Charleston and she wore her hair cut very short, just like a man's. Every teenager the world over had to see *Flaming Youth* or bust. Mum was away on a holiday, Auntie Lizzie was looking after us. The film was showing at Randwick. Dared we ask Auntie Lizzie to take us?

We braved it and Auntie Lizzie agreed. She sat back grimly throughout the film, if not disapproving, obviously unimpressed. It was a very mild sort of picture, really, despite all the fuss. Lizzie said afterwards she could not for the life of her see what was so wonderful about it. We loved it.

A girl arrived at school with the new short haircut. The nuns were aghast. By eleven in the morning the girl had received the message that the Reverend Mother wanted to see her. Why had she cut her hair like this? Reverend Mother wanted to know. What had possessed her? The girl was stunned. She blurted out that her mother had cut her hair; she had had nothing to do with it. The nuns rang her mother who said that girls everywhere were cutting their hair short now. Reverend Mother digested this. The Eton crop could stay, it was decided, but it was a near thing.

'She has a grotesque sense of humour which takes away from her a spirit of refinement,' was a comment on one of my school reports. About the same time as the midnight feast misadventure, I adopted a pseudonym. I fancied myself as a wit and wrote funny stories. I wanted to start a school newspaper. The nuns frowned on the idea, but I painstakingly made up a few copies at home and secretly distributed them.

'The Grey Ape of Clarendon' was the name I used for this venture. Clarendon was the name of our block of flats in Botany Street; where the Grey Ape came from I don't know.

When Noel Hackett went to boarding school at Riverview, he wrote me some schoolboy love letters, more to keep face with the other boys, I suspected, than out of passion. Perhaps he was lonely.

Dutifully I answered his letters and included some of the Grey Ape's literary efforts to lighten them up. I also promised Noel a comic opera, but it was never written and I still have a letter from Noel saying how disappointed he was that the Grey Ape hadn't come to light with it.

Like all schoolgirls, I had crushes which ranged from the sublime to the ridiculous. To look and love was enough, and all my lovers were equally unobtainable. There was Lord Byron, dark-haired, white-faced and passionate, every schoolgirl's ideal romantic hero. Rudolf Valentino, who deserves a chapter to himself, was my other great love. Women the world over were mad about him and we were no exception at Kincoppal.

One of the prefects, a clever, meek and mild girl who never put a foot wrong, became his most ardent devotee. She turned her bedroom at home into a shrine, lit two candles in front of his photographs and had fresh flowers arranged around it. If his name was mentioned, she went into a trance. 'Oh, Rudi,' she would sigh, rolling ecstatic eyes.

In the school holidays, my sister Molly and her best friend Lila Logan went to see Rudi in *The Sheik* at a cinema in George Street. Lila was another absolute devotee. She spent the entire holidays at the cinema. The first session started at eleven in the morning. Lila would be there and stay until the last session ended at eleven at night.

The Sheik was a silent movie. A man dressed as the Sheik came out on stage before each session to entertain the audience.

'Pale Hands I Loved Beside the Shalimar', he used to sing, and 'Less Than The Dust'.

Less than the dust beneath thy chariot wheels,
Less than the rust that never stained thy sword,
Less than the trust thou hast in me thy lord,
Even less am I, even less am I.

Lila lapped it up; we all did. It was our favourite song. While the boys and men professed only scorn for 'the green dago' (so-called because his pale skin looked sallow and sallow skin can appear green), they still to a man grew side levers just like Rudi's.

The woman who lived in the flat above us at Randwick was named Joy. She was a healthy blonde with a beautiful complexion and long hair and she looked like a Venus by Rubens. She must have weighed about fifteen stone. Starring with Valentino in *The Sheik* was the Austrian actress Vilma Banky. She was as blonde as Joy, but there the resemblance stopped, for Vilma Banky was as slight as Joy was full of figure. Joy, however, saw herself as a facsimile of the Sheik's petite object of desire.

If the prefect at school had a shrine to Valentino, Joy had a temple. She made a pair of Turkish trousers and a little sequinned top (why the Sheik's wife should wear Turkish clothing was a mystery known only to Joy). She draped the lounge room like the inside of a tent, put cushions on the floor and bought incense.

After she had done the housework every day, Joy lit the incense, lay back on the cushions in her Turkish attire and read the book of *The Sheik* which she had bought. It was her idea of sheer bliss.

Margaret as a tall teenager, standing on the present site of the University of New South Wales

Secrecy about sex was not confined to Yass. It was the absolute key word all my adolescent years.

The nuns at Kincoppal simply never mentioned sex. We had no sexual instruction. My first period came as a complete surprise to me.

Once they had a Redemptionist priest at the school to give a retreat. We listened agog to his endless ranting and raving about purity. He was not invited back; the nuns felt that the Redemptionist was too much for us innocent girls. Probably it was too much for their own gentle souls as well.

Except for Noel, boys of my own age were a bit of a non-event. Spending my holidays at Yass meant that I missed out on parties with my friends in town. But one holidays when I was staying at Grandma's, I was asked to Ursula Cusack's birthday party. I was thirteen. My cousin Pauline was also asked.

The Cusacks lived at the other end of Cooma Street from Grandma's. Lenny Cusack was my brother's best friend in Yass and there were plenty of boys and girls at Ursula's party. We played the piano and danced, we never thought about the time. When the party was over, we trooped out from the Cusacks' in a gang of about twenty. We walked everyone home from the party. Pauline and I, one of the Cusack girls and three of the Cusack boys were walking hand in hand. We went up Cooma Street, round the hill behind Yass in a giant circle back down to Cooma Street so we arrived last at The House.

Suddenly the clock struck two and I realised how late it was. Our entrance had better be discreet. We whispered, 'Goodnight' to the Cusacks and Pauline and I took off our shoes and started to creep into the house.

Pauline was a giggler; once she started, there was no stopping her. I, too, was prone to giggling attacks but it was Pauline who started that night. Frowning as hard as I could, I mouthed for her to be quiet, but to no avail; she couldn't stop.

As I opened the front door to step into the hall, Pauline dropped her shoes, bang, bang, on the stone step. The sound reverberated through the house. Like clockwork, Auntie Linda came out of the drawing room, her head wrapped in a white towel because she had taken off her wig.

'Do you know what time it is?' she demanded.

I was also laughing by this time; we were both hopeless cases. Linda was outraged.

Grandma was away in Sydney buying for the store that week and her absence gave Linda added vehemence. How dared we come home so late? Linda glared at us. When she told Grandma what we had done, Grandma would send Pauline and me straight back to Sydney because we couldn't be trusted. She went on and on. Half an hour later, our ears ringing with Linda's invectives, Pauline and I slunk off to bed.

We didn't appear at breakfast and waited until Linda had gone about her business before we got up and went into Annie's room looking for sympathy.

'Auntie Linda is most upset about you,' Annie said solemnly, with a twinkle. 'She doesn't know what on earth you could have been doing at that hour of the morning. She's going to make your father have a talk to you.'

I thought about this. 'Why didn't Dad or Uncle Luke come and

get us?' I asked. It was only a quarter of a mile down the street to
the Cusacks'; if they were so worried they should have come and
fetched us. We seemed to have logic on our side.

Dad and Uncle Luke, in fact, had never given us a second
thought. Dad had been to the Soldiers' Club, come in and gone
straight to bed. Uncle Luke came in later than Dad and also
promptly retired. Only Linda had sat up waiting and worrying.

When Grandma did come back next day, Linda subsided. As
usual, she was not really brave enough to tell tales to Grandma;
Dad certainly wasn't going to say anything because it had been
his fault, not ours, and so the party passed over. But Linda gave us
hell all the day before Grandma's return.

I had my first crush on a real person when I was fifteen. I fell in
love with a blond tennis player named Paddy who lived at the end
of the street. I followed him everywhere, which wasn't very far
since I was away at school all week but on Monday mornings I
made sure I was on the same tram. I tried to stand as close to him
as possible and I stared at him with longing across the crowded
tram. I was far too shy to talk to him; I couldn't begin to open my
mouth in his presence.

Molly had left school by then. She used to hold Friday night
card parties at our place for her friends. She knew Paddy and
occasionally he was asked on Friday nights. I wasn't invited but
hung about all night swooning in the background.

My swooning must have been more obvious than I realised.
Paddy had a friend called Bill. One Monday morning Paddy
wasn't on his usual tram, but Bill was. Bill was a tease, he came up
and chatted to Molly and me.

'Paddy tells me you've got a crush on him,' Bill said with a wink
to me. I glared at him, humiliated beyond measure. I was furious
that my love for Paddy should be a joke and that he should know
the way I felt. He could hardly have failed to notice the way I
haunted him, but such is schoolgirl passion. Paddy's appeal
diminished rapidly after that.

Having a photo of the person with whom you were in love was
very important. I developed a passion for another of Molly's
friends. I didn't have a photo of my new crush, but he reminded
me irresistibly of the picture of an ape in a *Cole's Funny Picture
Book* so I cut out the drawing and gazed fondly at that. My

infatuation with the ape also failed to develop into anything more serious.

About this time, my cousin Joe from Riverview and I had a perfect day together. Grandma had been away with Kathleen on a cruise, Joe and I went in early one Saturday morning to meet their ship near Darling Harbour.

Grandma stayed at the Hotel Metropole whenever she was in town. She would ask us in for a meal with her. After the meal, she would reach into her black bag (Grandma's big old-fashioned black handbag was a part of her) that contained an endless supply of two shilling pieces, and give us 2s each as a present.

This particular morning she was buying for the shop, so instead of taking Joe and me to the Metropole, she gave us each £1 and told us to enjoy ourselves. This was a fortune.

First we treated ourselves to a breakfast spread of bacon and eggs, tea and toast with jam. Breakfast over, we headed off to an eleven o'clock session at the pictures but before we went in we had enormous green and pink ice cream sodas in tall glasses. More ice cream soda and sandwiches followed for lunch. Then we saw the afternoon session. When we came out and counted our money, we had only our tram fares back to Randwick and enough to buy one copy of *Smith's Weekly*. So we bought *Smith's Weekly*, sat down in Hyde Park and read it together from cover to cover. We laughed at the cartoons and caricatures, and read the jokes out aloud. With our last fourpence we caught the Randwick tram home. It was a day to remember.

Molly was eighteen now and in full social swing, going to parties and dances every weekend and I was in awe of her and her friends. One of her girlfriends came to stay with us on a Friday night. Mum had put a folding bed down in the middle of the big bedroom that Molly and I shared. I was locked out while Molly and her friend dolled themselves up. They came out looking wonderful, I was suitably impressed and envious. The friend was said to be the best dancer around. She was a thin girl with a surprisingly large bust for such a slender body. Her hair was puffed out over her ears in the style of the moment. She and Molly swept off into the night.

About two in the morning, I was woken by their giggling. As I lay in bed watching them undress and listening to their gossip, I was startled to see Molly's friend pull out two pads that held her hair so fashionably puffed. Out of her camisole came two more pads; her beautiful bosom. To my horror, finally she proceeded to remove her teeth, which were also false. Her teeth had all been extracted because of an infection. It made an indelible impression on me.

However, Molly's friend was soon engaged and married, and lived happily ever afterwards. She must have danced her way into her boyfriend's affection.

We wanted to have a party at home, King and Molly especially, but Mum wasn't keen on our having parties. The flat wasn't suitable, she would say. It wasn't big enough.

She was right, but when she went up to Yass for a holiday, Molly and King decided to hold a party to end all parties. We moved the entire contents of the second bedroom into the back yard, dressing tables, wardrobes, beds, the lot, and prayed it wouldn't rain. The boys even took up the carpet and sanded the floor for dancing.

Lila Logan came to stay. She helped Molly to prepare the food. They did the cooking on the day of the party. Lila and Molly were beside themselves with excitement and made strange, high-pitched little whistling sounds to each other when it got too much for them. They made trifle after trifle for supper.

Streamers festooned the drawing room, hanging from corner to corner and cascading from the light bulb in the centre. The excitement had reached fever pitch; we had just finished putting up the very last streamer when the doorbell rang. It was Uncle Barney with John, a young cousin of ours. Barney's eyes lit up as he took in the decorations.

'You're having a party,' he said.

Could Mum have sent him to check on us? we wondered, panicking, or was Barney being genuine? Molly acted quickly.

'Yes,' she replied. 'Would you like to come?'

Barney's eyes positively shone. 'I'll have to bring John,' he said.

'That's all right,' we answered. It was not all right, but we didn't find that out until later. John was only twelve, and we banished him to the kitchen.

Determined not to spend the evening there with John though I was only a year or so older, I searched my mother's wardrobe for an evening dress I could wear to the party. Long dresses were fashionable. I was as tall as my mother, but I was skinny. The gown I chose hung about me like a flag without wind, its hem trailing on the floor. I must have looked a sight.

Joy from the flat upstairs came to the party on her own; her husband Bill was working as a dancing instructor at the Palais Royal and didn't finish till late. A tall, awkward, angular youth, a friend of King's, was immediately besotted with Joy. Early in the evening they both disappeared into my mother's bedroom.

About midnight, Bill arrived at the party. 'Where's my wife?' he asked in a loud voice.

Joy emerged smiling from the bedroom, the angular youth nowhere to be seen. His whereabouts remained a mystery.

Barney enjoyed himself immensely; I can still see him reciting poetry to an admiring circle in the drawing room. John had a good time, too, as Molly discovered when she went to serve the supper. He had eaten all the trifles Molly and Lila had so painstakingly and lovingly prepared.

Dancing continued in the second bedroom until early in the morning. There were not enough chairs to go round, and people either danced or leaned against the wall. Towards the end I was shocked to see a fat man sitting on the floor, with his pudgy legs stuck out in front of him and a tankard of beer in his hand. He seemed extremely gross to my youthful eyes.

When the last guest had gone, the gramophone finally wound down. The angular youth appeared from under the double bed in Mum's bedroom, where he had flung himself in terror at the sound of Bill's voice.

Next day the furniture was moved back inside. We cleaned up, washed the dishes, took down the streamers and everything was in place as Mum arrived home. She took one look around the room.

'You've had a party,' she said.

A shred of streamer was stuck to a tack in the corner of the ceiling. The trouble that ensued was nothing, we felt; the party had undoubtedly been a triumph.

*

We had exams at Kincoppal, but there wasn't the emphasis on them that there is today; the school was too small to bother with formal examinations. Trix called me in at the end of the year after the Intermediate exam and told me that if I wanted to do the State Leaving exam, she would send me to Rose Bay convent for my final year.

Again, I resorted to tears, though not of joy this time. I didn't want to go to Rose Bay, I pleaded. I couldn't bear to leave Kincoppal because I loved it so much. Besides, I wanted to leave school so I could become an artist. (I thought that once I was out of school I would become and artist in a few weeks. As it has turned out, being an artist has taken me half a century.)

So I stayed at Kincoppal for another year, without exams. My last year was a good one. I studied the history of art and worked on my art lessons with Dattilo-Rubbo. We had a few painting lessons now, as well as still life drawing. I did a painting in oils of the harbour from the school grounds and for the first time Signor Rubbo praised my work.

Four or five young boys also attended Kincoppal. Their classes were held in the stone stables behind the nuns' house. A funny beginning for them, I thought, coming to school in the convent with the grown-up girls and the strangely dressed French nuns.

I taught the boys art that year. One boy, who had a crush on me, bought me a series of presents, first rosary beads, then he shyly pressed a two shilling piece into my hand. I didn't want to take the two shilling piece because I didn't know if he had stolen it from his mother's purse. I didn't want him to get into trouble, but he was so insistent I should keep it that in the end I did. They were nice little boys; I liked them. I don't think there were any older than six years.

Trix was still hoping I would be able to wear the blue sash of merit, but it didn't come my way until about three months before the end of the year. It was a beautiful cerulean blue silk ribbon with a wavy water mark through the silk. As soon as I had the ribbon I did something wrong; I can't remember what, but the sash was in jeopardy. I do remember that only the intervention of Mother Percy-Dove, the nun who always had a twinkle in her eye even when she was upbraiding me, saved the ribbon. To Trix's relief, I finished out the year besashed.

There was no caning or corporal punishment at Kincoppal; we were simply expected to live up to their ideals and any girl who did not was out. I managed to survive their regime of prayer and discipline. All those years at Yass helped; to me religion was just another part of life. But I always had an inner conviction that I was going to be an artist no matter what, and that sustained me.

I was sixteen years and nine months old when I left school. I had been at Kincoppal for seven years. On my last day I was presented with a prize for art history and I won an 'O'Grady Says' display competition. Just before I left, Reverend Mother called me in to see her.

God, what have I done now? I wondered desperately.

'Margaret, you are not crying?' Reverend Mother looked at me hard.

'No.' I stared back at her apprehensively.

'The girls always cry the day they leave school,' Reverend Mother continued. Oh, no, I thought. Surely I won't get into trouble for *not* crying.

'I believe you are happy to be leaving school, Margaret,' Reverend Mother said, shaking her head at me.

'Yes,' I said, 'I am,' bowing my head and hoping that the wrath of God would not descend upon me. But Reverend Mother merely shook her head again and dismissed me.

I was happy at Kincoppal. I had loved those seven years but I was glad to be leaving. I was going to be an artist.

5

In the Good Old Summertime

Margaret at the beach

They were happy days at Randwick the first year after I left school. Amber Hackett and I were partying, planning our next party, playing tennis (at which I wasn't good), or just lazing about. If I wasn't with Amber, there was plenty going on at home. Molly, King, Jack and I were living together as a family for the first time since I had been a little girl at Yass. We went out to friends' homes and to dances. It was fun.

On Tuesdays I went to Dattilo-Rubbo's classes in the city and when I wasn't going out, I practised drawing at home.

My mother seemed quite thrilled about my being an artist; there was never any question of my doing something else. Besides, there was the legend of Jack Flanagan, my second cousin. He had left Australia at the age of twenty and gone to New York, where in the space of ten years he became one of America's highest-paid black and white artists (he was allergic to oil paint), illustrating stories in such magazines as *Cosmopolitan*. When I said I wanted to be an artist, the family hoped I might become as rich and famous as Jack Flanagan. I don't think they really believed it, but at least Jack Flanagan's success encouraged their positive feelings about artists. I, of course, was obsessed by the legend; the drawings I did at home were always in black and white because I was trying to be like Jack Flanagan.

The artist George Lambert had a studio in Randwick, where the Prince of Wales hospital is now. Soon after I left school, I saw him

Jack Flanagan at work on an etching

A family portrait. Back row: Dad and King. Front row: Jack, Margaret, Mum and Molly

riding down Botany Street, looking magnificent on horseback. I rushed inside to tell my mother so she could see him too. After the bright sunlight, I was blinded in the dark kitchen. I crashed into the door and regained consciousness on the kitchen floor with Mum bending anxiously over me. My eye came up like an egg before it discoloured. I often saw George Lambert riding round Randwick after that, but never with such painful results.

Friends of mine arranged for me to visit a relative of theirs called Alf Coffey. Alf Coffey lived by his art; he was a painter and an etcher. We spent a week at his Wyong studio house. I was enthralled, watching a real artist work.

Mum's brother Joe O'Dwyer came to stay with us. After tea he read aloud from Dickens and the Canadian writer Stephen Leacock. Stephen Leacock's *Nonsense Novels*, as his short stories were called, had us laughing all night. We liked 'Gertie the Governess' who made herself a ball dress out of old newspapers, but by far the most hilarious story was 'Boarding House Geometry' with its rules such as 'any number of meals produced in a boarding house does not equal one square meal'. We loved those family evenings. We were really getting to know each other.

My brother King, slim and athletic with chestnut brown hair, worked in the bank. Jack was red-headed and made wirelesses; Molly had curly black hair and very blue eyes. She worked in the Taxation Department.

Molly was a perfectionist in her dress. Gloves, shoes, handbag: everything had to match. I was much more haphazard with clothing. When I left school I cut off my long hair and tried to wave it, but my hair was never in place like hers.

I had big black freckles, which I hated. While I was at school, I started smothering myself every night with a thick, greasy, mercury-based cream called Thorburn's. I anointed my freckles nightly with Thorburn's for years; I think it did eventually tone them down.

A friend of my mother's had another remedy. Freddy her son was so pale-skinned and fair that even his eyelashes were white. He was covered in freckles. Every night as he slept his mother dabbed his face with urine. She assured me that this was the best way to remove them, but I could never face Freddy's mum's freckle treatment.

King and I used to go swimming early in the mornings. We would get up about five, walk to the top of Coogee Bay Road then run downhill all the way to Coogee beach. King was a good swimmer. I wasn't, but I loved our expeditions, the exhilaration of the run, the freshness of the surf. Sometimes we went to Wiley's baths on the south side of the beach. After our swim we caught the tram back to Randwick; it was too strenuous to run up the hill. The tram fare home was twopence.

The Coogee aquarium was at the end of the line where the tram stopped. When we were children it was an indoor swimming pool; later they turned it into the aquarium that featured in the famous shark arm murder case.

The Coogee picture show was up the other end of the beach. The day the outdoor amplifier arrived at the picture show was a tremendous occasion. Peals of bells re-echoed across the sand and out blared 'If You Were the Only Girl in the World'. Coogee was ringing with the song. So excited were the proud proprietors that they played it night and day. There was nothing like it in Sydney.

King was a lifesaver. He joined the Coogee club because Dad's brother Frank had been a foundation member. The lifesavers took it in turns to keep watch in the shark tower on the beach. King was alone, doing his stint in the tower, when he saw a shark cruising and rang the alarm bell. Everyone left the water immediately, but King could see one man left out in the surf. He couldn't understand why the man didn't come out. At last someone came to relieve King and he raced into the water and swam out to the surfer. The sound of the ringing bell had paralysed the man; he literally couldn't move for fear.

Shark attacks were quite common then, before they put shark nets off the beaches. A shark killed the Randwick postmaster's son and I knew another boy called Jack Dagworthy who was attacked by a shark. Late one summer evening Jack Dagworthy and a friend went down to Coogee for a swim. Walking past the Coogee picture show, they saw a poster for a film showing a shark attack.

'That's not the way a shark tackles,' Jack Dagworthy said. While they were swimming, Jack Dagworthy was mauled by a shark. He lived, but only just.

King was a lifesaver most of his life. He told a funny story about a swimming test he had to do when he was getting older. King knew he was really too old for it, but wanted to try. He had to swim round a buoy in the surf. About halfway out, a bluebottle wrapped itself round his leg. King started swimming faster than he had ever thought possible. He passed the test with flying colours and remained a lifesaver for another year – thanks to the bluebottle, he always said.

Amber Hackett and I were almost inseparable that first year after school. The Hacketts had a beautiful house in Milford Street, Randwick, with parquet floors for dancing and a tennis court. The verandah had a view overlooking Randwick right down to Coogee.

They had two small fluffy Pomeranian dogs. Every time the front door bell rang, there was a chorus from these two. Yapping madly, they seemed to dance on the tips of their toes with curiosity. The dogs were cared for by Old Bob, whose sole function this appeared to be. Old Bob was a bit of a mystery. I never knew who he really was; we called him Bob to his face, Old Bob behind his back. Jim Hackett had brought him back from Bourke. We didn't know if Bob was a relative, an old employee, an ancient chauffeur or a business friend. He was treated with great respect by the Hackett family and lived with them until he died.

Three times a week I had my evening meal at the Hacketts' with Amber and Noel. Every night was like a party. Noel loved dancing, Amber always had a couple of admirers hanging about and the two girls from next door came in. The gramophone would be wound up and we danced the Charleston. 'Chicago' was the big song. I would stay until ten o'clock then I ran home. It was two minutes from Milford Street to Botany Street.

The blond heart-throb tennis player Paddy appeared again. Amber and I were both in love with him this time. The Hacketts used to call for me in the white Rolls Royce when I was going to dances with Amber. Amber and I sat in the back with Paddy between us.

Paddy would be alternately squeezing my hand then Amber's all the way to the party. We were totally jealous of each other, but we kept a stiff upper lip because neither of us wanted to admit that she cared so much about Paddy.

The Palais Royal in Moore Park was the popular spot for dances and balls in Sydney. Peggy Dawes and Jim Bendroit gave dancing exhibitions there before they married. Afterwards Jim Bendroit opened the elegant Prince's restaurant in town. We also went to the Ambassadors. The Ambassadors had a specially sprung floor which moved, or seemed to move, as we danced. The waltz and the foxtrot were what everybody danced, and the tango. I was very proud of being able to tango. Charities held dances to raise funds, as they have fetes now.

Boys asked girls to go with them to dances. Molly had plenty of invitations, but often we bought our own tickets and went in a party. As well as public dances, people held smaller private dances in their homes. I didn't have nearly as many dance dresses as Molly. Mum, who made all my clothes, taught me to sew and I ran up my few dance dresses myself – simple frocks with full skirts, the fuller the better, a straight bodice with straps, a large rose or posy pinned to one shoulder, and some floating tulle.

My only bought dress, a present from Mum, was made of white georgette: it had a pleated skirt with gold ribbon running round the hem – sounds garish, but it wasn't – and a little gold lamé jacket to go with the dress. It was the nicest frock I ever had.

I didn't make my debut, though mosts girls did, including Amber. The year I left school, Grandma broke her hip. We all believed Grandma was immortal and the news caused consternation in the family. She refused to be hospitalised and spent six months with the leg in traction ruling the roost from her brass bed in The House. I felt Grandma's broken hip was sufficient commotion without my 'coming out', as they called it. My mother was secretly relieved; Molly's coming out had been enough drama for her.

Although she was clever, Molly didn't win a scholarship to university. She would have liked to go, but higher education cost money we couldn't afford. She won a teacher's scholarship, but she didn't want to be a teacher so she took a job in the Taxation Department.

Molly was making her debut at the Catholic ball at the Palais Royal and was determined to have a night to remember. She spent weeks working out the design of her frock, which she had specially made. Little handmade white satin roses were sewn to lattice work across the bodice.

The great day arrived but when Molly went to clock off from work at the regular time of a quarter to five, the boss informed her she had to work back. They had been working overtime in her section, but Molly was convinced that the boss knew about her debut. He was making them work overtime deliberately because he was jealous, Molly fumed. She tried to get off at a quarter to six, but he wouldn't let her go. Molly was frantic. It was Friday night and we were sitting around the dining room table in the flat living every minute of it with her. Molly was on the phone every five minutes.

'Nark, he's doing it out of nark,' she repeated hysterically.

Mum laid out her dress on the bed and had everything ready for her. At half past six, Molly and her colleagues were meant to collect their tea money and have a meal break. The boss told them they had to come back afterwards.

'I'm going out tonight,' Molly pleaded. 'Can't I go home now? I'm going to a ball; I'll never be ready in time.'

'No,' the boss replied. 'I can't make exceptions for anyone.' Molly was furious now, as well as desperate. She picked up her tea money and came home. By the time she arrived at the flat the tears had set in. Mum had to bathe her face, wash her eyes, get her into the coming out frock, help with her hair. It was nine o'clock before Molly left for the ball. We heaved sighs of relief and went to bed exhausted.

Molly and I went to the Hackett's wonderfully extravagant, never-to-be-forgotten New Year's Eve party. French champagne was flowing; nothing but the best for the Hacketts. We were quite unused to such style. The waiters kept topping up our glasses.

Suddenly I noticed Molly had vanished without a word. Noel and I went looking for her. We found her out on the lawn not exactly unconscious, just lying face upwards gazing at the stars,

Molly finally makes her debut

the two Pomeranians licking her face. She normally drank very little and the champagne and excitement had been too much for her.

She came to and we slipped off home. Molly was a long time recovering from what she felt was a terrible disgrace. Dad was still in Yass with Grandma. Hopeless with money, he continually disappointed Mum. Mum wanted her own house but there was no way Dad would ever be able to provide it on Grandma's wages.

By some miracle Dad had managed to save some money that first year after I left school and Mum was hoping that at last he might put a deposit on a house. But Dad decided pianolas were the thing. He would invest his money in them and make his fortune. He bought up a whole stockpile, planning to sell them door to door on time payment. Mum looked stricken when she heard about the pianolas. Dad gave us one for the flat. The last thing in the world Mum wanted was a pianola.

It drove her mad. Dad would come in, sit himself down and pedal with vigour. The keys flew, music churned out. A wide selection of hymns came with the pianola, as well as popular tunes. 'Faith of Our Fathers' was Dad's favourite. The flat resounded with 'Faith of Our Fathers' whenever Dad was in town.

The pianolas sold all right; the trouble was that, as the Depression was beginning, no one made payments on them. They were a financial disaster.

This was heartbreaking for my mother; her dream of her own house receded even further. The rest of us, though, were happy enough in Botany Street.

Mum's other dream was to go to Russia. Back when we had been staying at the Coogee boarding house, the Villa Taormina, a man named Jim Quinn was lodging there. He was a builder and a member of the Communist Party, which we didn't know at the time, who left a vast fortune to the Communist Party in his will.

Every time I met Jim Quinn, he would say, 'How's your art going?'

'Very well,' I answered dutifully.

'Ah,' he would intone, 'art is a weapon.'

He lived a solitary life and became very attached to us during our stay at the Villa Taormina, particularly to Mum. His endless talk of Russia, I think, inspired her with this wish to travel there.

Our cleaning lady in Botany Street was Russian too, which might have fuelled Mum's fantasies. This woman had been a dresser with the Russian Ballet before the Revolution and her husband was a strong man in the circus. They had walked across Siberia to Vladivostok to escape from Russia and come to Australia.

Until she was a very old lady, Mum talked about going to Russia one day. But she never did.

Molly was born on Melbourne Cup Day. She loved racing and she loved horses. Being so close to the racecourse, Randwick was full of racing stables, and Botany Street was in the midst of them. Jerry Carey lived two doors up. O'Connor's were three or four doors away; Jameson's, a New Zealand trainer, were up the street and Jack King's big stables were at the end of the street opposite where the entrance to the University of New South Wales is now.

When we first moved to Randwick, I used to pick bunches of boronia and other wildflowers on the university site, which was a big paddock. I think the wildflowers thrived on the sandy soil. Soon they started quarrying. The quarry left a huge pit which, to our horror, became a tip. The smell of garbage used to waft up the street to the flats, but the hole was filled and they turned it into a small golf links. None of the locals could believe that the university was to be built over the old tip; they said the university would sink into the quarry. But it seems to have survived.

Irish old-style racehorse trainers, the Paytens, lived on the corner of the block and opposite the Paytens lived another trainer, Grafter Kingsley. Grafter Kingsley weighed over twenty stone and used to ride down Botany Street in a tiny sulky drawn by a very small horse. From the back, the sulky almost touched the ground under the strain of the Grafter's immense weight.

George Lambert and Grafter Kingsley lived within a few hundred yards of each other. It fascinated me that two such different worlds were so close, yet they couldn't have been further apart.

Molly lived for the races. For days before the big spring and autumn meetings we heard of nothing else. The phone rang hot with tips for her. You could always rely on Molly for a sure tip at

Randwick. 'That horse can't lose', 'That horse will lose all right', 'That horse can only come last'; 'That horse is a surefire winner'; I can't tell you how often I heard those phrases.

I took it all with a grain of salt, but Molly was deadly serious about her predictions. She would be positive her horse was going to win and, if by some mischance it lost, she had every excuse off pat.

Easter, down at Inglis's stables, they held the yearling parade. The yearlings were led round the yards with great pomp and ceremony. Dad used to come up from Yass to spend Easter Sunday with us and he and Molly never missed a yearling parade.

Mum's younger sister, Aileen, also used to stay with us at Easter. Aileen was a champion rider who came down from the country for the high jump events at the Royal Easter Show. She used to share my room and I remember her waking up once at about four in the morning.

Mum's sister Aileen at the Wagga Wagga Show, 1924

'Listen to the horses' hooves!' she said excitedly. The race-horses were setting out for their early morning training gallops. We were accustomed to the noise and slept through it but Aileen, being a visitor, was awakened instantly. She jumped out of bed and stared through the window. She couldn't understand why we weren't up watching them, too.

The racing atmosphere in Randwick was contagious; even Mum, who was not a gambler, sometimes had a bet on. She would often dress up on a Saturday afternoon and walk round to the races with Molly.

I didn't share Molly's passion for horses and like Mum, I was not a gambler, but I did watch the races from 'the hill'. From the top of the sandhill where the university now is, there was a clear view of the race track.

Every Saturday afternoon, a mixed crowd gathered on the hill, mostly down-and-outs, old soaks, a few children and teenagers. Bets were in twopences and threepences, but a smart bookie could still make ten shillings on a race. If he was overextended or couldn't make his payment, he just used to disappear, so as soon as a race was over everyone would make a circle around the bookmaker to ensure he didn't run away.

The Little Sisters of the Poor were familiar figures in Randwick on race days. Since most of the trainers were Irish Catholics, they virtually supported these nuns, whose order, many years later, cared for both Bea Miles and Dulcie Deamer before they died.

The trainers were Irish, Catholic and highly superstitious. A trainer had put his hat on ready to take his horse to the track, when a Chinese who went round selling fruit and vegetables from a cart came by and wished him luck.

The trainer's horse won the Summer Cup that afternoon and the trainer said 'the Chinaman' had brought him luck. He arranged to have him call before every big race and wish him luck after he had put his hat on.

The back of our flats adjoined Jerry Carey's stables. His apprentices came from the country; often they had just arrived in the city. They were boys of twelve and thirteen, small for their ages. Because they took the boys so young, the trainers were responsible for their welfare. Stable boys led a strictly disciplined life.

One night we heard screams followed by the sound of someone being sick. The lights in the stables went on, a boy's sobbing was heard.

'Will I die, Mrs Carey? Will I die, Mrs Carey?' he whimpered. It was surreal. 'Don't worry, it's all right. One of the older boys took him to a party and got him drunk, that's all,' another voice shouted over the fence. Next thing we heard was Jerry's voice booming out to the older boy, 'Now pack your bags and go!'

King bought himself a punching bag, the sort you hit as if you are boxing with someone. King wanted to build himself up, and pounded away at the bag on the first morning he got it. That evening Jerry Carey came round at the flats.

'Mr Coen, I'm sorry to tell you this,' he said. 'The horses were nearly driven crazy with the noise this morning, so if you don't mind you'll have to stop using that punching bag.' Jerry said it nicely, but sounded as if he meant it; King didn't use the punching bag again.

One of the Careys' horses took a fancy to a cat I had, and horse and cat became inseparable. The cat still came home to me for dinner, as well as filling up on extra tidbits at the stables, but that was all I saw of my cat after it met the Careys' horse.

At Danny Lewis's stable, they bought a milking goat for the children. The goat and a horse fell in love. The goat did everything with the horse except accompany it onto the track.

That was racing Randwick: something special.

My brother Jack loved everything electrical. In Jack's bedroom, we had to pick our way through red wires, blue wires, half-made wirelesses, crystal sets and 'cats' whiskers', a name that always intrigued me. I don't know how Mum ever fought her way across the room to make his bed. Jack never made his own bed. Even the floor underneath the bed was covered with paraphernalia. Jack's bedroom was his workroom. When he managed to hear a strain of music or a few words on a wireless he was making, he emerged, wildly excited, and dragged us in to listen to his new set. Jack not only made wirelesses that worked, he sold them too, which impressed us no end.

Giving us electrical shocks was part of Jack's experiments. He would drop a penny into a basin and run an electric current through the water. We had to line up holding hands, then he made one of us try to pick the penny up. The resulting shock was quite something; the current ran through all of us. One person only had to touch the water; you couldn't get anywhere near the penny. The family tolerated Jack's shocks in much the same way as they put up with my wanting to be an artist.

Jack enjoyed fiddling with anything electrical. Joy's husband Bill from upstairs, the dancing instructor at the Palais Royal, used to get home at about one o'clock on a Saturday night and he often brought a group of friends back with him. A dozen or so people would party on upstairs almost until daybreak. Mum got tired of the racket. She said she wasn't feeling well; perhaps she was just fed up with the sound of other people's parties. She was never a party person and anyway, the dancing on the floor above our bedrooms was very noisy.

One Saturday night, Mum said to Jack, 'Go upstairs and fix them.' Jack disappeared outside and disconnected their fuse box. The flat upstairs was plunged into darkness. We could hear the expressions of surprise and dismay that ensued and the guests departed rapidly. Mum slept soundly. On the Sunday morning, Bill came downstairs very apologetically to ask Mum if Jack would be so kind as to have a look at their fuse box.

Jack, who could keep a poker face, said he would be delighted. He went upstairs, restored their box to order and accepted their thanks without the slightest twitch of a smile. Party nights did decline a little after that.

King and particularly Jack had a bad time of it in the Depression. People couldn't afford to be too choosy about where they worked. Jack was sacked from various places as they closed down; that's why he ended up working for himself, making wirelesses. In the bank, King was at least secure.

One day King bought a motor bike with a sidecar. We woke up and there on the front lawn was this dreadful, decrepit machine. He hadn't said a word about it to anyone except Jack. The bike wasn't secondhand, but about twentieth hand; King paid £15 for it and Jack chipped in so he could have a share. I don't know how they even lifted it inside the front gate.

It took King weeks of tinkering to get it going. Amber and I used to drive around Bondi beach during the day like princesses in the chauffeur-driven Rolls, then after tea Jack or King would come around to the Hacketts with this old bike. We would pile in, about six of us squashed into the sidecar, and go for a bone-rattling drive around Randwick before we went home.

King had a girlfriend, Mary Frost, who used to go everywhere with us. She was like one of the family already. We thought she was the most beautiful girl in the world, with her black hair and eyes and complexion the colour of pink carnations.

The bike needed a run. King decided one long weekend he would take Mary to Goulburn to visit some relatives of hers. Mary, rugged up with blankets, scarf and hat, was installed in the sidecar and they set off. Goulburn was quite a distance away. A begoggled King concentrated on the road and the bike, while Mary bumped along beside him for hours. Just before Goulburn, King turned to say something to his passenger. To his horror Mary was gone. There was no sidecar, no Mary, nothing.

The sidecar had dropped off along the road about ten miles back, King discovered, and Mary had been left sitting by herself on the roadside. King wondered if Mary would ever forgive him, but she did. Soon afterwards they announced their engagement.

Life had its ups and downs. Some cousins had a weekend house at Cronulla, which they let us have at Christmas and for weekends through the year. Usually about twelve of us stayed there, mostly King and Molly's friends. Mum made it a condition that we did the work, otherwise she said the holiday only meant extra chores for her.

On one occasion eight of us, four boys and four girls, including Mary Frost, rented a boat. The boys took it in turns to row, as we made our way across the glassy flat sea to Point Hacking. A sudden southerly blew up and on the way back the boat seemed to stand on its head every time it went over a wave. It would drop down again before going up and over the next wave. We were terrified. Molly was weeping, Mary and I were in the back of the boat saying rosaries out loud in between exhorting the boys to row harder. We were going to drown, this was the end, I thought.

Molly started calling on St Jude, patron saint of the impossible. St Jude came good. The boat finally seesawed into Cronulla and safety. Mary and I said another rosary in gratitude.

The bank suddenly transferred King up to Bundaberg. He wasn't exactly overjoyed; we had just scraped together enough to

Mary Frost's engagement portrait

buy a new gramophone for the flat. Music was very important in our house.

'Just my luck to be moved away when we get the new gramophone,' he groaned.

After a few months, he came down for a weekend. Like everyone else, King hated the dentist but he had a bad toothache, and wanted to see our family dentist in Randwick, Clarrie Hughes. Unfortunately, Clarrie couldn't see him until Monday morning.

Saturday night King tramped around the house, unable to keep still because of the pain in his tooth. Then he disappeared onto the back verandah. Mum went to see what had happened. She was shocked to find a huge tooth covered in blood. King had used an old pair of rusty forceps to pull out the tooth out himself. He tore his jaw to pieces in the process and Clarrie spent hours patching it up on Monday morning.

I don't like the dentist myself. As a child in Yass, I was climbing on some rafters mother had declared out of bounds when I fell and broke my tooth. Because I was so frightened of the dentist, I didn't tell her about the tooth. Instead I tried to keep my mouth closed and I developed a dreadful, lopsided smile that stayed with me long after the damage to my tooth had been rectified.

King came down again the next year. He and Mary Frost were

married and Mary went back with him to Bundaberg. Our family was splitting up again.

About this time, I received my first proposal of marriage. A heavily built and swarthy Greek Orthodox priest used to come calling on his flock down Botany Street. Mum always asked him in for a cup of tea. There was something contrary in Mum's nature; she never asked the Catholic priest in.

Mum liked the Greek priest. She said she felt sorry for him having to go round on foot in such hot weather collecting for the church. She used to make him a cup of tea and a sandwich and give him a shilling for the church, for which the Greek priest was suitably grateful.

One day when Mum was entertaining the Greek priest she called me into the sitting room; I could see her eyes were twinkling.

'Father Constantine has a proposition for you,' she said blithely, and stopped. Father Constantine took over. His eyes were glowing and he waved his hands around as he explained.

'Margaret, my child, I have found a nice husband for you,' he said. 'A nice Greek husband. The boy is here in Sydney, the marriage will take place in a few months. You will be very happy with him.'

Father Constantine was very happy. I was furious. I had not the slightest interest in an arranged marriage with anyone, not even a nice Greek boy. Father Constantine took my refusal badly. He wanted Mum to intervene. But Mum said the decision was up to me, since it was my arranged marriage.

The Greek priest went off in a huff. I don't know if he was paid to arrange marriages, but I think not. Probably he was fond of mother because of the cups of tea and thought he was doing us both a favour by providing a husband for me. No more tea and sandwich visits to the Coens for him.

I received another equally strange proposal at about the same time from wealthy family friends, a married couple about Mum's age, who seemed quite elderly to me. The man picked me up as I walked down Botany Street and said he would drive me home. Instead we drove off and did a circuit of Centennial Park. Then, in the most matter-of-fact voice, he asked me if I would consider becoming his mistress. He didn't touch me. It was as if he was offering me a business proposition.

'What about your wife?' I stammered out.

'My wife understands,' he said calmly. 'She thinks it would be a good arrangement.'

I was terrified. I wasn't at all convinced that the wife knew anything about it. I didn't know what sort of maniac he was.

'I don't think so. You'll have to ask me another day,' I said, stalling for time.

We did another circuit while he coolly elaborated, telling me that he had been watching me and how much he liked me. He had no intention of leaving his wife if I became his mistress, he added and concluded by saying that I would be very well looked after financially.

I wasn't going to be this man's mistress any more than I was prepared to accept a Greek husband I hadn't met. The man and his wife were childless and I often wondered afterwards if they had wanted me to produce a child for them.

If you say you are going to be an artist, the first stumbling block for religious people is that you have to draw from the model. It shocks them.

It doesn't matter that every artist who ever painted drew from the model; they are still shocked. In my case it began with Auntie Ina before she entered the convent, when I was a child and she was still living at The House. For reasons best known to myself, I had undressed a doll, but my doll appeared mysteriously dressed again. Miffed at this intervention, I undressed the doll as before; again mysteriously she was re-dressed.

Then I caught Ina in the act. I was cross with her for interfering in my games, and she in return scolded me for daring to be so bold.

'Cranky Ina' I called her. The name stuck. She was 'Cranky Ina' for many years thereafter.

During my first term at Rubbo's art school, I took a selection of my work up to show Grandma. It included a few studies of the nude. I hadn't quite made up my mind if I would show them to her or not. In the meantime they were safely stowed away in my bedroom. Or so I thought.

Ina, who had now long been a nun, was back at Yass for a holiday. She went investigating in my room and managed to fossick out the hidden nudes.

'Is this what they teach you in art school?' she said in shocked tones.

'Unless you draw from the model, you will never be able to draw the human figure,' I replied defensively.

Ina quailed. Nothing more was heard from her about the nude. Annie and I giggled about it in the kitchen, Annie agreeing that Ina shouldn't have gone snooping around my things in the first place.

Not only Catholics carried on about drawing the human body. One of Doug's strictly Anglican uncles was visiting us long after we were married and living in St Ives. The house was hung with nudes, mostly by Norman Lindsay. A nude that Norman made out of plaster of Paris stood on the mantelpiece under a painting of a nude in oils, while a bronze figurine made the centrepiece of the dining table.

Uncle Wallace looked askance at all this nakedness, his wife pretended not to notice. After two whiskies and a few glasses of wine, Uncle Wallace recovered from his initial shock at seeing unclothed females adorning the house, and even grew a little lecherous.

'I've never seen so many,' he confided over dessert.

'Well,' I said, 'when you finish your lemon meringue pie you'll find another.'

The dessert dishes were hand painted by Arthur Murch. At the bottom of Uncle Wallace's pudding plate was a curvaceous mermaid. Uncle Wallace scraped away at his pie with a gleam in his eye.

I was drawing the model as soon as I started Rubbo's art class. Usually Rubbo's pupils had to spend twelve months in another room drawing 'the antique' before they were allowed anywhere near the model. This meant drawing from a series of famous plaster busts and bodies, starting with a head of Homer, moving on to the hideous bust of Voltaire, the bane of every art student's life, then on to the 'Drowned Girl of the Seine' with such a calm expression on her face. A life-sized plaster torso with the skin stripped off to show the muscles came last.

Rubbo might have taken into account the years of drawing lessons I had from him at Kincoppal, but for whatever reason I escaped the antique. Later, at the Royal Art School, I was not so lucky.

Despite my delight at having left school and becoming a serious art student, the first time I saw the model I nearly died. I knew I would have to draw from the nude and thought I was prepared for anything, but I was still surprised when I saw our model. She was not a young woman. She had masses of black hair which looked dyed to me, naturally dusky skin with a pinky glow and although she had a slim figure she must have been about forty – I was, I suppose, expecting the model to be like the women in Botticelli's 'Primavera'.

My mother was as alarmed as everyone else when I started the life class. 'Do the models have any clothes on?' she asked. 'The men wear vees,' I told her. 'The women have nothing on, but during the rest breaks they go behind a screen and put on a dressing gown and slippers before they sit down with the rest of us.

'Come in and have a look for yourself,' I said to her. 'See how absorbed everyone is, it's almost like being in church. The invitation was sufficient to quiet Mum's concern. She didn't come to the art classes and she didn't say any more about drawing the nude. What I said about the religious atmosphere was true; in a life class you can hear a pin drop, the students concentrate so intently.

Rubbo's studio was on the seventh floor of a building in Bligh Street. The lift up to his rooms was cramped and creaking, but once you arrived, the space was quite airy. Sun streamed in the front windows. Up to the left was the Hotel Metropole; directly opposite, in an old-fashioned sandstone building with Doric columns across the porticoed front, was the Union Club. In spring and summer, the jacaranda tree that grew in the small strip of garden down the side of the Union Club was covered with mauve blossoms and the members' wives held garden parties there. We watched them with amusement arriving in elegant frocks, big hats and white gloves. The back windows had a view right across to Circular Quay.

Not that we had much time to stand and stare with Signor Rubbo. We always had to call him 'Signor'. 'Perspiration, not inspiration' he told us was his motto. 'Work, work, work!'

The Tuesday class I attended was made up of women pupils only, mostly of my own age. There was Elsa Russell, Janna Bruce and tiny pretty Dora Jarret, very proud of being half French. 'The Jarret' Rubbo used to call her.

Janna Bruce

Rubbo gave everyone pet names. Janna was 'Brucie', the other two girls were 'Woy Woy' and 'Goldfinch'. Irene Marr was 'Titianella', which I thought was wonderful. Irene had red hair and the fair complexion that goes with it. When Rubbo criticised her work, we could see the blush run up her face. Alison Rehfisch he called 'Gorgeous'. 'Gorgeous' was Alison's favourite adjective; Alison herself was gorgeous too. Golden-haired and blue-eyed, she was a little older than the rest of us. She had been married and used to bring her little daughter Peggy to classes. Peggy called me 'Auntie Margaret'.

My name was 'Gunner', which I didn't find nearly as attractive as 'Titianella'. Rubbo said it was because one day I would go 'boom boom'. I didn't know what he meant then, and it's no clearer to me now.

Signor Rubbo was in his mid-fifties then, still handsome, still wearing the green Borsalino low over one eye. With his curly black hair, he reminded everyone of Frans Hals' 'The Laughing Cavalier'. Often he wore a red tie, like a communist, to make him look dangerous. As he grew older, he became more sober about his dress and would appear in a double-breasted suit, a white collar and dark tie. Even in his most flamboyantly bohemian attire Rubbo was never untidy or ill-groomed.

Rubbo's head and hands looked slightly too big for his body.

He should have been a tall man, but both his legs had been broken in some childhood accident, which impeded his growth at a critical period. His hands were beautiful, though; sensitive and artistic with the smoothest olive skin.

Numerous stories about how and why Rubbo came to Australia passed round the class. The one most often given as the truth was that he set out from Naples for South Africa but as a prank his friends put him on the wrong boat and he ended up in Australia.

When Rubbo first arrived here, Norman Lindsay had a studio next to him in Rowe Street. There was only a thin partition between them; Norman could hear Rubbo talking aloud to himself, lamenting his lack of recognition. Norman used to give an amazing imitation of this; you would swear Rubbo was in the room. 'Rubbo's soliloquy', Norman called it.

'The great Rubbo is dead,' it began. 'Nobody knows who this great man is. They will come, they will find him on the studio floor, they will see the masterpiece on the wall.' Of course Rubbo was dramatising; he never suffered a fate like this. He was well loved and cared for until the day he died.

Rubbo had a secretary in Bligh Street, a tall, skinny woman who wore navy blue suits with flaring skirts nipped in at the waist and very high heels, on which she tottered around. Her hair was done up on top in a bun that looked as if it never came down.

Her duties included preparing Rubbo's lunch. She was no cook and as she grew older, her culinary skills declined. Rubbo would set up a table in the antique room at which they sat and ate, or tried to eat, whatever inedible mess she had concocted in the cubbyhole kitchen off the side of the two classrooms.

Poached eggs were her *pièce de résistance*. She would break the eggs into strenuously boiling water, wait a few seconds, then dish the whole lot out onto a plate. Rubbo would stare down with horror at the uncooked eggs swimming in water before him. Eventually his wife sent his meals in.

Besides drawing from the model, Rubbo made us do character studies of old men; Rubbo loved painting old men. He would scour Hyde Park for derelicts and persuade them to come up and pose for us. (I presume he paid them for their services.) After he had arranged his subject on the dais, or the model's throne as it was called – usually a table with the legs cut down – Rubbo put a shovel or pick next to the old man to add a touch of authenticity. But the warmth of the sun coming through the windows sent the derelicts straight to sleep. In retaliation, Rubbo kept a pocket full of gravel; as soon as the model nodded off, ping! With deadly aim Rubbo threw a pebble at the peacefully somnolent sitter. Rubbo drew them very well. He was deeply sympathetic towards them. Later one of these old derelicts actually lived at his house.

The male models in the life class were a sorry lot. I don't know how the boys felt about drawing from the female models, but as far as we were concerned, the men were no temptation. Old Mack, looking like a Roman emperor gone wrong, was almost always tipsy. Ten minutes into a pose his mouth would sag open; not a seductive sight.

We had to draw the model in the same pose until we knew it inside out. Sometimes we drew the one model for six weeks. Being stuck with Old Mack was punishing.

Then there was Petit, who claimed to be the descendant of kings. He was a very short man with an immense moustache. Anything less romantic than Petit would be hard to imagine.

We had a favourite story about Petit. He was posing for the Women Artists, a sketch club of prim and proper elderly ladies. Petit picked up the wrong pair of trunks when he was changing and came out to pose in vees belonging to a much larger man. The lady artists stared at him aghast, none more so than Mildred Lovett, who finally broke the silence.

'Petit, your person is showing,' she said. Her words became legendary. Every art student had heard about Petit's person. It was hard to suppress the smiles when Petit appeared to pose.

After a class began, there was no chattering or mucking about. Rubbo insisted on utter silence while we worked. He would stalk round the room, criticising our efforts in turn.

We waited in fear and trembling for Signor Rubbo's appraisal. If he didn't like a drawing on the board in front of you off it came, a habit with which I was already too familiar from my days at Kincoppal; it was still devastating. To work on a drawing for a whole day, or three days, or three weeks, then to have it suddenly vanish with one whisk of the feather duster or Rubbo's handkerchief was more than we could bear. In desperation, we gave up charcoal and started drawing in soft pencil. 'Rub it out, rub it out,'

Rubbo would mutter furiously, but at least he couldn't take to it with the duster.

Attention to detail was what he taught, not emphasising detail as such, but learning to show every detail in its correct relationship to the whole, tonal differentiation being the key.

I didn't use colour at all in those days. When I wasn't drawing in charcoal or pencil, I was doing pen and ink still lifes. It seemed that I laboured over each one for hours. Pen and ink is a finicky medium, but I was desperate to become an illustrator like Jack Flanagan. I didn't work as hard as I do now, though. Now I hate to waste time, but it takes years of learning to become really industrious.

My mother had a large collection of my early drawings in the flat at Randwick. When she was taken ill and had to leave the flat, the drawings were bundled up and destroyed. Just as well, I think.

Our neighbours had a daughter, Mary, whose mother thought, since I was an artist, I should paint Mary's portrait.

Mary wore glasses. I was nervous about drawing them so I suggested she take them off. There was no need for her glasses to be in the portrait, I argued. I produced a reasonably good pencil likeness, except for the eyes. I worked on them for a couple of days, but they still looked wrong. My mother came to inspect the portrait.

'Good heavens,' she whispered reprovingly, 'you needn't have made Mary so cross-eyed. She may be cross-eyed in real life, but you could have left it out of the drawing.'

Mum was right. I had forgotten. Mary had one eye that looked straight ahead, while the other looked out to the side (not strictly speaking cross-eyed, but we always called her cross-eyed). That's what had been worrying me as I tried to draw her. If I had roughed out the head properly from the start, I would have noticed at once.

When you're drawing a head, you rough it out first, you do a circle where each of the eyes is to go. You don't draw it feature by feature to begin with, as I had.

Rubbo himself fell into that trap once. Doing his usual round of the class, he swooped on one unfortunate girl working away at the model. 'Why are you drawing one toe, two toes? Here you have drawn six toes,' Rubbo scolded, busily wiping the drawing off the board.

'But, Signor Rubbo,' the model spoke up, 'I *have* six toes.'

Rubbo also taught at the Royal Art Society, and towards the end of the year I started going to classes there four nights a week. I chose the Royal Art out of loyalty to Rubbo; there were other art schools in Sydney, including Julian Ashton's and J. S. Watkins's. By then Watkins was a very stooped old man who gave lessons in his studio. Janna Bruce went to an etching class at Syd Long's, which he conducted separately from his Royal Art classes. The East Sydney Tech didn't have the stature it later did; nobody studied there much because the course had no diploma.

Going to the Royal Art Society meant that I became much more serious about my art. My Randwick party life with Amber gradually declined. Being an artist was most important to me now, although I still loved dancing. If there was any party in the offing, I was eager to be dancing.

Amber had become involved with a boy (not Paddy the tennis player). She spent an enormous amount of time talking to him on the phone. When I did go round to the Hacketts now, the phone would inevitably ring and Amber would disappear for hours. They didn't marry for six years, but he was a constant presence in the meantime.

Even though that side of my life was fading away, Amber and Noel always treated me with the greatest respect as an artist – not that I had done anything to justify that title – and they believed in me totally. Noel gave me my first commission. He asked me to do two black and white drawings as a wedding present for a friend of his.

I was thrilled pink. The finished product, I'm afraid, was not verty original. It bore a close resemblance to the work of an artist named Harold Clark, who had illustrated an edition of Edgar Allan Poe's *Tales of Mystery and Imagination*. I was an ardent fan of both the stories and the illustrations.

The Royal Art Society was two floors up a rickety staircase at 75 Pitt Street on the Circular Quay side of Martin Place.

Syd Long was my teacher two nights a week now; Rubbo still taught me the other two. Syd was easier to get on with. He didn't seem to take teaching as seriously as Rubbo did. Small and quiet

Sydney Long

with grey hair, Syd was a bit grey all over but he had a pleasant, rather inquisitive expression and a gentle smile. He would stroll round the classroom, humming as he looked at our work.

'That's nice,' Syd would say after he had inspected a drawing, then reach into his pocket and hand over a boiled lolly. Syd always had a bag of lollies in his pocket and he always hummed 'In the Good Old Summertime'.

Friends of my mother's wanted to buy some of Syd's etchings and they asked me to introduce them to him. I set up an appointment with Syd, took them along, did the introductions and left. That night at the class Syd handed me an envelope. Inside was a £5 note.

'That's your commission,' he said. He had given me 25 per cent of the £20 worth of his etchings they had bought to take back to the country. I was surprised and delighted. Syd Long could do no wrong in my eyes after that.

The Royal Art rented a whole floor of the building, consisting of two classrooms (one for the life class, one for the antique) and an office. A notice in the life room said, 'Silence is requested while the model is posing', which someone had changed so it read, 'Silence is requested while the model is dozing'. We thought this was a great joke.

Alison and George

Mr Oxnard Smith, an elderly man with a drooping white moustache, presided over the office. On his desk were copies of a German magazine called *Jugend*. On the wall hung a male nude, a pale, thin, ordinary-looking man, also with a drooping moustache but beautifully painted, by a Belgian artist, I think. It mysteriously disappeared in one of the Royal Art's moves.

George Finey was one of the first people I met at the Royal Art. A little timorous, I arrived to find George clad only in shorts and sandals prancing around on top of the long table in the secretary's office where the board of directors held their meetings. George, with his false teeth on a plate pushed up the front of his mouth, was grimacing fearsomely as he pranced. It was the weirdest sight, a strange first meeting.

Jack Mills, Bob Gunter, John Santry and Hilda Townsend were new friends for me at the Royal Art, and, of course, Alison's best friend George Duncan.

George Duncan was the guardian angel of the Royal Art. Big, blond, blue-eyed obliging George – if anything ever went amiss in the place, we said, 'Let George do it.' 'Let George do it' was the class catchword.

George did meticulous academic drawings; it was a long time before he attempted any painting. He and Alison were absolutely devoted to art and to each other. Alison and Janna Bruce had come along with me to the Royal Art from Rubbo's day class. When Rubbo's son Sydney was interviewing us forty years later, Alison described how Rubbo had introduced her to George.

'George, this is Alison. I want you to look after her,' Rubbo said at class.

'And,' Alison concluded, 'George has been looking after me ever since.'

Arthur Murch was overseas on a travelling scholarship with John Eldershaw, Rah Fizelle and E. A. Harvey when I began at the Royal Art, but his drawings, including a typical rounded luminous pink nude, were hanging in the Royal Art office. I was impressed by the beauty of the work. Murch, when I did meet him, was blond and chubby like one of his own paintings. He and Harvey (Harvey was his surname but everyone called him 'Harvey' as if it were a first name) started a sketch club in a studio down near the Haymarket. Fizelle had his own studio in lower George Street, near Grace Crowley and Thea Proctor. Thea Proctor was much older than the rest of us and well established as an artist. She dressed as elegantly as she drew, and rarely mixed with students.

A clattering on the dilapidated Royal Art stairs would announce the arrival of the Lindsay boys, Ray and Phil. Everyone waited with bated breath to see what would happen next; the Lindsay boys were supposed to be wild young men. They would tumble in, falling about, causing uproar. Phil was short with long fair hair. He wore an ancient green velvet coat that was far too long for him and it trailed on the floor. He was always tripping over it, or tripping over something else.

Ray was tall and dark, quite different-looking from Phil, but also long-haired. The Lindsays wore long hair before anyone else. I don't think they ever drew at the Royal Art, they just dropped in to collect their friends for another night on the town.

Monday, Tuesday, Thursday and Friday I went to the Royal Art. A short, blonde woman in a rabbity fur coat used to catch the same six o'clock tram from Randwick as I did. She had a swollen look about the eyes. I thought she might have a night job in the city. She did, but not what I imagined.

The classes finished about nine or nine thirty. One night I was on my way to Elizabeth Street to catch the tram home with John Mills and a couple of the other boys when, fur coats flying, high heels clacking, suddenly a dozen women came running like gazelles down Martin Place. Among them I glimpsed the face of the woman I used to see on the tram. Following close on the women's heels were the police. The women were prostitutes, the boys told me. King Street was their regular beat. Every so often the police felt obliged to chase them off.

I met a girl called Rosalie Humphries at the Royal Art. Since my move into art circles, I had lost touch with my close friends from school such as Genie Devlin. I was longing for a friend with whom I could discuss books and literature. One night at class when we were discussing poetry Rosalie asked me if I had ever read *Hassan* by James Elroy Flecker. I hadn't, so Rosalie lent me a copy. I had always liked poetry; at school I learned long poems like 'The Ancient Mariner' off by heart. Hassan enchanted me; the magic and mystery of the romantic verse play with its hints of Oscar Wilde, Aubrey Beardsley decadence and sadness. I loved the character of the carpet maker who wove borders of black for death around his patterns.

Rosalie brought me in more books of modern poetry to read. Eagerly I devoured everything she lent me; we had long conversations about poetry and art. Rosalie learned fencing, which I envied because it seemed so romantic. I wished I could afford lessons myself. She had an old bomb of a car and quite often drove me home. We rattled our way out to Randwick, enthusing over books, swapping ideas, planning our careers.

Rosalie invited me to a luncheon party at her parents' home; her father was a doctor at Killara. The table was elegantly set, every place setting had a finger bowl and in each bowl Rosalie had put a scarlet poinsettia petal.

The grilled racks of lamb were arranged in a circle on a serving plate. In the centre was a mound of mashed potato and around each cutlet was a little white paper frill. It was all just like Mrs Beeton's cookery book, more stylish than our meals at home and quite different to the cheap snacks we snatched before the Royal Art classes.

To my distress, a few weeks later Rosalie announced that she had accepted a physical culture teaching position in Tasmania because she wanted to get away from home. I was stricken. I missed our talks and the rides in her funny little car. Rosalie was a kindred soul, I thought.

From Tasmania, Rosalie wrote saying that she was off to try her luck in England. A year passed before she came back to Sydney, but it was only a brief visit before she went back to England for good. I saw her off at Central station; she was catching the train to Melbourne and taking the boat from there.

I remember walking back along the platform crying my eyes out because I thought I would never have such a good friend again. Rosalie had been my mentor.

The classes at the Royal Art being mixed, I had my share of invitations and romances with the boys, but I was very wary of entanglement. I hadn't gone to art school for a husband and I thought that if I married I wouldn't be able to be an artist. Besides, art students didn't have any money for grand nights out. Molly was off every night of the week to dinner or the theatre. She would come home laden with corsages and boxes of chocolates. I used to sneak a few of the chocolates as a small consolation for my lack of rich admirers.

John Mills was a special friend of mine among the boys at the Royal Art. He did a charcoal drawing of me, which I still have. If the model didn't turn up at class, one of the students sat on the model's throne and the rest of the class did a portrait of him or her instead.

One night it was my turn and John gave me his drawing, the first time anyone had ever drawn me.

John had a part-time job looking after a yacht and he took Bob Gunter and me out on the harbour with him. I'll never forget it; the yacht was so quiet. I was caught up in the spell of the water as John dashed about changing ropes and we wended out way across the harbour with the wind.

The Royal Art boys used to take me for a cup of coffee after classes to Mockbell's in Castlereagh Street. Mockbell's was a chain of coffee shops, the haunt of the literary and artistic. The men used to play chess at the long, marble-topped trestle tables and the waitresses wore black dresses. You could sit there for hours.

Kitty and Joan Britten, two German girls who were models in the life class, were always at Mockbell's. Artists used to draw at the tables, someone always had a sketch pad out. I loved looking at the Mockbell's habitués but I never stayed long. If I was home late, I had such a deal of explaining to do to Mum that it wasn't worth it.

We had christened an ex-sailor who attended classes 'Bloody Politeful'. Bloody Politeful was a misfit at the Royal Art. Painfully shy, he went bright red whenever he spoke. He was always inordinately polite except for occasional lapses into ripe seagoing language – hence the nickname. Bloody Politeful wanted desperately to be my friend. He was tired of the sea, he told me, and lonely. He had joined the art classes in the hope of meeting some nice girls.

Bloody Politeful took to accompanying me to the tram after class. Next thing I knew, he arrived with a huge box of chocolates, not very nice chocolates either, and asked me if I would be his girl.

'No, I'm sorry,' I told him as gently as I could, 'but it's out of the question.'

That was the end of the romance. I think he eventually drowned in the harbour.

My next would-be consort was Luigi Nobili. He was an Italian nobleman, an artist who fled from Italy because he couldn't bear the thought of being called up for Mussolini's military service. Rubbo brought him down to the Royal Art and introduced him to the students. No one knew if Luigi was really an aristocrat or if the Nobili surname had people fooled. Anyway, Luigi took an immediate shine to me.

Luigi was a stylish dresser. He wore tailored suits and silk shirts with his initials embroidered on them. Nothing ragged or bohemian about Luigi. He was a little shorter than me, which was a worry – at eighteen those things seem important.

Luigi inveigled me up to his Rowe Street studio for a black coffee. Black coffee made in a percolator was very avant-garde and exotic, not to say decadent, in those days. He serenaded me on the mandola, an instrument that looked and sounded like the mandolin. After a few more visits to his studio, I decided to invite Luigi home to Randwick, to meet my family.

Luigi was delighted and asked if we could stop off on the way at the famous Centennial Park he had heard so much about (not from me, after my Centennial Park experience with the married man).

The Coogee tram went up the Anzac Parade side of the park. The tram stopped at a bushy part of the park where there were lots of native plants. It was also boggy. Luigi wanted to see the rose garden in the centre of the park. I guided him across the marsh until we came to a stream with only a plank for a bridge.

'Don't cross here, Luigi,' I said apprehensively, glancing at the immaculate pale blue coat and trousers he was sporting that afternoon. But Luigi the gallant insisted on leading me across the plank. The inevitable happened. Luigi went head first into the narrow but surprisingly deep little stream and emerged covered in mud from head to toe.

He was upset, not so much at the dunking, but he kept asking where he could have his suit cleaned. I suppressed my smiles. I

Luigi Nobili   *Margaret Coen*

found him a tap, cleaned him up as best I could and then we made our way to Botany Street.

'Luigi had some bad luck,' I said when we arrived. Luigi did look bedraggled, his clothes still damp and mudcaked. 'He fell off a plank at Centennial Park.'

My rotten, unfeeling family laughed their heads off; almost the final straw in an afternoon of calamities. However, Luigi forgave my family's barbarities; he survived the expedition and our courtship continued.

Among the paintings hanging on the walls of his studio was a landscape of a lavish Italian garden, with red spots strategically positioned over it. Luigi told me he had been in love with a beautiful young girl in Italy. She had been the love of his life, but her parents had arranged for her to marry a man twice her age. The painting hanging on the wall in Sydney depicted the grounds of the flash hotel where the couple had honeymooned.

During the honeymoon, Luigi and the girl had met secretly in the shrubbery of this garden and the red dots marked the sites of their assignations. A most romantic tale, I thought.

Luigi was finding it difficult to earn a living as an artist in Australia. He decided that the answer to his financial problems was to open a country art school in Goulburn. He packed his bags, took up his easel and a stack of his canvasses and headed off to make his fortune. Out of sight, out of mind, I'm afraid, as soon as Luigi departed. I forgot about him. But when I was at Yass for the holidays, I remembered that he was toiling away in nearby Goulburn and wrote to him.

Annie used to collect all the mail for The House in the morning from the Yass post office. Grandma would distribute it while we were sitting round the table at dinner time.

'I think this one must be for you, Margaret,' Grandma said, handing me a letter – we were both Margaret Coen and that's why she had thought it was for her. The letter was from Luigi; as I read I nearly died.

Dear Margaret, So it is because you are amongst the blacks and the old people that you think of your friend Luigi . . .

Had Grandma read any further than the 'Dear Margaret'? I never found out but I prayed she hadn't. What could she have thought?

The letter went on to say that I must come and visit him in Goulburn, but my love affair with Luigi Nobili was over. Luigi had vanquished any romantic notions I had of him with this thoughtless introduction.

The story of Jim Leape, a student at the Royal Art, was much sadder. He was about my age and did very skilful pen and ink drawings. One Friday night as I was catching the tram, he asked if he could come home with me. We caught the Randwick tram and he showed me a book he had made of Coleridge's 'The Ancient Mariner', filled with his own drawings of the cursed seaman and the unlucky bird. After we alighted, he wanted to walk down to Botany Street with me.

'I like walking,' he said when I hesitated, thinking it was too far out of his way.

The further we walked, the more passionate his declarations became. He made no physical advances, just verbal declarations of his infatuation. I knew we liked each other, but I had no idea his feelings about me were so strong.

At the flats we said goodnight. Jim Leape said he would see me on Monday and set off into the darkness. From Botany Street, he was going to walk to Coogee, where he lived.

At the Royal Art the following week, someone asked me for two shillings.

'What for?' I asked.

'For a wreath,' Percy Norton told me.

'Who for?'

'Jim Leape.'

I was stunned. Jim Leape had died of a heart attack at the weekend. I found out later that he was only sixteen and that rheumatic fever as a child had weakened his heart. His death troubled me for a long time afterwards; I couldn't help but wonder if our long walk had had anything to do with his death.

At the end of my first year out of school, I went as usual to Yass for my holidays. I stayed on after Christmas and frittered away the time until the end of January. Then my father came into my room holding a letter.

'Your mother wants you back in Sydney,' he said. 'Jack Flanagan has come out from America.'

Jack Flanagan

Frantic with excitement, I packed my bags and was on the next train back to Sydney. My idol, Jack Flanagan the artist, the American success story, here! I couldn't wait to meet him.

Jack Flanagan was tall, fair, blue-eyed, good-looking and a stylish dresser; I remember him always in a grey suit. He was only thirty-three, a great dancer and very recently divorced, which added enormously to his sex appeal in the 1920s. Women were mad about him.

In Sydney for an exhibition of his work at Rubery Bennett's gallery in King Street, he was staying at the Hotel Australia on the corner of Rowe and Castlereagh Streets. The Hotel Australia was the place to stay in those days.

Jack invited me to have dinner with him there. I was thrilled beyond measure just to be in his company. He introduced me to a cocktail called the Clover Club, which he said everyone drank with dinner in New York.

He filled my head with stories of famous artists and writers, such as Scott Fitzgerald, whom he had actually met in New York. He worked as an illustrator for the same magazines as the writers wrote for and he talked about the Salmagundy, the famous club where they all met. My eyes were out on stalks. How I envied him.

His studio was where the English artist Augustus John had stayed when he was in America; West 67th Street, the Hotel des Artistes. Jack's studio was on the top floor and he had a giant skylight cut into the roof for extra light while he worked.

As well as illustrating stories, Jack did advertising work for a French shipping line. He loved the East and the Middle East, and in return for doing a series of beautiful black and white drawings he travelled on their line free of charge.

The East was the source of much of his inspiration. Some of his most famous works were illustrations for *The Story of the Other Wise Man*, the tale of a fourth wise man who visited the infant Christ.

I dreamed about New York after that night. If only I could go to America, all those wonderful things might happen to me, too. Meanwhile in Sydney, Jack was lionised wherever he went, and there were parties thrown for him all over town.

Jack showed a marked preference for my company, which miffed some of the relatives. Cousins of ours held a big party at Mosman for him and I wasn't asked; Molly was, but not I. I stayed at home moping.

'Where's Margaret?' Jack asked as soon as he arrived at the party.

'We didn't ask her,' they said. 'But Molly's here.'

'I know,' Jack replied, 'but I want to see Margaret.'

He stayed for half an hour at the party, then came back to the Australia and rang me up.

'Come in and have a Clover Club,' he said.

I was in like a shot, brooding forgotten. This was a great feather in my cap. I went to many places with him after that. I was wildly jealous when a society writer on one of the papers took a fancy to him and started to chase him.

Rubbo had taught Jack before he went to America and the Royal Art gave Jack a sendoff party. Jack told me on the side as he was leaving that he was glad to be returning to America. He was a bit tired of Rubbo's enthusing.

'He keeps calling me "Jacka",' Jack said. 'It makes me feel like a bloody kookaburra.'

At the end of a fortnight's hectic socialising, Jack sailed out of my life, bound for the East on a ship called the *Malabar*. I went to see him off. Life seemed suddenly very flat.

Somehow, I vowed, I would get myself to New York. I would have my own studio. I, too, would make a fortune as an illustrator. I could think of nothing but Jack Flanagan and New York. I became obsessed. I wrote Jack miles of letters and lived for the postman bringing a letter back from him. When a letter from him finally did arrive, I was mortified beyond belief because I had misspelled his name. It was not 'Flannaghan', but 'Flanagan', like the Irish kings, he pointed out. I never was a good speller.

A beauty contest was advertising a first prize of a trip to Hollywood. If I could make it to Hollywood, I felt sure New York would be only a stone's throw away. I entered the contest under the name of Perdita Adams and sent in two portraits taken by a studio photographer. Very appealing I looked, gazing soulfully up at the camera, my hair cut short and waved. The photographer carefully concealed my heavy black freckles.

On the strength of the photos, I made the finals. It was more than a beauty contest, though; the contestants were supposed to be able to act. We had to appear on stage at a Kings Cross picture show for the last judging.

I didn't really think I had much chance of winning, but I was determined to go along. I had nothing to wear.

'Do you think Molly would mind if I borrowed her new frock?' I asked Mum. Molly had just finished paying off a layby on a frock for the Randwick spring meeting and Mum and I knew very well that Molly *would* mind. She worked hard for her clothes and, as

Royal Art party for Jack Flanagan. Margaret is on the right in the front, next to the dinner-suited special guest

she had to pay rent at home (which I didn't), every new dress was precious. An outfit for the spring meeting was sacred.

My mother agreed not to breathe a word about my borrowing the dress. Aunt Mary Carter, my mother's closest friend, lent me a pair of shoes with high heels. I didn't wear high heels myself; I wore flat, woven, Spanish-style sandals from a shop at Circular Quay. I was really happiest in no shoes. Aunt Mary's shoes were two sizes too small for me, but I forced my feet into them, donned Molly's dress and took myself off to the Cross.

We had to walk across the stage of the theatre and say a few words as if we were in a play. I got stage fright, as I had in the Yass school concert many years before. I completely dried up. I couldn't get a word out. Perdita Adams came nowhere in the beauty contest, but at least Mum kept her word and Molly never found out about the dress.

There was, of course, no hope of my being able to leave Australia. Going to America took weeks and weeks by boat and cost a fortune. Most girls didn't go off by themselves in those days; even if we could have afforded it or if I had won the Hollywood prize, I doubt if I would have been brave enough to set off alone.

To cheer myself up, I sent one of the Perdita Adams photos to King in Bundaberg. Perdita was a winner up there; King showed the photo to his mates in the bank, who were most impressed. King wrote back enthusiastically saying he hadn't realised how good-looking I was.

The postscript, however, was a jarring note. 'P.S.,' King added, 'for God's sake never come to Queensland.' He didn't want to lose face with his mates; he knew the glamorous girl in the photograph didn't quite match the freckle-faced reality.

America was a dream. I worked much harder at being an artist after Jack Flanagan's visit; I struggled to get out of the antique into the life class at the Royal Art. Jack Flanagan's visit also inspired me more than ever to be a black and white artist. I resolved to take the first commercial art job available.

Perdita Adams

Margaret, ready for a job

6

Our Talented Master

I answered an advertisement in the paper. 'Wanted: apprentice for commercial artist', the ad ran. This sounded like me, so down I went to Angel Place where Mr Angus, the commercial artist, had his studio.

Mr Angus was a tall, thin, sharp-featured man with a pointed nose, a mouth like a piece of string and ice-blue eyes behind rimless round glasses. As it turned out, he was also extremely mean.

Being Mr Angus's apprentice meant that I wouldn't receive any salary but, he promised, I would learn everything there was to know about black and white reproduction. It could be my entree to Jack Flanagan's world, the beginning of my career as a black and white illustrator. I signed up with Mr Angus.

A World War I fighter pilot hero, Mr Angus found difficulty adjusting to civilian life after the war and more difficulty still in attempting to earn his living as a commercial artist. He hit on a simple solution: let other people do the work and don't pay them. The scarcity of work towards the end of the 1920s made this easy for him.

Mr Angus's artwork consisted of advertising commissions. He had an extensive filing system, a huge library of drawings cut out of magazines and filed under various headings such as a day at the beach or family picnics, on the golf course and jockeys and horses at the races. Mr Angus was always keen on including animals.

When a commission came in the three apprentices – myself, another girl called Bessie and a boy, Stanley – had to search the files, find an appropriate drawing and carefully trace it onto paper. The tracing was then reversed and rubbed down onto a sheet of clean white paper. The finished product looked like a well-done pencil drawing. Mr Angus himself never drew anything; he couldn't draw and his sole contribution was to ink in our traced pencil work. His pen and ink technique was crude. Apart from Jack Flanagan's work, I studied every black and white artist I came across and Mr Angus didn't measure up.

Not only was he exploiting our artistic abilities as fast as he could and not paying us, but he was mean with materials. It added insult to injury in our eyes. Our pencils had to be used right down to the stub. When one was too short to hold, Mr Angus devised a holder into which the stub was fitted, like a pen nib. Every pencil was used until the last bit of lead was gone.

Stanley grew more mutinous by the day; Mr Angus had taken me on as the new apprentice, knowing Stanley would soon quit. Stanley frequently took the day off. He was clearly fed up with Mr Angus and his school of hard knocks. Finally he vanished for good. Bessie stayed on for a few months and I stuck it out for almost a year, slaving away at the wretched tracings.

After I finished work four nights a week, I still went to the Royal Art Society. To fill in the time from five or five thirty until the classes started at seven, I used to walk up from the Angel Arcade to the public library and read. I got through a lot of books there. I was addicted to reading and in winter the library was always warm and comfortable, an additional benefit. Mum kept dinner for me at home on top of a saucepan on the stove and it was usually about ten when I ate. Sometimes I had a sandwich with one of the boys from the Royal Art on the way to class. Bob Gunter also read at the library; sometimes I would meet him there and we would share a snack together before class.

One summer's night, Bob and I came out of the library starving. We sat in the Domain to eat our tea. Bob had a pie and I had a slab of chocolate.

The most hungry-looking dog in the world approached us. He sat down in front of us and just looked, occasionally giving a feeble half-wag of its tail. Bob, always kind-hearted, was the first to weaken. He tore off a piece of his pie. One gulp and the pie was gone. Immediately contrite, I gave the dog half my chocolate. A second gulp and that was gone, too. The remainder of Bob's pie went next, followed by the other half of my chocolate. We were rewarded by much tail-wagging. The dog's dinner had made the dog's day.

Everyone was hungry then.

I loved the library as much as I did reading. I was determined to have my own library. There must be thousands of books at home now, but then I was only beginning.

I started buying World Classics, a series that cost sevenpence halfpenny each at Anthony Horderns, a big old-fashioned city department store, on my way home from school in my last year. World Classics included authors like Victor Hugo and Guy de Maupassant. Maupassant's short stories delighted me. I read the first volume standing up in Angus and Robertson's bookshop in Castlereagh Street. The paper was poor, the print atrocious, but I had quite a collection of World Classics.

In my last year at school I discovered a book that I really coveted. It was *The Painter's Anthology* by the artist Arthur Watts, a collection of his favourite poems – Shakespeare, Browning, Blake, Keats and many others – all illustrated by himself. There were eight colour plates, eight black and white plates and fifty black and white line decorations. I was longing to buy it.

Grandma used to send the family £10 every Christmas. Mum used to take £5; the rest of us got 25s each. Mine usually went on a book, or a couple of books. *The Painter's Anthology* cost 17s6d, expensive for me.

I told Mum about it, hoping she might advance me my share of Grandma's £10. Mum said, 'I'll see if your father will give it to you for Christmas.'

'But I'll have to put a deposit on it now, or it might go,' I begged.

Mum went into town and actually bought the book for me, then she wrote to Dad saying that this was what I wanted for Christmas. To Mum's surprise, Dad sent up the money for the book straight away and she was reimbursed. I cherished that book, and I still have it today.

Back at work, Mr Angus became more demanding. I had to run

messages for him, not just work messages, but personal errands. He wanted me to do his household shopping. I don't know what his fat French wife was doing; resting at home, I supposed, while I did her work. I was very angry with Mr Angus by now, angry that he didn't pay me for the endless tracing, angry that he didn't pay me an office girl's wages for the other chores he made me do, and angry that he could teach me nothing about black and white drawing because he knew nothing.

My dissatisfaction came to a head when Mr Angus decided to move offices. He presented me with a list of premises to inspect. I was to report back on the condition of the buildings, what the office space was like, and measure up the interior. There were also groceries to be picked up, including meat from the butcher's. The butcher's errand finished me. I took the instructions, didn't say a word, put my hat on and walked out. I didn't go back.

Mr Angus rang Mum at home, very disturbed and most upset. What could I be thinking of? he shouted down the phone. How could I be so ungrateful after he had taught me so much?

My mother wasn't fooled. She was fully aware of his perfidy, and she took him severely to task in reply to his barrage.

'Anyway, she'll never be an artist,' Mr Angus retaliated as he hung up.

Fifteen years later, I was on the judging committee of the Watercolour Institute and some works came in from a Mr Angus. It was the same Mr Angus, who, in his retirement, had turned his hand to watercolours, still traced, I was sure, from an English magazine.

My brief description of Mr Angus and his methods of commercial art ensured that the committee promptly put his dreadful paintings out as they deserved. It gave me the greatest satisfaction.

I received no money from Mr Angus during the year I was with him. The fees for four nights a week at the Royal Art were not expensive but in 1930 there was almost no money around. I knew I should try for another job immediately, a proper paying job.

Besides, Trix, my godmother at Kincoppal, was worried about me. I think she thought I was spending too much time with artists and mixing with a wild crowd. Cloistered away at Kincoppal, how

Trix knew or could possibly suspect what I did was a mystery. Nun or not, however, she was a smart woman.

The phone rang; Trix wanted to have a talk with me. She had been talking to the Reverend Mother at St Vincent's, Trix began innocently. Without pausing, she continued that, as a very special concession, the Reverend Mother had agreed to accept me as a trainee nurse. 'Everybody knows how difficult it is to get into St Vincent's; you know what a favour it is,' she rattled on.

Dismay filled me. A nursing career, for me who was going to be an artist?

'Trix,' I pleaded, 'I couldn't do such a thing. It's ridiculous!' All those lessons wasted, all those nights coming home late to warmed up leftovers, a whole year of Mr Angus for nothing! Trix gave me a reprieve.

But her offer (or threat) certainly speeded up my efforts to find work after quitting Mr Angus. I answered an advertisement by a woman called Phyllis Seymour. She had a commercial art studio in Bond Street and was looking for assistants.

Phyllis was the sister of the Seymour whose bequest to the University of Sydney many years later resulted in the present Seymour Centre, but there wasn't too much money floating around Phyllis in those days. My new job was colouring in photographs of Persian carpets.

Five days a week, nine to five, for £1 a week, three of us girls worked with our heads down colouring in the endless, intricately patterned Persian carpets. It was exacting work; if nothing else it taught patience.

The carpets had been photographed in black and white. We rubbed them down with French chalk, then laboriously hand painted them to match a series of colour plates. The French chalk was a powder that took some of the gloss off the photos so the paint would stick to their surface.

Working for Phyllis had one completely unexpected result. For years I had been hearing about and wanted to meet the artist Norman Lindsay, because he had taught Jack Flanagan. But Norman's world was as far from mine as Jack's America, or so I thought.

Dick Hore, another commercial artist, had a studio in the same building as Phyllis. I was chattering on to him about Jack when suddenly and quite casually Dick said he knew Norman Lindsay and would take Phyllis and me up to Springwood to meet him.

I was bowled over. Anything to do with pen work still fascinated me. I hoped that maybe Norman would teach me, as he had my cousin.

Dick, Phyllis and I caught the train to Springwood from Central station on Saturday morning to stay with the Lindsays for the weekend. Springwood in the Blue Mountains isn't far away, but the train jolted and jerked its way up the mountains, stopping at every little station: Glenbrook, Warrimoo, Valley Heights. I thought we would never get there. It seemed an age, but at last we arrived.

Rose, Norman's dramatically handsome wife, met us at the station. On the front of the big car sat a sphinx, a little figurine Norman had made specially for the bonnet, an exciting beginning to our visit.

We sped up the main road for a couple of miles before turning off, down a rough track through dense bush. Rose, who was a forthright woman, commandeered the conversation. Dick made polite and appropriate responses. Phyllis and I sat in the back, straining our eyes to see something of the house.

The car bumped and wound its way through the bush, up and over a slight incline. Then the car swung round to the left and we were confronted by a large square sandstone house with a columned verandah. Norman had made these Romanesque pillars that adorned the verandah, as well as the colonnaded walkway covered in wisteria alongside the house. Lawns surrounded the house. Satyrs and nymphs at play adorned the garden, as well as larger statuary versions of the sphinx on the car. Phyllis and I were thrilled.

Norman rushed out to meet or rather greet us. I had the immediate sensation of someone tremendously alive. Blue, blue eyes blazed above the fine aquiline nose. He was like quicksilver, constantly moving, with an extraordinary lightness about him. He walked almost like a dancer, his feet hardly seeming to touch the ground. His extreme lightness gave the impression of a much smaller man than he actually was; Norman, in fact, was quite tall. His enthusiastic welcome that became so familiar to me over the

years we found astonishing on that first visit and we were swept along as inevitably as the tide.

Later, Phyllis and I sat for him. Norman did a watercolour head of each of us. I was fascinated by Norman's watercolours; I had seen people using watercolour at the Royal Art, but not as he did. Norman used tubes of watercolour paint instead of little pans. He squeezed the paint out onto small white saucers before touching the paper with it. When he started to paint, the floods of pure colour plus the perfect control held me spellbound.

Norman showed me how to put a wash down. I had already bought some watercolours for myself because they were cheaper than oil paints and canvas, but no one had shown me how to use them.

'Margaret,' he instructed as we were leaving, 'you do some watercolours. The next time you come up, bring them with you and I'll see what your work's like.'

I had gone to see Norman expecting to learn about black and white; I came away determined to become a watercolourist.

After two days in Norman's company, coming into work and colouring carpets on Monday morning was certainly coming back to earth with a thump.

On our second visit to Springwood, we arrived on a Friday night and stayed until Monday morning, which was even more of a treat. A crowd of us went with Norman and Rose to a charity dance in Springwood on the Friday night. Norman had done the backdrop for the dance stage, an enormous oil painting of Pierrot and Columbine under moonlight. The painting seemed to cast a spell that lasted the weekend.

I felt very weak at the knees when I produced my feeble paintings, but Norman told me what was good about them, where I had gone wrong, and above all encouraged me to keep on with watercolour. A student can go to art school for ages, but if someone takes an interest in you, as Norman did in me, it makes such a difference. In those two short visits, he ensured I was seduced by watercolour for a lifetime.

On my second visit, too, Norman gave me a copy of his novel

Norman Lindsay at Springwood

Redheap, which I read and loved. The furore in the press about *Redheap* was just beginning. It was such a harmless novel about country life in a country town; the agitation it caused amazed me. The papers were full of complaints that the characters were based on real people and the book was eventually banned. I think the 'wowsers', as Norman called them, just felt bound to object to anything he did. I cut out and kept everything in the papers to do with the novel. Reading the clippings again now, all the flurry seems so silly.

The carpet colouring for Phyllis continued week after week. Eventually the supply petered out and so did my job. Not that I minded. I had seen enough carpets.

Dick Hore the commercial artist once again intervened in my life. He suggested I go along to Celebrity Pictures, where they wanted an artist to do black and white illustration.

Celebrity Pictures' Pitt Street office was totally strange. In the office, a row of white-gloved girls sat running film through their fingers between two spools. They were film examiners. If there was any catch in the film, they had to stop, cut it out, rejoin the film and wind on.

Celebrity Pictures was an agency for British films. When a film arrived here from overseas, the accompanying publicity had to be changed. This was my job. I might do a black and white or a wash drawing of an actress for an ad in newspapers or alter the lettering under an advertisement to fit the Australian season.

I came in hopefully at nine every morning and stayed until five, but there was very little work to do.

Celebrity Pictures were slowly going broke, which hardly helped. They were run by an Englishman, Mr West, a kindly man without much business sense. However, he gave me a tiny room with a desk so I could work on my own things while I was waiting for commissions. I wasn't given a weekly wage, only paid for whatever work I did, but it was the Depression and any money was better than none.

Despite the business slackness, Celebrity Pictures was the most entertaining place I ever worked.

Maureen, the girl on the switch, wrote novels. She had the room next to mine and sometimes business was so slack that the phone wouldn't ring all morning. Maureen was unperturbed. She busily filled notebook after notebook with wildly romantic prose. Barely sixteen, almost illiterate, Maureen had a head crammed with ludicrous characters and highly improbable situations. Would the lady of the manor succumb to the charms of the handsome villain and be ruined? Will the purer-than-pure young wife of the alcoholic spendthrift discover his infidelities? Dare the prim and proper spinster run away with the mysterious stranger in town? What is hidden in the spinster's past?

Maureen used to lend me her novels to read and they cheered my periods of idleness and unemployment no end. When she wasn't writing, Maureen regaled us with stories about her family, whose extraordinary goings-on almost equalled her imaginary tales. The sex-mad cousin made good listening. The whole office knew about him. He was sixteen, too, and had interfered with everybody in the family – *everybody*, Maureen darkly hinted, males and females – until he was sent off to gaol.

'He'll be coming out soon, interfering with all the girls again,' she concluded with relish; the prospect seemed to delight rather than to worry her.

Maureen's family was poor. She was supporting the lot of them by working at the switch, and was the only one who managed to hang onto a job; she could see that fading away, too, with the demise of Celebrity Pictures.

Two sisters, also victims of the Depression, worked at Celebrity Pictures. The older girl was employed as a senior typist, then, when she was sacked because they couldn't afford to pay a senior's wages, her fourteen-year-old sister Muriel came on as a junior. Muriel was paid £1 a week and they both lived on that. Their mother had died when the girls were still at school. The girls brought a friend home from school for the holidays. Their father fell instantly in love and married her. The sisters were disgusted and didn't want to have anything more to do with the father and they left home immediately to struggle on together as best they could. Muriel was plump with golden curls, and really did look very young. She was one of those baby-faced women who would probably look young at sixty.

Celebrity Pictures obtained an agency for American films, which was cause for jubilation. Things might look up financially now, we hoped. An American was coming out to take charge of the business and smarten up the office. He was given a welcoming party on the day he arrived, and it rapidly developed into a real Australian beer-swill. Inhibitions flew away as freely as the beer flowed in. Muriel's sister had come from home to join the celebration. As the evening progressed, she grew as loquacious as Maureen from the switch. In hushed tones that rang round the room, Muriel's sister revealed that Muriel wasn't fourteen. She giggled then whispered solemnly that Muriel was actually twenty-four.

Next day, no one higher up appeared to remember the sister's revelation. Perhaps they were too busy with the American's antics to be concerned with Muriel's masquerade and none of us was going to dob her in. Muriel remained fourteen as long as I worked at Celebrity Pictures.

Before the new boss arrived there was great rivalry among the girls about who was to be his secretary. The immaculate Miss Jones, always so neat and tidy, won the sought-after position. But Miss Jones soon ceased to be the envy of the typists' pool. The new American boss had a health problem. He suffered from catarrh. From the first day he hawked incessantly and spat onto the new carpet which had been laid in his honour. Miss Jones and Mr West, himself a fastidious man, watched in horror as the new boss rubbed phlegm into the carpet with the heel of his boot.

By the end of the week, Miss Jones would have given her new job to anyone who wanted it. Gradually Mr West and Miss Jones resigned themselves to the new regime, which fortunately didn't last too long. The American was despatched to spit on fresh carpets.

As well as entertaining us, Maureen kept tabs on the whole staff. She told us there was a skeleton in the cupboard of the nice-looking young man who came from the wealthy family in Randwick. He had a freak in his family; a fat girl, as big as those you see in sideshows. The young man married and the office hummed with speculation about his wife. Even Maureen was unable to fathom any information.

Only a few weeks after the wedding, the young man took to the bottle. A couple more weeks went by, then one Friday his wife came in to collect his pay. There was nothing unusual in that – lots of wives did – but in front of our mesmerised eyes stood an enormous figure. The fat girl in the family wasn't his cousin or his sister: she was his wife. His drinking worsened and the nice young man lost his job. Mercifully, perhaps, the marriage didn't last long afterwards, Maureen somehow found out later.

Casimir, a Russian boy whom we called Cas, also worked with us in the office. Like Mum's cleaning lady, his mother had escaped the Revolution by walking across Siberia to Vladivostok. She had had a tribe of little children with her, one of whom was Casimir.

Cas used to bring pots of face cream to work and try to sell them to us girls. He said the cream was very special; the recipe had been given to his mother by a lady-in-waiting to the Czarina. All the women at the Russian court, including the Czarina herself, had used this very same cream. The wonder cream didn't cost very much. We bought up and waited in high hopes for the miracles it was going to perform.

One Friday, Casimir's mother appeared to collect his pay. She was as wide as she was tall. Her complexion was swarthy, and long hairs sprouted from little lumps in her face. The women in the office took one look and felt sick, especially Miss Jones, unlucky again. She had treated herself to a lavish supply of Casimir's cream.

No more orders were taken for the Czarina's beauty cream.

When Cas was eventually retrenched he refused to leave, continuing to arrive punctually every morning and staying to the end of the day as if nothing had happened and he was still being paid.

'I just want to work,' Cas pleaded. 'I will help the firm out by working unpaid.'

It was pathetic. He was so desperate for work, so anxious to please that he practically lay down on the floor for people to walk over. Occasionally they found him some office work; the rest of the time he followed us round like a shadow. We understood, though. Spending all day every day at home with his dumpy Russian mother would have been a daunting prospect for the strongest soul.

I found out that Hilda Townshend, a friend from the Royal Art classes, was working for a signwriter on the floor below Celebrity Pictures, which also made my days there more bearable. Slight, with curly dark hair and hazel eyes, Hilda was passionately devoted to being an artist. 'When this Depression is over,' we consoled each other, 'one day we will really be artists, with our own studios, doing nothing except painting.'

Also working for the signwriter was a tall, handsome man whose burning ambition was to win the Archibald Prize. Hilda and I thought it was sad because he had a young family and was making very little money; his chance of having any time for painting was slim. Once he came into the office and showed us a large parcel of beautiful red parrot fish he had bought cheap at the markets.

'I ought to be painting these, not eating them,' he said wistfully. 'What a still life they would make!'

An offer of work in Brisbane came through for him. He packed up his family and shifted to Queensland, his art career abandoned. The price of the times.

I managed the black and white drawings at Celebrity Pictures when there were any, but lettering had to be done with the advertisements. Spelling was my downfall. I would toil away, finish the job, then discover I had misspelt a word; of course I then had to redo the whole thing. Advertisements became an ordeal. I have never been a good speller and it's very easy to misspell a word when you're hand lettering, because you're absorbed in each letter, not the spelling of the word.

A publicity man who worked for Celebrity Pictures on commission handed one of his outside assignments on to me; a label for a lemon cheese bottle. The makers wanted a drawing of lemons and lettering underneath. I designed a label, drew some nice lemons, did the lettering right, but made one spelling mistake.

The publicity man came raging into my room. The label would have to be scrapped, he shouted. My design was useless; he would have to get somebody to design a new label. I offered to alter the label, but he wouldn't have that. It would have to be redone.

A week or so later Maureen, who was always poking her nose into everything round the office, saw the label I had designed on his desk, printed up. He had altered my design himself, then gone ahead with the printing. More infuriating, he never paid me. If I could earn five guineas for a commercial art job in those days,

I thought I was made. To miss out on any payment was disaster.

Oddly, however, lettering led to my next source of employment, if not of income. A commercial art school opened down from the Royal Art in Pitt Street and the Royal Art recommended me to teach lettering and rough drawing. Spelling aside, lettering wasn't my forte, anyway, but still I took the job.

Rough drawing was right; no battles with the antique, no subtleties of life class studies. It was strictly commercial art, meaning that the pupils learned as little as possible while the man who ran the school made as much as possible. Twenty-five shillings a week I was paid for teaching two afternoon and two evening classes. The first couple of weeks I was duly paid each Friday, then four weeks went by without payment.

The school depended on a continuing cycle of enrolments. Pupils were joining all the time. As soon as a new pupil paid up, my employer would disappear for a couple of hours, reappearing later with a red face and smelling of whisky. He would blunder round the school for half an hour, then stagger off home, leaving me to run his art school. The fees were drunk as rapidly as they came in. Pupils stayed a while, then drifted off disillusioned as new victims signed on.

Teaching was impossible. I either kept starting the classes again for the new ones, so the others were bored, or kept going and the new students were left in the dark.

After another month without wages, I tackled my employer. A few days later he presented me with £5 and I subsided. After three months, a brochure appeared which referred to me as 'our talented master'. I thought this very funny and so did the girls at Celebrity Pictures. Every time I put my head in the door, they chorused, 'How is our talented master today?' Another month passed without salary. I pleaded for some remuneration.

'I don't think I should give you any more money. You don't seem very interested in your work,' my employer replied. No money was forthcoming, and our talented master dug in her heels. A friend gave me some legal aid and I sued my employer in the Court of Petty Debts and secured another £5 from him before leaving the school.

The next excitement was the artist Harvey asking if he could paint my portrait. I was very flattered. Like Arthur Murch and the

Alison and Dora out painting

rest of us, Harvey was very short of money and he was hoping to win the Archibald Prize with the portrait.

Another artist, Miriam Moxham, lent him her studio in Margaret Street to work on the portrait. Miriam was older than the rest of us and lived with her family at Roseville, but she said it was impossible to do any work at home, so kept a studio in town. Miriam's studio was in an old building next to Pfahlert's hotel and overlooking Wynyard Park. Because the building was condemned the rent was cheap. It was full of artists; J. S. Watkins, Dorrit Black, Joe Hollaway's Sketch Club, Myra Cox and my friend Hilda from the Royal Art all had studios there. A studio meant a bare room, an easel, a few chairs, perhaps a gas ring and kettle, maybe some matting on the floor; they were strictly rooms for painting.

I made my own clothes because I couldn't afford to buy them. I used to embroider them to make them more attractive. A high-waisted dress of dusty pink and black was my favourite; it had black cross-stitch on the pink bodice and pink cross-stitch down into the black skirt. I kept that dress for years. I also used to buy

'Margaret Coen' by Harvey

white voile and make it up into blouses which I also embroidered and wore with a black skirt. I wore one of the embroidered voile blouses for Harvey's portrait.

The glass beads were a present from a friend of Molly's who

had been overseas and had come to dinner wearing some glass beads like grapes she had bought in Venice. I couldn't take my eyes off the dark green and clear glass clusters.

'Your beads are so beautiful,' I said. She took them off and gave them to me as a present. They were the most beautiful beads; people fell in love with them. At a party, a man stared at them all night as he talked to me. A couple of days later, he rang me to arrange another meeting.

'Your beads are haunting me,' he said. 'I've been thinking about them all the time. I've even dreamed of them.'

I think Harvey himself provided the paisley shawl which is draped across the background of the painting.

Harvey worked at the portrait for quite a while. His method of painting – partly traditional, partly distinctively his own – was slow and meticulous. After each sitting, he carefully covered the canvas with newspaper to pick off any surplus paint before the next session.

One Saturday afternoon, Harvey and I thought we were alone in the building when we heard an extraordinary noise. Tramping of boots, bangs and crashes, the commotion seemed to be coming from the studio where Joe Hollaway had his sketch club.

We went to investigate. The police were going through Joe's studio. They were looking for someone, not an artist, but someone they wanted to question whom they thought might be hiding in the building. Not that they had much respect for artists; artists were the lowest of the low, in their opinion. The nudes, done by Joe's students and tacked to the walls, confirmed their suspicions. Naked women, they guffawed. Artists! What a den of iniquity!

Next to the nudes, the students had stuck a front page of the *Sun* with the photograph of a suspect in a grisly murder case. This further incensed the constabulary. As if naked women weren't enough, what sort of people would put such a photograph up on the wall? Artists! Empty-handed, still sounding off, the police force departed.

Harvey's painstaking work paid off. I thought the portrait was wonderful. It was finished and entered for the Archibald Prize. We both had our fingers crossed. On the days the prizes were announced, a downcast Harvey came to see me.

'Margaret,' he said sadly, 'someone called Henry Hanke has won the Archibald.'

'What!' I exclaimed. I had never heard of Henry Hanke and found it difficult to believe Harvey's work had been passed over.

Henry Hanke won the 1934 Archibald Prize with a self-portrait. He had been doing relief work for a local council to earn a living and the prize was very important for him because after it was announced he started to receive commissions and was able to work full-time as an artist. But it was a hard blow for Harvey.

For us students, the great thing in those days was to have work accepted for one of the exhibitions put on by the Society of Artists, the Royal Art or the Society of Women Artists. We had to work for years before getting a painting hung in an exhibition.

I knew it was a long time off for me. The only money I could earn was from commercial art jobs and anything else I could find in the same line. Even before my ventures into the commercial art world, every Christmas after I left school I had made black and white calendars with little silhouette drawings of crinolined women in full swinging skirts and children at play, to try and earn money. I used to wear my shoes out walking round town trying to sell these, but nobody took any.

Aunt Mary Carter came to my rescue – Aunt Mary Carter who had lent me her shoes to wear in the beauty contest. As soon as I showed her my calendars, she ordered about three dozen. Her friends and her sister Beatrice all received calendars that Christmas and for Christmases to come.

Aunt Mary Carter wasn't really our aunt, but that's what we called her. When Mum and Dad first married and were living in Nowra, Aunt Mary Carter was married to an hotelkeeper named Walters in nearby Bomaderry. Walters was cruel to her, and their marriage ended badly. One night Mary had to flee for her life; she climbed a gum tree to hide from her husband and spent the entire night up there in her nightgown, while Walters prowled around with a revolver, looking for her.

Mary Walters divorced her husband after that. She went to Western Australia to start afresh and married a man named Carter. But Mum and Mary Carter stayed in touch and when Mary's second husband died and she came to live in Sydney, she and Mum were best friends.

Diminutive, neat, brisk, intrepid Aunt Mary Carter was a darling, and we all loved her. She never had any children of her own; perhaps that's why she spoiled us so much.

She took me to see Pavlova dance at the Theatre Royal while I was still at school. We saw *Swan Lake* and *Autumn Leaves*, sitting right up in the gods. Even so far from the stage, Pavlova totally captivated me. Aunt Mary and I went round to the side door in Rowe Street after the performance to see her as she left. Pavlova was so fragile I couldn't believe it; like a fairy. At the stage door, she looked as though she would be blown away by the slightest breeze, yet on stage she was magic.

Aunt Mary had a younger sister Beatrice who used to stay with her down at Nowra. Aunt Mary often talked about her sister, but as children we never met her and Beatrice McCaughey was a bit of a legend to us. The McCaugheys were a famous family of graziers from Narranderah. Beatrice was the second wife of John McCaughey, who was seventy-five when he married her. He had a daughter older than Beatrice by his first wife. He lived for another ten years and his death left Beatrice a wealthy woman.

She had a suite of rooms on the seventh floor of the Hotel Australia, the poshest hotel in Sydney where squatters and socialites swanned. Having a permanent suite was amazing swank. Beatrice also had a chauffeur-driven limousine which she didn't use much. She sent my mother down to Yass in it once when she had been ill.

Aunt Mary had been telling Beatrice tales of my hard luck, how I was struggling to be an artist, how hard it was to earn any money from commercial art, how trying the teaching job was, and what a fraud it turned out. Beatrice asked me to bring some paintings to show her at the Hotel Australia.

She was small, impeccably dressed and beautiful, with silver hair, grey eyes flecked with green and perfect skin. She led me into the pale green, soft-carpeted drawing room, almost claustrophobic in its femininity and prettiness. It had Louis Quatorze furniture and the couch and chairs were upholstered with a print of bunched primroses.

Bedroom, bathroom, kitchenette, pantry (even though Beatrice didn't cook, having her meals sent up) – all the rooms in the suite showed the stamp of Beatrice's personality. The balcony outside ran the length of the hotel and looked down into Castlereagh Street. I was overawed at such a style of living.

Beatrice took a lively interest in my paintings, studying them closely and asking me questions. Nothing more happened for a while, then she rang up to invite Molly and me to dinner at her flat in Edgecliff. She still kept her suite of rooms at the Australia; they were her headquarters, so to speak, but she and Mary moved into a luxurious flat in Ocean Street, Edgecliff, to keep each other company.

Molly and I arrived. At each of our places on the dining room table was a huge box of Personality chocolates, the best. The boxes were tied with lilac ribbon and on top of each was a giant purple and white orchid. Molly and I had never been treated like this in our lives, and it was just the start. After dinner, Beatrice made an announcement.

'I have a surprise for you, Margaret,' she said softly. 'I have decided to pay the rent of a studio for you and buy your materials so you can continue painting.'

A studio of my own! It was like a dream come true. John McCaughey had begun this tradition of helping people; he had put a number of students through medical school, and Beatrice carried on his generosity. However, I had no idea she intended to do this for me.

Getting a studio of my own was, of course, a major event in my life. I rented a large room in the same Margaret Street building where Harvey painted my portrait, I was so excited. The rent was only about fifteen shillings a week, but it would have been beyond my means without Beatrice's assistance. I thought I was made.

7

Circolo Isole Eolie

Margaret in costume for an artists' ball

Circular Quay was a world of its own in those days, a world of artists and bohemians. From Martin Place to the Quay was like a rabbit warren, so many artists either rented rooms to paint and even lived there. Moving into my own studio in Margaret Street meant that the Quay, its character and its characters, quickly became familiar to me.

I might meet Percy Lindsay on the steps of the *Bulletin* newspaper offices; Perc with his rosy complexion, shiny white hair and alert blue eyes was an unmistakable figure dressed in white tropical suit and white solar topee. Percy had a cold shower every day of his life, which perhaps accounted for his particular sparkle.

I might see Bea Miles jumping off a tram; a young, boyishly pretty Bea, also always in white, white frock and white beret. She had a round face and short brown hair.

Everybody seemed to know everybody else. Artists and their friends congregated at the Royal Art, which had moved from Pitt Street to lower George Street and at the other half dozen or so sketch clubs round the Quay, such as Rah Fizelle's.

Rah Fizelle, whose elbow had been shot away in World War I, was nice but highly nervous and intense. He began painting quite traditional watercolours but after travelling overseas, his style changed drastically and he produced the modernistic nudes for which he became famous.

Dora Jarret's studio was in the same building as Alison and George's, number 4 Dalley Street. Dora painted Sydney street scenes long before anyone else. Grace Crowley and Thea Proctor had studios in lower George Street. The grapevine on the roof of Grace's studio ran about half the length of the street. Doreen Hubble, the artists' model, used to laugh about Thea Proctor's yellow bath tub. Thea loved to paint Doreen, with her red hair and creamy skin, either sitting or standing in this tub.

Rubbo was still ensconced in Bligh Street but Julian Ashton's art school was in lower George Street and so were Parker's, the framers, and Smith and Julius, the printers who published *Art in Australia*.

Two doors down from the *Bulletin* offices in George Street, close to Bridge Street, was Mockbell's coffee shop where the *Bulletin* push consumed quantities of coffee, night and day, when they weren't drinking in the pub on the corner. One of the *Bulletin* crowd, a man called Jim Emery, drew beautiful maps.

Percy Lindsay sometimes drank at a wine bar further down George Street, and in between this and the *Bulletin* pub was Leo Buring's wine shop. Women didn't go into wine bars or pubs. They were strictly masculine strongholds.

Next door to my studio at Pfahlert's hotel, older-established literary and bohemian figures hung out in the bar and grill room. I never ventured in but it added to the atmosphere.

J. S. Watkins, Dorrit Black, Miriam Moxham and my friend Hilda were still residents of Margaret Street when I moved in, but I think Joe Hollaway was about to shift into rooms above Mockbell's. The room I rented was big and empty with bare boards. My furnishings were sparse; not that I minded. Painting was what mattered.

I already had an easel. Making a model's throne was easy. I cut the legs off a large table so it was about ten inches off the floor. When drawing from the model, or painting a portrait, if the subject sits on a throne like this, it gives a better perspective. On Newtown Road, where there were lots of secondhand shops, I bought myself a marvellous old mirror, the sort that used to hang over sideboards. It made my already large room look twice its size.

The Australian agents for Vaseline rented the rooms below me, and their office was filled with red cedar shelving. Because the building was condemned, all the offices were gradually being vacated and when the Vaseline people departed, I asked if I could buy some of their red cedar. The request was granted. I took enough to make a long shelf and a desk for my studio.

As I was still living at home, I used to help Mum with housework in the morning, but I was in at my studio without fail by nine thirty or ten. Lunch was a packet of sandwiches from home; dinner was reheated on the top of the stove after Royal Art classes.

I busily painted still lifes, particularly my first love, flower pieces. I kept on with black and white for a long while, but was now more interested in colour and gradually abandoned pen and ink work.

The flowers I painted came from anywhere I could get them. Mum grew a few flowers and around the corner from us in Randwick friends of hers who had a proper garden gave me some of theirs. Florists were cheap. I did buy some flowers but I'm afraid as great as my passion for painting flowers is my passion for stealing them.

Mount Vernon, a lovely old home in Botany Street, had a beautiful garden with a pink camellia tree by the gate. Very occasionally, if I was painting a flower piece that really needed a pink camellia, I would take a flower from this tree.

'Do you want some camellias?' suddenly a voice challenged me. An elderly man almost bent in two emerged from the other side of the bush.

'I suppose you think I'm a thief, stealing your camellias for no good reason but I'm not, not exactly. I'm an artist. I paint flowers and I want to put your flowers in a painting,' I said. I didn't know if this explanation would help or not, but it was worth a try.

'When you come by tomorrow morning, look in the tree,' he answered, to my surprise. 'I'll leave you some flowers. Don't let anyone see you taking them. I'd get the sack if they saw me picking the camellias, let alone giving them away.'

As long as the camellias were out, I would walk past Mount Vernon in the morning, quietly put my hand into the tree and take out the bunch of camellias waiting for me. The stems were only about four or five inches long, tightly tied with string so they made a real little bouquet. I was very grateful to my ancient gardener friend for his gifts.

Sometimes for a change I painted landscapes. I would catch the ferry to Balmain from the bottom of Erskine Street and get out at the various wharves on the way to paint the harbour. I painted Balmain from the Darling Street wharf, looking up the hill to the church spire pointing into the clouds. Nancy Keesing has one of these early Balmain watercolours.

Balmain appealed to me; I would have liked to live there. I was in love with a small sandstone cottage set in a rambling garden. Balmain seemed so peaceful, compared to the constant bustle of Darling Harbour, which I also painted, sitting on the grass at Observatory Hill and looking down through the elephants' feet trunks of the Moreton Bays. I took the bus to Pyrmont and painted the railway and the quaint old rundown houses there.

My efforts were rewarded. The Fine Arts Society, a small group of artists to which Arthur Murch belonged, hung two of my paintings. A portrait of my mother and a fanciful black and white drawing of a mermaid surrounded by seaweed tendrils and shells were shown in a private exhibition at Burdekin House, a long, low colonial building in Macquarie Street. My first exhibition and my first sale. Right at the opening, a man wanted to buy my mermaid. A red spot! Over the years, how important became the red spot that means a painting is sold! My painting in the Fine Arts Society exhibition was hardly expensive – two guineas – but still a red spot. I was beside myself with excitement.

A box of violets arrived for me through the mail next day. My buyer lived at Moss Vale, he had picked the flowers at home and posted them up; a romantic gesture, but the money for the painting was what interested me. He rang and asked me out to dinner. All very well, but where was the cheque?

The show closed; still no cheque. I decided I had better accept his dinner invitation.

The Hotel Clovelly was the setting for our dinner date. He picked me up at the studio in a flash car. The hotel dining room was swish, wine flowed and as the meal progressed he grew more and more friendly. I was increasingly edgy; no sign of cheque book and pen.

Glasses were filled again, the music swelled, his advances

became openly amorous. Paying for my painting was obviously the last thing on his mind. Best to make my escape while I could, I thought.

It was late. I hadn't told my mother I was having dinner with him because she would have been asking me all the questions in the world. If I didn't leave now, I would certainly be in trouble one way or the other. I made one last effort to secure my two guineas.

'I haven't received my cheque yet.' I came straight out with it. The wine had loosened my tongue.

My suitor cooled off quickly, annoyed at my mercenariness, as he called it. Not a word was spoken as we drove back to Randwick. He dropped me at the top of Botany Street as I asked and drove off without a backward glance. Four days later a cheque for two guineas came in the post with a cold little note.

The portrait of my mother, the other painting in the show, disappeared. I don't know what happened to it, but I never saw it again. The show had turned out to be a disappointment, but then the Australian Watercolour Institute accepted a painting of mine and the Royal Art hung one in their annual exhibition. My career was under way.

Hilda used to supplement her income from the signwriter by doing suede work. In her studio, she made suede cushions, travelling bags, notebooks and calendars, which she decorated by burning designs into the suede with a poker.

The poker looked like a copper pencil and was heated up over a methylated spirits burner. We drew the designs into the suede with the hot poker. She used Australian designs – waratahs, gum leaves, native bears. I drew some birds for her. It was difficult work, but Hilda needed the money for her fees at the Royal Art.

The tenants were gradually moving out and Margaret Street was becoming empty. No one came round for the rent. Weeks went by and my conscience nagged me so I visited the architect who was to be in charge of the demolition and construction of the new building that would replace it.

'I think I owe you some rent,' I said reluctantly.

I needn't have bothered. He didn't seem to care who was living there. He hadn't the slightest interest in collecting rent and let me off most of mine. I don't think the other artists in the building paid any rent.

There was no caretaker and I often saw strange people wandering around the building. The weekends were especially eerie. I had been there about eighteen months and was one of the last tenants to leave. It was hard, working away on my own; I used to hear strange noises coming from an empty room upstairs.

Rats, I thought. Natural enough in an old, deserted building.

The police came round again; this time they were more successful than they had been in their previous raid on Joe Hollaway's studio. A wanted criminal was holed up in the empty room above mine. He had been there for weeks, perhap months. So much for the rats.

That terrified me. I bought a huge padlock and every evening as I left I bolted my door on the outside. I wasn't taking any risks. I didn't want any desperate characters camping overnight in my studio.

I started looking for another studio soon after this episode and soon moved into 38A Pitt Street, right in the thick of Circular Quay life.

The Quay itself was lovely. It had no overhead railway, that was the big difference. Towards the end of Pitt Street near the harbour was a spreading fig tree, not a Moreton Bay but a smaller branching Port Jackson, under which was a fruit stall. The outline of the stall and the tree in front of the open space of the Quay looked so pretty.

The words, '*Circolo Isole Eolie*' were handwritten on a piece of paper in a cafe window at the Quay. I loved the sound of those words. I had no idea what they meant, but the rolling vowels conjured up endless romance in my imagination. After about a year, I found out that the words meant 'The Aeolian Islands Club', an Italian social club, but '*Circolo Isole Eolie*' was far more appealing.

Other names at the Quay intrigued me. Mischa Burlakov and Louise Lightfoot seemed appropriate names for dancing instructors. They gave dance demonstrations at parties. Another couple danced the tango together and even gave recitals at the Conservatorium. Over the years, the woman partner grew too heavy and in the end the man was struggling to lift her off the floor for their finale.

A shop at the Quay sold every sort of pie: rabbit, pork or beef, apricot. Pies were a staple of our diet. Round the corner in George Street was Plasto's hotel, where women could safely have a beer in the upstairs lounge. Old Nick's was another cafe in George Street with plates, cups, saucers all printed with a grinning devil and pitchfork. We could have chicken cooked any way we liked – steamed, boiled, roasted – for 2s6d there.

Maniaci's, the Italian fruit shop, arrived later at the Quay. Before that, there were two Chinese fruit and vegetable shops opposite each other in Pitt Street. Fruit wasn't so varied then. We never saw an avocado or a pawpaw, but the Chinese fruit shops did sell rice whisky on the side. They couldn't have had a licence but nevertheless they dispensed a fierce alcohol that burned a fiery track down your inside. Chinese whisky came in full, round-bellied bottles with a brown glaze. Each one was a bit different, a bit crooked-looking, because they were hand-made. There wasn't a studio in town that didn't have a Chinese whisky bottle for still lifes.

A woman ran a little grocery shop at the Quay which, despite the gallons of disinfectant she and her husband poured over the floor, always smelt of mice and rats. This woman spoke fast, and her turn of phrase was so very Australian it was like a language of its own. 'Bran' new, never been worn before, tore it on a floggin' nail' was her vivid description of tearing an apron which I never forgot.

The Quay yielded other delights. A Chinese ship was in town and as I was walking down from Plasto's hotel, I saw a line of sailors from the boat. They had been fishing at Circular Quay and were walking hand in hand along the street. Every second one was carrying an octopus. It looked so Oriental.

When a Dutch ship docked on Queen Wilhelmina's birthday, Dutch sailors wandered round, wearing necklaces of yellow flowers in honour of their queen's birthday.

I'll never forget another sight I witnessed going down to Rah Fizelle's studio another night. A tall, thin blonde girl ran out of an hotel, bleeding from the mouth and with blood on her chin. A sailor was running after her.

I stopped, horrified, wondering what was going to happen next.

But the sailor took the girl in his arms and they kissed passionately and kept on kissing, the blood still pouring down her chin. Even though I felt I should move, I couldn't stop looking at them.

The harbour fascinated me. I suppose this was because I grew up in the country and hardly saw any water except when the river flooded, until I suddenly discovered the harbour that first summer in Sydney.

The most romantic night I ever spent in Sydney was on the harbour, and it began at the Quay.

Dora Jarret had been to Paris. This was romantic enough. We were thrilled and envious when she set off. We all dreamed of going to Paris and studying art; in fact, we took French lessons from a Madame Henri who taught at the Conservatorium. Later she even came and gave classes to about eight of us in Alison and George Duncan's studio.

Coming back to Australia on a French ship, Dora had a love affair with an officer and arrived home engaged. She invited Alison, George and myself to meet her French fiance. At sunset on a summer evening, sailors from the ship rowed over to Bennelong Point and picked us up. The ship was moored off Kirribilli and we had to climb a steep, almost perpendicular ladder up its side. The harbour at night had always entranced me. Our night with Dora was totally captivating. Even the food was special, fillet steak with champignons. I had never eaten a champignon before; even ordinary mushrooms were rare. We drank French wines, champagne with dessert and liqueurs. Then we sat up on deck looking out on the city lights like distant jewels across the inky indigo water. Dora's officer had a gramophone in his cabin and afterwards we danced. None of us wanted the night to end. But at midnight the sailors rowed us back to Bennelong Point, thrilling with the splash of oars resounding across the silence.

The French ship went on to Brisbane, the officer's attention wavered. He turned to new conquests in new ports, and the romance broke up. Dora was heartbroken.

Dora was usually involved in whirlwind affairs of the heart, engaged one minute, unengaged the next. Eventually she married a Chinese doctor, but her love life kept us perpetually in suspense and surprise.

Number 4 Dalley Street, where Alison and George had their studio, was also a condemned building (owned by the Electricity Commission) so Alison and George paid cheap rent for a large room, plenty big enough for parties, except that the caretaker made it almost impossible.

The caretaker was a crabby old man who used to shut the outside door at six o'clock and refused to let anyone in. One Saturday a few of us from the Royal Art came round for an evening with Alison and George. We banged and banged on the door, to no avail. The caretaker wouldn't let George open the door. 'Nobody's having a party here tonight,' he snapped.

The studio was on the third floor, the top storey. George had a brainwave. He put his head out the window and lowered a long string – it must have been a whole ball of string – with cooked frankfurts down to the street. We were having a downgrade party that night; punch parties were upgrade, frankfurts and beer were downgrade. Beer bottles followed on another string and we had our party sitting outside in the gutter.

At last the caretaker grudgingly let us in after much sweet talking from George. But as soon as the party warmed up and we started dancing on the bare boards, the caretaker was back, thumping on the studio door for quiet.

'Mad artists!' he shouted through the keyhole. This was his favourite refrain.

George later found out the cause of the caretaker's obsessive fear about opening the door after six. The back lanes between Bridge Street and the Quay were frequented by sailors and men off ships. They went on shore leave drinking sprees after the pubs closed at six o'clock, and there was nowhere else for them to go. Back lanes saw savoury and unsavoury action of all sorts. Two sailors had been sick on the steps of 4 Dalley Street. The caretaker ordered them off. The sailors wouldn't budge; they were happily sprawled across the steps, singing. The caretaker went into his room and fetched a kettle of boiling water which he poured under the front door.

Boiling water got the sailors moving all right; it scalded them.

It also made them angry. They swore they would come back and do for the caretaker. That's why he kept the door closed after dark; he was frightened of the sailors returning.

Often after a party, I would catch the tram home from the terminus at the Quay. The Coogee, Bondi and Maroubra trams all left from Circular Quay. Each tram had a different-coloured light in front. The Coogee tram was green. One night I was up in Phillip Street waiting for its green light to appear. I waited and waited; there was no sign of a tram. A taxi came by and stopped. The driver asked me what I was doing.

'You've missed the last tram,' he said. 'I wouldn't hang about here if I was you. I'll take you home.'

I don't have the money for a taxi,' I answered. This was the truth.

'It doesn't matter. If I had a daughter, I wouldn't want her standing round late at night. Hop in, I'll take you home for nothing,' he said, and he did. I didn't know whether to trust him or not but something about his face told me he was honest, and he was most fatherly on the trip out to Randwick.

Alison and George moved to a studio in Bridge Street. Their new studio was as spacious as Dalley Street. It still had three flights of stairs to climb, but there was no cantankerous caretaker to contend with. Number 8 Bridge Street became famous for its innumerable bohemian parties.

That was where I saw the last of my old flame, Luigi Nobili. Luigi rented himself a room on the top floor of a building in Dalley Street opposite Alison and George's new studio. To Luigi's consternation, he caught the mumps and no one would go near him, especially the men. It was quite a bad case and Luigi's face had to be swathed in bandages. Alison could see up into his room; she used to wave across, trying to cheer him up.

Luigi's idea of convalescence was to paint his self-portrait. My last image of the Latin lover is a swollen-faced figure busily at work before a large easel, reproducing his bandaged self.

My own studio at 38A Pitt Street was also a largeish room. Along with the rest of my paraphernalia, I successfully shifted over my red cedar shelving and my mirror from Margaret Street. Miriam Moxham, who had found the building, rented a studio there, too.

The rent was cheap at 12s a week, but we did have a caretaker now, a woman. I had seen Alison and George's sufferings at the hands of their caretaker and 38A Pitt Street was my initiation. Caretakers were always most suspicious of artists. I was lucky to have escaped so far.

Our grey-haired, lard-complexioned, many-times-a-grandmother caretaker Queenie refused to give either Miriam or me a key to the front door. We had to rely on her letting us in, which was infuriating when we wanted to paint at night or on the weekend.

Queenie had what she called 'SP-ing' at the back of the building. She ran an illegal betting establishment and had a room lined with telephones to take bets. This meant she didn't like anyone being in the place on Saturday afternoon or Sunday, in case it attracted the attention of the police.

A constant battle of wits went on between us and Queenie. We had one laugh on her, however. Miriam came into my studio almost choking with laughter.

'Has Queenie told you about her operation?' Miriam spluttered.

'No,' I said. 'Why?'

'She's just given me a blow-by-blow description,' Miriam shrieked. 'She told me she had forty-six stitches in her penis.' Miriam, normally rather proper, shrieked with laughter again. 'Forty-six stitches in her *penis*, my dear!'

'Miriam, you can't be serious.' I was as much astonished at Miriam at the revelation.

'Yes, I am serious,' Miriam replied. 'That's what she said. I don't know what she meant, but that's what she said.'

Maybe she meant forty-six stitches in the place where her penis would be if she were a man; that's as far as we dared hazard a guess. Queenie herself never shed any further light on her predicament.

Each studio party had its own special name. Alison and George's 'loincloth party' was held at 8 Bridge Street.

The guest of honour was a professor of anthropology, a well known celebrity round Sydney in those days and a bit of a dandy with long hair and a monocle. He was to entertain the party with a demonstration of ethnic dancing, for which purpose he brought along a gramophone and a loincloth.

The guests streamed in, some sedately dressed in street clothes, others in more fancy dress. Dora Jarret came as a pierrot in a pretty dress with a frilled neck and Alison's cousin wore a grass skirt in honour of the professor.

A frail, delicate girl who wrote fairy stories and lived in a tiny room at the top of number 8 was enamoured of the professor. Most of us were; he was very good-looking. The fairy story writer arrived at the party decked out in a long trail of orange, green and brown georgette. Her long, dusty red hair hung loose to her waist. I asked her what she had come as.

'An autumn leaf,' she answered. An autumn leaf was just what she looked like, an autumn leaf, newly dropped, ready to be bowled along by the wind. The professor was nice enough to everyone, but I don't think he gave her a second glance as she wilted around, desperate with unrequited love.

It was a hot night and after two or three glasses of George's powerful rum punch, the party was away. The professor emerged wrapped in a scrap of material from New Guinea. Very fetching, very exotic. As soon as he started his South Seas dance routine, the party became out of control. Everyone was stripping off, though the girls didn't undress as much as the males.The men grabbed the drapes off the models' throne and improvised their own loincloths, much briefer than sarongs. Hardly there at all. Amid gales of laughter, we dubbed it 'the loincloth party'.

The men cavorted in their loincloths, doing more island dancing. George was wrapped in a piece of curtain netting embossed with pink and green roses. My sister Molly had come to the party with me. Her eyes opened wide when she saw George in his netting.

'I don't mind him *wearing* it,' she whispered agitatedly in my ear. 'But I don't think it ought to be net. George is such a *large* man.'

I don't know if it was the net or what she glimpsed under it that was upsetting Molly. Perhaps she would have preferred George in chintz.

The professor was in his element, undulating round the room, monocle miraculously in place, equally charming every woman. I used to consider myself a bit of an Isadora Duncan. I did a dance at studio parties to the 'Pagan Love Song'. I Isadoraed away the night. The loincloth party was a raging success.

The party started to wind down about two or two thirty. Molly and I had well and truly missed the last tram.

'Not to worry,' the professor declared gallantly. 'I will escort you home in a taxi.'

We left about three and made out way up Pitt Street, Molly, the professor and I. The professor, who had thrown a black opera cloak over his loincloth, seemed to have entirely forgotten or abandoned his ordinary clothes.

We went up to the Café de Fairfax, an all-night cafe on wheels frequented by reporters and newspaper staff, on the corner of Pitt and Hunter Streets, outside the *Herald* building. When we had finished devouring pies as if they were the greatest luxury around, the professor grandly hailed a cab. He sat in the middle of the back seat with a fond arm round Molly and me on either side of him.

Somewhat to our alarm, he dismissed the cab outside the flats in Botany Street and came tiptoeing after us. To make matters worse, we had lost our front door key. We crept up the path: me first, then Molly, with the professor in the rear. Molly put her finger to her lips.

'Don't make a noise or you'll wake our mother,' she mouthed at the professor. We were going to be in enough strife coming home so late if Mum caught us without having to explain a professor in loincloth and opera cloak. Cautiously I opened the window of the downstairs flat in which we were living and scrambled in. Molly followed. The professor was about to do likewise – his hand was on the sill – when Molly slammed the window shut.

'Go home, you must leave, our mother is awake,' Molly mouthed again through the safety of the window glass.

The professor made frantic gestures of protest from the lawn, but Molly ignored his pleas. He stared through the window, staggered at this rejection. Thank goodness he was too much of a gentleman to break the glass. Eventually we heard him making his way off down the path. Molly and I looked at each other, rolled our eyes, heaved sighs of relief and stole off to bed.

The next day I went in to help Alison and George clean up the studio before the afternoon sketch club and George recounted the aftermath of the professor's ride to Randwick. He couldn't get a cab in Botany Street or anywhere in Randwick, so he had to walk back to the city from Randwick. He arrived at the studio at about five in the morning to collect his clothes. Several items were missing and the professor was in a state. George had been cleaning up. The party debris was already in rubbish bins outside. George hastily went through the bins and retrieved the professor's belongings, including his singlet and a fob watch of which he was very fond.

The professor had sobered up and was suffering from post-party remorse. He was terrified that some hint of his behaviour might leak out to the papers and besmirch his social standing.

'I hope there were no gentlemen from the press at the party,' he kept repeating nervously to George. No gentlemen from the press were present at the party, George assured him. The professor's reputation, if not his dignity, remained intact.

Janna Bruce knew a group of artists who lived, or rather squatted, in Elizabeth Bay House. Wallace Thornton and Wolfgang Cardimatis were two. Elizabeth Bay House was very rundown. They had no right to be there, but the alcoholic caretaker turned a blind eye and they lived for nothing amidst the ruins of colonial splendour. The upstairs bedrooms had a wonderful view straight out across Sydney Harbour, the only disadvantage being the loose floorboards.

Janna went to a party there. The electricity had been cut off so the guests took their own candles for light. The party was a success, despite the caretaker's being drunk as usual and screaming abuse at them, but not doing anything to stop the party. There was an awful lot of noise but surprisingly the neighbours didn't complain. At midnight they were deciding to disband the party when suddenly every candle burnt down at the same time and they were plunged into blackness. It was terrifying, Janna said, having to pick her way across the holey floorboards, then make her way down to the ground floor, clinging to the curving staircase.

Soon afterwards, the artists in Elizabeth Bay House were kicked out and moved to a large terrace house in Jersey Road, Woollahra. Many parties were held here, too. The drawback to the new residence was a nearby garbage dump. Janna said she

could practically hear the cockroaches crawling up the cliff face
and marching up to the house.

I never went to these parties. This was a different crowd from
my friends. I started giving my own parties at 38A Pitt Street, a
couple of punch parties a year, usually one at Christmas. My
Christmas punch party became a real institution.

My punch set came from Leo Buring's wine shop. Leo Buring
not only sold wine in bottles; customers could also have a glass of
wine to drink downstairs in the cellars, and there was a selection
of glasses for sale. This is where I bought my punch set. The
heavy china bowl and eight goblets that I bought were a rich
vermilion colour, decorated with greeny-grey clusters of grapes.
The colour first attracted me to the set; I thought it would be
good for still lifes. I put a layby on the bowl and eight glasses; it
took me quite a while to pay the ten guineas off.

The Leo Buring man came round to my studio about four days
after I had scraped together the last payment and told me they
had found another four goblets to make up a dozen, but I was too
broke. I've regretted it ever since. Later I bought a green
wineglass from the shop because it exactly matched a green-
topped wineglass in my reproduction of a Vermeer painting.

My punch, based on red or white wine, was much subtler than
the rum and ginger brew George made for his and Alison's
parties. I started preparing the morning before the party. First I
put in a pound of castor sugar, then poured in four bottles of
claret or hock and let it stand until the afternoon, when I added
six bottles of soda water, a glass of brandy, a smaller glass of some
liqueur like curacao and fruit. For a claret punch I stewed up
black cherries, letting some of the syrup go in with the fruit; for a
hock punch, I used sliced peaches and a few cucumber rounds.

With punch parties, the danger is the guest who brings the
extra bottle. The vodka or rum flask tipped into the punch for an
extra kick will have guests reeling in no time.

Just getting bright people together made those studio parties.
Alison and George always came to mine, as did my friend Hilda,
Dora Jarret and Ellen Grey who married Dattilo-Rubbo's son.
Ellen did very modern dancing, way beyond my Isadora Duncan
'Pagan Love Song' efforts. Another guest was Clarence Murphy,
an actor, whom we called Murph. Murph was a great dandy, very

funny at parties. He worked with Doris Fitton and we went to see him in *And So to Bed*, her production of a play about Samuel Pepys. Murph was in his element.

A man called Joe Collins, a friend of Hilda's who worked for the printer Smith and Julius, often came. So did Geoff Blunden the writer and his wife Mick, a dear friend of mine; even John Young from the Macquarie Galleries would drop in. Later the literary ones from the *Bulletin* came; Ron McCuaig and his wife Beryl, Guy Howarth from the English Department at Sydney University and his wife Lillian, and still later Beatrice Davis from Angus and Robertson. But that was after I met Doug.

One Christmas punch party, the Blundens, Hilda and I intended to finish the evening by going to see Mo at the Tivoli. We came out of the building. Somebody wanted something from the grocery shop about three doors down, so we crammed into it. A display of tinned peaches was built into a pyramid on a shelf. Out of merriment or mischief or both, I pretended to knock the pyramid down. The grocer was incensed at such skylarking in his domain and jumped out from behind the counter.

'Don't do that! You can't do that,' he blustered.

I must have had my fair share of punch.

'Oh, yes I can,' I replied swiftly.

Then I really did kick his precious tins of peaches, but the cans were empty. It didn't take much of a kick; one nudge from my toe and the whole pyramid came tumbling down. We cleared out swiftly, the grocer's threats and insults ringing in our ears as we raced down Pitt Street.

At the Quay we dived into the safety of Plasto's hotel, up to the lounge for a last beer before heading off to the show. By the time we arrived at the theatre, it was so late we had to sit on the steps in the gods. Still, the look of outrage on the grocer's face as his carefully arranged cans came down round his feet was worth it.

Bea Miles loved the Tivoli; we would often hear her calling out in the middle of a show. If Bea had something to say, she said it regardless, in the Tivoli or the Playbox Theatre in Rowe Street. Once, to the horror of the audience, she interrupted a very serious play at the Theatre Royal.

Artists' balls were altogether different from our studio parties. Everybody went to the artists' ball: Dulcie Deamer in her leopard

skin, George Finey in a baby's napkin fastened with a safety pin, everyone. At my first artists' ball, we students from the Royal Art painted scenery right around the Town Hall. If we volunteered for scenery painting, we were given free tickets. The Theatre Royal lent us their stage painting brushes and paints. The paint was mixed up in big jerries and it was very funny working away brush in hand, dipping it into an old po. To collect these jerries, the brushes and the paint, we went to the theatre and climbed up to the flies, where the stagehands prepared the scenery. Five of us decided to stay and watch the show for free. *The Ringer*, a thriller by Edgar Wallace, was playing. We concealed ourselves in the heavy folds of drapery and settled back to enjoy the performance. Halfway through the first act, the actors realised we were there and they were not happy.

At interval, pandemonium broke loose. The management came swarming up the ladder. I crawled off and hid among the electrical wiring. It's a wonder I didn't electrocute myself. I could hear an angry voice shouting at the others.

'Come down here!' the voice ordered. 'If you're not down in two seconds we're calling the police and we'll have you arrested.'

The word 'police' sent me into a state and I froze. I could see myself being hauled off in the paddy wagon, my career as an artist ending in ignominy and disgrace, so I stayed hidden. When the second act was under way, I managed to extricate myself and sneak down the ladder. I had almost made it to safety when I was spotted at the stage door. I was out the door and up the lane beside the Theatre Royal at top speed. Not pausing to see if my pursuers were in fact pursuing me, I tore up King Street where I could see the Coogee tram stopped at the corner of Elizabeth Street. It started to move off just as I reached the stop. With a last desperate spurt of energy I took a flying leap and flung myself onto the running board. Everyone on the tram cheered. Despite this narrow escape, I was still as keen as ever about the ball. I felt I had earned my ticket by now.

Mum didn't want me to go. I pestered and pestered but she was

A Royal Art Society fancy dress party. Margaret is in the front row, wearing a dress with a flounce around the hem

adamant; she wasn't having me traipsing off on my own to any artists' ball. But Jack, my brother, said he would take me and Mum relented. My opinion of Jack shot up instantly.

Jack and I set off in high spirits. I did have a few nagging doubts, though: what was he going to do all night? Whom could I introduce him to? Please God, don't let him be too bored, or too shocked or both, I offered a brief prayer. But I need not have worried.

'See that clock up on the wall?' Jack pointed inside the Town Hall. 'I'll see you back here at two to take you home.' Two o'clock was when the ball finished. I didn't see Jack for the rest of the night.

A touring Russian dance troupe dropped in after their theatre performance. Resplendent in national dress, especially the men in embroidered and braided waistcoats, they thronged around the bar. I couldn't take my eyes off one handsome man in silky pants gathered at the ankle. He seemed to be staring back at me.

I ventured closer and he came up to me. Conversation was at a minimum, but our glances spoke volumes. Suddenly he broke into a wild Cossack sort of dance; squatting low on his heels, then almost jumping over our heads, he sprang round the room. My eyes were riveted to the leaping figure in his silk costume. The next moment, the clock struck two and Jack appeared. He didn't say what he had been up to, but from the look on his face, he had enjoyed the artists' ball as much as I had.

Fancy dress was the norm at the artists' ball. The next year I was more fully into the swing of bohemian life. I wore my Kincoppal school uniform, complete with navy blazer and basketball pocket. The nuns would have died, I think, if they had seen me. Percy's son Peter Lindsay still gleefully recalls the sight of me in my school uniform at that ball. William Dobell was there, too; the uniform must also have impressed him because he danced with me most of the night.

I was more decorous in other years and hired costumes from J. C. Williamson's, the theatrical suppliers. I went as a Restoration lady in a heavy white wig which made my neck ache. It felt as if I was carrying the most enormous weight on my head.

In 1934, there was inordinate excitement because Smithy, Charles Kingsford Smith the famous aviator, arrived at the ball

Left: Margaret ready for an artists' ball in a hired costume
Right: The Spanish look

fresh from his first flight across the Pacific and was mobbed. My feet were sore for weeks afterwards from being trodden on in the crush around him.

Alison and George shifted studios when rooms at 12 Bridge Street became vacant. Number 8 was three floors up; 12 was on the second floor, but Alison thought the move would be worth it. Their friends were seconded into helping with the shift. It took us all weekend.

Furniture had to be carted down three flights of stairs, carried along the street, then lugged back up another two lots of stairs into the new studio. The tables and chairs from Alison and George's sketch club seemed endless. Tables, chairs and donkeys, up and down, up and down. Donkeys were primitive easels with seats that could be straddled as we drew. The paper was attached to the timber upright in front. Donkeys were part of every sketch club. As well as the furniture, there were the usual studio props artists accumulate. Even when artists can't afford the rare and gorgeous objects they may covet, they still manage to collect a mass of cheaper treasures. Anything that will look good in a still life is saved – stone ginger jars, an old green Benedictine bottle, the Chinese whisky bottles.

My first recollection of 12 Bridge Street was sitting on the floor of the studio with my back to the wall, feeling very tired and very dirty (the studio needed a lot of cleaning; that was Sunday's chore), eating sandwiches, drinking beer, and thinking what fun life was. I never dreamed how much a part of my life the studio would become.

Alison and George started a new sketch club at number 12. The sketch club met on Wednesdays because there were no classes at the Royal Art that evening. I usually went to 12 Bridge Street on Wednesdays because their nights were so lively. We had dinner, a cheap meal consisting of pies or frankfurts – we seemed to live on frankfurts. After tea we drew from the model.

Someone was flush one night and we had a lobster party. The lobsters were cooked in the studio, which was quite a feat. I think we skipped sketching that night. After lobster salad and beer, we danced.

An elderly gentleman attended every Wednesday night most conscientiously. He drew devotedly, scarcely raising his head from his work. Totally absorbed he appeared, and we marvelled at his dedication until we discovered his secret. Our elderly gentleman wasn't drawing the model. Or rather, he did an initial study like the rest of us, then his imagination took over. He began adding underwear to his drawings. Naughty lacy camisoles, frilly panties, wicked-looking suspenders and silk stockings and high heels. Hardly surprising that our elderly gentleman was always so loath for class to finish.

About this time we had a marvellous bearded male model; beards were unusual then. He had come out from England but was supposed to be French. Klayber Klaus was his name. Klayber liked posing naturally. He was a nudist and so was his wife.

When they first came out to Australia he and his wife had a little farm up in Queensland, where they wanted to start a nudists' colony. Their little boy used to wander around with no clothes on, scandalising the locals. The neighbours used to dress him themselves and send him home.

The bigotry of Queensland was too much for Klayber and his wife. They moved to Sydney, hoping the city would be more tolerant. Klayber had worked as a model in London and decided to try it again. Alison and George were thrilled about him posing naturally, and had him round at their studio for the sketch club. His physique and beard kept Klayber in demand and he posed as all sorts of characters. He turned up in one exhibition as John the Baptist; we thought he really did look like John the Baptist, as if any of us could know. I enjoyed going to exhibitions and recognising the models we knew in paintings with weird and wonderful names.

Then the Klauses had a daughter. Klayber's wife used to rub the baby down with olive oil each day and put her out in the sun. None of our mothers would have dreamed of doing this, but the baby looked fine and grew up to be a dancer. About a week after the baby was born, Alison, George, Dora Jarret and I were invited to dinner at their home in Paddington. We didn't know what to expect; they had very little money and posing was very poorly paid.

Klayber met us at the door in a short toga and we sat cross-legged on the floor, the food spread out in front of us. A huge wooden platter was made up with fruits and raw vegetables, potatoes, carrots, pumpkin and cabbage all chopped up fine or grated. They were also vegetarians.

Klayber eventually worked a fruit stall near Anthony Hordern's at the Haymarket end of George Street. I used to see him there for years. In a blue shirt and a tanned face, he always looked remarkably healthy.

I struck up a new friendship. A nun from St Patrick's school, Church Hill, the steep hill off George Street on the way to the bridge, rang me up at home. I don't know how the nun knew of me, but she asked if I would do the artwork for notices they wanted printed at the school. I didn't want to charge her anything when the work was done, but the little nun insisted on paying me. Someone had given them money for the notices, she said.

'Is there anything I can give you?' I asked. 'A present I can buy you?' I thought she should, at least, have a share of the money.

'There is one thing I love,' she replied. 'Honeycomb in the jar.' So honeycomb in the jar was what I bought her and she was delighted.

I visited the convent again after the nun had commissioned more work from me. I was waiting for her in a tiny room. The room contained a small table and two chairs, in one of which an enormous cat was asleep. My friend couldn't see me straight away and asked me to wait ten minutes.

'Don't touch the cat,' she admonished, poised at the doorway. 'It's Sister Pauline's cat and that's his seat. He hates to be disturbed. He gets most upset,' she concluded.

'I wouldn't dream of disturbing Sister Pauline's cat,' I assured her hastily, but I was speaking to thin air; she had already vanished into innumerable convent corridors. I sat glued to my chair.

'I don't know how anyone could be as fond of a cat as Sister Pauline,' my friend remarked after her return, as we walked off to her classroom. 'You know she picks him up when she comes in and kisses him on the mouth. I don't like to criticise, but I think it's dreadful, kissing a cat on the mouth. It's not hygienic.'

Cat lovers wouldn't think anything of that, I tried to placate her. Inwardly I, too, had misgivings about Sister Pauline. I am very fond of cats, but I have never in my life kissed one on the mouth.

The little nun and I became great friends and I often visited her with jars of honeycomb. One day when I arrived, she was extremely agitated. 'You know the dear old nun who did our cooking?' she said. 'We've had to send her away to a hospital.'

'Why, what happened?' I said, expecting to hear about an accident or a heart attack.

'Well, she was getting forgetful, but the other night she made us a steamed pudding. We like steamed pudding, you know; it's a bit of a treat.' What in the world was this leading to? I wondered.

'The currants were very sharp, we thought, as we took the first mouthful,' my friend went on. 'Instead of putting currants in the pudding, she had emptied a box of tacks into it, and that's why the currants were sharp. It's very sad, but we were really quite frightened for her. The only thing we could do was send her somewhere they can look after her.'

My nun was in tears by the end of the tale. I kept a straight face and consoled her as best I could, trying not to think of the nuns sitting around the refectory table with mouths full of tacks until I was out of her company and could smile in safety.

Other characters round the Quay I knew so well by sight that they seemed like old friends. A pensioner couple, probably in their eighties, used to sit in Macquarie Place. Early in the evenings I used to see them, a small man and a small woman approaching each other from opposite directions. He always carried a brown suitcase like a school case and she had a shopping bag. They would sit down on a bench together. The man would take out a parcel from the brown case and the women would produce a package from her bag. His had bread and butter, hers usually hard-boiled eggs or occasionally slices of cold meat. Solemnly they shared the food out. The meagre repast over, they talked animatedly for a while, then went their separate ways into the night. Their rendezvous were so regular, the couple were like clockwork figures. I loved to speculate what their story might be.

Then there were the cat women. City strays appeared by the score from the Quay's back lanes. I became friends with Mrs Bultitude and Mrs Royston, who fed the cats in Macquarie Place. A third old lady fed more cats up behind the Conservatorium, but I wasn't on speaking terms with her.

Mrs Bultitude was a big woman, Mrs Royston was skinny and scraggy. Mrs Royston had seen her fill of life, I felt. Mrs Bultitude was worried because Mrs Royston didn't believe in God. She had tried to convert her, but without success. Mrs Bultitude lived at Kensington and made a most circuitous journey into the city to feed the cats. Kensington via Redfern was her daily route. She bought cheap cats' meat at Redfern, chopped up and ready to dispense.

Mrs Royston lived in a room at Phillip Street and fed the cats rabbit innards which she bought from the pie shop at the Quay. She was furious about the cats at the Conservatorium. 'The most dreadful tomcats live up there,' she said. 'They rape the kittens.' A rape victim was hidden in her room. Poor cat, she was practically a kitten herself, with kittens of her own. 'She's only a child, dear.' Mrs Royston couldn't forgive the tomcats. 'Only a child.'

Cat and kittens were secreted in Mrs Royston's bed. Her

landlady wouldn't allow cats on the premises, but what could Mrs Royston do? The tomcats would attack the kittens as soon as look at them, and they had to be rescued.

Mrs Royston's face was dead white, her hair dyed blond and straw-coloured. No matter what time of night I went past Macquarie Place, I would see her face glimmering palely like moonlight among the Moreton Bay fig trees. Bedecked in dilapidated finery, she would sit all night in Macquarie Place. It was too hot, she said, in her little Phillip Street room to sleep on summer nights.

Mrs Royston's wardrobe was extensive. She wore embroidered evening dresses with a feather boa or rhinestones. I remember seeing her elbow deep in a basin of blood sorting rabbits' insides. She looked as if she were wearing long red evening gloves to match her ensemble. The cats thought she was wonderful. Macquarie Place was full of them, mewing around Mrs Royston as they waited for their rabbit. The Lands Department next to Macquarie Place had a fat ginger cat that must have belonged to the caretaker. Every night the ginger cat arrived for its share of food, along with the waifs.

Sometimes late at night Mrs Royston roamed the Quay. One hot summer's night she met a man who had just missed the last ferry to Neutral Bay. Mrs Royston struck up a conversation with him because he had 'such nice socks, dear. You can always tell a gentleman by his socks.' I don't know what she could see of his socks in the middle of the night at Circular Quay, but Mrs Royston invited her new-found gentleman friend up to her room in Phillip Street for a cup of tea.

'He must have been lonely?' I asked.

'*Lonely*, dear?' Mrs Royston replied. 'Lonely, dear? He was desperate.' So might Mrs Royston have been.

At the top of Bridge Street was a piece of vacant land with a few trees growing on it. One year there was a plague of case moths. The case moths hung off the trees in their little bags like flowers. An extraordinary sight, city trees blooming. But their flowering was brief. The moths hatched and the trees were ruined. I've never forgotten the sight; it all happened so rapidly.

8

A Pocket
Venus

A nude study by Norman Lindsay

I hadn't seen Norman Lindsay since he fled to America in 1930 at
the height of the *Redheap* drama. Now, four years later he was
back, busy setting up the Endeavour Press to publish Australian
novels. I met him in the street outside the Wentworth hotel
where he was staying for a few days. Norman always stayed at the
Wentworth when he was in town.

He asked me if I knew of any studios available because he
wanted to start painting from the model again. Up at Springwood
he was restricted, he could only have the model to stay for two or
three days. If he had a studio in town he could have the models
call every day and embark on a series of large oil paintings he had
planned.

George Duncan had gone off to try his luck in England. Alison
had stayed behind and kept the studios on alone. But they were
such a devoted couple that Alison couldn't bear being away from
George. She was about to join him in London. 'Number 12 Bridge
Street's vacant,' I told Norman.

I took him round and introduced him to Alison, who arranged
for Norman to take over the studio as soon as she left. So Norman
Lindsay became the new tenant at 12 Bridge Street.

Numbers 8 and 12 Bridge Street were both dark brown, three-
storeyed buildings. Number 12 had a big solid carved front door
that opened onto a wide cedar staircase. The studio on the
second floor was next to Isa Lorrimer's rooms. Isa was a petite

redhead who taught children dance and ballet. She lived in one room and had another fitted out as a dance studio, complete with mirrors and practice bars.

Stella Kidgell lived on the third floor. She was a draughtswoman with the Lands Department, the only one, I think. Various old ladies had previously lived in the building, including an elderly aunt of the poet David Campbell. A steep ladder like a ship's ladder led from the third floor onto the roof, and as the buildings adjoined each other, once on the roof one could have walked the length of Bridge Street.

The studio was actually two rooms. Alison and George hadn't lived there, but Norman did. He worked and slept in the huge, high-ceilinged front room, and used the back room for storing materials, easels, canvasses, drapes for the models. The bathroom he shared with Isa Lorrimer was out on the landing.

The front room had a tiny stove hidden behind a screen Norman made. It was the tiniest stove I ever saw, about a foot square, with a griller on top, and more jets below which could be used like an oven, even to cook roast beef.

The plywood screen was painted with enamels and had a rich lacquered appearance. A mass of female forms swirled around it, from a neat little sphinx-like figure, lotus-positioned, to a giant vermilion-saronged and turbaned black woman. There were bookcases along one wall, with cupboards underneath to hold drawings. Norman's bed was in another corner of the room. He slept on a couch with boxes in the bottom, a divan, really. His bedclothes were kept neatly folded in one of the drawers and I never saw any sign of a bed when I arrived at the studio in the morning.

The model's throne was in the centre of the room, with various other chairs scattered around. Norman was always very keen on home-made chairs. The large windows down one side let in plenty of light. Often Norman allowed Hilda and me to draw the model with him; sometimes Dora Jarret came and the three of us would be drawing away while Norman painted. His son Ray also dropped in to draw. They were great days.

When you knocked on the door Norman would answer, his eyes sparkling with pleasure.

'Come in and have a cup of tea,' he would say. The tea would be already made and his palette laid out.

Norman was fifty-four when he moved into the studio, frail-looking but relentless as far as work was concerned. He liked to start at ten; it upset him if the model was late. He would be ready, waiting and charged up at ten. Wasted time made him angry.

Sunburned models also annoyed him. If a model had been sunbaking and came in with contrasting white and brown skin he would do a drawing and send her away. You couldn't paint skin that wasn't all of a piece, he said. It's true – any artist finds it difficult to paint a banded model.

Norman hated interruptions. He would rush to answer a knock on the door, brush in one hand, palette in the other. 'Sorry, old man, I'm working,' he would say and shut the door in the caller's face.

He stopped only briefly for a light lunch, then worked on until about three thirty or four. Afterwards Hilda and I would clean his brushes and tidy up the studio. We didn't mind doing this work for him; in fact we loved doing it. I also did any shopping Norman needed. Hilda, Norman and I sometimes strolled down to inspect the ships in the harbour, down George Street, round the Quay, Norman talking non-stop, up Pitt Street and back to the studio for a reviving cup of tea.

Norman taught both of us an enormous amount; Hilda about oils, myself about watercolour. He showed me in detail his own special method of putting down a wash and how to improve my technique. He criticised my paintings constructively and I came away feeling elated, believing I might really be an artist.

Towards the end of the afternoon, the visitors arrived. I usually came over about this time if I hadn't been drawing at the studio during the day. I first met Norman's brother Percy in the studio. Percy in his spotless white was charming and gentlemanly. He won everyone's heart. The brothers were similar in appearance and mannerisms, particularly the rapid way they spoke, but Perc was stronger-looking and far more easygoing. Beaming, full of good humour and stories, Perc was always relaxed.

The literary *Bulletin* boys would appear for a cup of tea. Norman never drank; alcohol disagreed with him, he said.

Norman's flame burned too bright, I think, for him to need extra stimulants. A cup of tea and talk would light up his eyes as fast as any alcohol.

Everyone was writing a novel in those days, it seemed. I would stay spellbound listening to the talk until six and could hardly bear to leave. Norman had boundless enthusiasm for new projects. Words spilled out of him; he loved encouraging any artistic endeavour.

Brian Penton was a late afternoon regular, a slight figure with black hair and very black, wicked eyes; his malicious, lively expression marked a wit as black as his eyes. He had already written his novel, *Landtakers*, and was beginning a second, *The Inheritors*.

Brian was keen that the Endeavour Press would succeed because he was fed up with his career in journalism and wanted to become a full-time writer. But when *The Inheritors* was finished, it didn't have the impact of *Landtakers*. He accepted the editorship of the *Telegraph* and the large salary and yacht that went with it. There were no more novels from Brian and the slim young man became the corpulent figure Dobell painted years later. But it was the slender young man, the passionate talker with the flashing eyes, who entertained us in the afternoons at 12 Bridge Street.

Brian came into the studio once and saw some studies for one of Norman's big paintings, 'Don Juan' or 'The Amazons'.

'Good heavens, Norman, you're painting Australian girls at last,' he exclaimed. Like many others, Brian thought that because Norman's settings were fanciful, the women in his compositions weren't real either, that the women Norman painted were figments of his imagination. Norman's women were all very much alive and real.

At Rubbo's soon after I left school, I first heard of a model posing for Norman Lindsay. A model named Peggy used to pose for Rubbo's class. Michael Arlen's book *The Green Hat* had taken the town by storm. Peggy intrigued us innocents by always appearing in an enormous green hat similar to the one worn by the woman in the story.

Rubbo was irate one day because Peggy was late for posing. She was due at ten, finally she arrived at half past eleven.

'Where have you been?' Rubbo raged.

Peggy told him she had been up at Springwood posing for Norman Lindsay. Coming down on the train, Peggy said, her green hat blew off. She had to get off at the next stop to retrieve it, hence her lateness. That was my introduction to Norman's models.

At Rubbo's I also met Doreen Hubble, red-haired and creamy-skinned. Doreen was a treat to draw after my struggling for six weeks at a time with ancient male models such as Petit. Doreen posed for everyone: Thea Proctor, Victor Mann and the Society of Women Artists who met once a week in the Queen Victoria building and who tastefully swathed her in tulle. She posed for us at Alison and George's sketch club and also for Norman up at Springwood.

Norman was not the only artist in Australia who painted the nude. A woman artist, Janet Agnes Cumbrae Stewart, did magnificent pastel nudes and of course Julian Ashton had painted the famous Chloe in the bar of the Adams hotel, a favourite bohemian hangout. A Melbourne artist, Charles Wheeler, had made his reputation painting nudes, but Norman said he cheated, since he only did back views.

Norman attributed his artistic inheritance to his grandfather Williams. Grandpa Williams was a Wesleyan missionary in Fiji who wrote and illustrated a book about Fiji. He drew the landscape and the women without any missionary qualms or scruples. Grandpa Williams's Fijian women were never overdressed.

When he was about five, Norman was taken to the Ballarat Art Gallery where he was shown a painting, 'Ajax and Cassandra', by an artist named Solomon J. Solomons. 'Ajax and Cassandra' deeply impressed the slight blue-eyed boy who stared up at the massive painted canvas – Ajax striding ahead with the flimsily draped Cassandra held high in his arms. Norman started drawing the nude after he saw that painting. He began at the age of five, and I don't think he ever stopped.

I knew all the models from the Royal Art and the different sketch clubs so when Norman took the studio in town I arranged for them to come in and pose for him. I didn't have the telephone on at 38A Pitt Street; if Norman was in a hurry for a model, I just went out to her home and fetched her. The models were so familiar to us, we were like members of a big family.

Rita was, of course, Norman's favourite and most famous model of this period. 'Buttery-coloured' he called Rita's skin tones. Rita's father was Chinese, her mother Spanish. Rita said he made her feel like the Queen of Sheba sitting on the dais surrounded by luxurious drapes. I didn't introduce Norman to Rita; she was posing at Joe Hollaway's sketch club and someone brought her round from there. However, I was at the studio the first time Norman drew her. She came with her mother.

Rita's mother liked to meet the artists for whom her daughter posed. The mother was just as beautiful as the daughter: older and a little careworn, but beautiful. I've always regretted that I didn't ask Rita's mother if I could draw her that day.

'Rita of the Nineties' is one of Norman's most famous paintings of Rita. Rita remembers Norman taking her up to Henderson's in

Percy Lindsay in a Roman toga with Margaret as a flamenco dancer

Pitt Street to buy the material for the dress; this was during the war and he had saved up his food coupons to pay for it. Henderson's store was well known for its speciality dress materials. Norman chose plum-coloured taffeta with enough for a matching hat. Rita later wore the dress to an artists' ball, the one to which Percy Lindsay came as a Roman in a toga.

As a wedding present Norman gave Rita a length of pink satin, which he had probably first used as a drape. With the material was a note telling her that she was too beautiful to be in a kitchen and to make herself something nice out of the satin.

Norman worked so hard that after a full session painting an oil of Rita he was exhausted at three o'clock.

Usually he did a pencil drawing or a charcoal study first, this was put down on canvas, then he started painting. He worked in two or three tones to begin with, a method called impasto. The lights are put on thick, the shadows kept thin. He would add a rich note of colour, say just a touch of pure vermilion, with the point of his brush.

Rita was his favourite model but there were many others. Norman never needed to look for models; they came looking for him. They weren't paid much, only a few shillings a sitting, but they loved posing for him.

Norman said you got the best out of a model by praising her good points. He never made a model hold a pose overlong, as they did in the art schools. If the word went round that Norman was in town, not just the regular models but girls who had never posed before appeared at the studio looking for work; a model's sister or her best friend would decide she, too, would like to pose for Norman.

I have kept a notebook with the names and addresses of Norman's models and it has one hundred and thirty names in it. Next to the model's name is a brief description in Norman's handwriting: 'Gloria, aquiline nose, fair hair.' Often underneath it reads something like, 'Jeannie, Gloria's friend.'

Norman didn't turn anyone away. If a girl arrived, she was given a sitting. He would make a pencil study but if he didn't like the girl, she was not asked back. He drew girls of all shapes and sizes, from Solly, the Nordic blonde with strong arms and legs and beautiful big feet who taught swimming at a harbour baths, to

Duck Sweetie, who was tiny and what Norman called a 'pocket Venus'.

Duck Sweetie wasn't her real name, but that's what we called her. 'Duck Sweetie' was the name of the shooting gallery where she worked at Luna Park. She had to stand posed or poised above a tank of water; if a customer hit a target he got to duck Sweetie, and she tumbled into the water. She was tired of constantly being ducked like this and catching cold so she decided to take up modelling. At least then she wasn't always wet.

Amber, another model, was Dalmatian, her people owned a fish shop in New Zealand. Amber was very beautiful. Her family expected her to marry someone suitable and carry on the family business. She had come to Sydney for a bit of a fling before she settled back to cleaning fish for the rest of her life.

The dark girl you see in Norman's paintings was little Olive. Olive was Ethiopian, born on the island of Mauritius and the most captivating creature. She had dusky skin with a sheen on it like a ripe plum, frizzy hair that stood out about ten inches around her head, a small waist, big hips and a funny husky voice. Everyone loved drawing and painting Olive, because her stories were so amusing.

Norman's favourite Olive story was the Ethiopian Prince. We all knew him; the Ethiopian Prince had been posing round all the studios. Very flash he was, dripping with rings and bracelets, and musical, too. He was a pianist and received many invitations to play at snob Darling Point and Vaucluse parties, or so he told us. He assured everyone that he was truly a prince and only posed on the side.

Olive came into the studio and Norman asked her if she had met the Ethiopian Prince. 'Met him!' Olive said scornfully. 'He's not an Ethiopian Prince. He's me uncle's brother.' I don't know why she didn't say he was her uncle, but 'me uncle's brother' the Ethiopian Prince became a standing joke with us.

Noreen, yet another model, came from an address in Woolloomooloo. There was nothing wrong with that, but Olive told us that Noreen's house was no ordinary house. In fact, her mother was a madam. Noreen was rather tough-looking; she could assume a ferocious expression. But she had beautiful tawny golden skin, and turned the loveliest Rubens-like back, with two dimples on her shoulder blades and two more above her bottom. Noreen's back can be seen in many of Norman's oil paintings.

Noreen regaled us while she posed with stories of Woolloomooloo life. When she was younger, her mother had locked her in an attic bedroom at night but Noreen used to open the skylight, climb onto the roof and walk along to a fire escape ladder. She would scramble down the ladder and go off into the night wherever she liked. In the morning, she climbed back to her room by the same means.

Norman returned to Springwood during the war, but still came down to the studio for a few days' painting. One night he was awakened by an urgent knocking on the outside front door. Norman hurried down the two flights of stairs to see what the matter was. On the doorstep stood Noreen, with a bashful and very young American sailor.

Noreen explained to Norman that the sailor wanted to marry her, but was insisting that Noreen should give him a reference first. (Norman used to shriek with laughter when he told this story.)

'What sort of reference do you want?' he asked.

'A character reference,' said the young sailor, who had suddenly found his tongue. 'Like when you go for a job.'

'Certainly,' Norman said. He was so tickled by the request he went upstairs straight away and wrote out a reference saying that Noreen had given excellent service when he had employed her; he thoroughly recommended her and wished her well in any future position.

Reference in hand, Noreen disappeared happily with the young sailor. We never saw her again, so we never found out if they married or not.

Norman also had some fine male models. Don Juan in his 'Don Juan' painting was Michael. Michael was intelligent and good-looking, but during the Depression modelling was the only work he could find. The Depression caused a lot of people to work as artists' models who in easier times might have found other employment.

When 'Don Juan' was exhibited at the Macleod Gallery on the top floor of the *Bulletin* building, Michael took his girlfriend, thinking she would be thrilled to see him looking so handsome in the painting. But instead of admiring his appearance, she slapped his face.

'To think you stood there posing with all those naked women,' she upbraided him, and ran out of the gallery.

This was unfair. Norman only ever worked with one model at a time. For 'Don Juan', as for his other large paintings, he did a series of pencil studies of the composition first, then each model in turn came to pose while he painted that particular figure. (Some people even thought he used to have the jaguars and leopards in paintings such as 'Crete' running loose in the studio. Norman went over to the zoo and drew the animals before he painted them in back at the studio.)

Michael came mooching round to the studio after the exhibition, hoping that Norman might be able to set things right by convincing his girl that Michael hadn't posed with any women, dressed or undressed. But his girlfriend couldn't be induced to visit the scene of the crime and Michael remained out of favour.

Michael's story didn't have a happy ending. When war broke out, Michael enlisted. He said goodbye to Norman the night before he left to fight in New Guinea. That was the last we heard of Michael. We supposed he was killed in the fighting.

Norman's other male model, James Robb, 'Old Rob', used to call himself 'Norman's Principal Pirate'.

Old Rob, who scrubbed Norman's floors as well as posing for him, was an ex-sailor. Norman was good at persuading people to tell him their life stories and he also encouraged them in any artistic venture. He had Old Rob writing his autobiography.

Rob had been a seaman in the days of sailing ships, which appealed to Norman, who had an overwhelming interest in any kind of ship, but especially sailing ships. He was always working on ship models, which ranged from an ancient Roman galley to copies of the cutters described in the novels of his beloved Joseph Conrad. Old Rob managed to get about one-third of his life story down in between posing and his other chores.

He loved pulling faces and play-acting for Norman. He was very proud of being 'Norman's Principal Pirate' and many of the male figures with fierce expressions are Old Rob.

The black-veiled woman at the back of 'Don Juan' was Joyce

Delamare. Delamare was an Irish girl with large violet-coloured
eyes and red-brown hair. She had been a showgirl in the famous
musical *Chu-Chin-Chow* which was written and first produced on
the English stage by an Australian, Oscar Asche. The play ran
from 1916 to 1921 in London. Delamare was in the back row of
the chorus because she was so tall. *Chu-Chin-Chow* was a hit
here, too. Everyone knew the songs from it; my brother King
used to stride round the lounge room of our flat singing in his
deep voice, 'I am Chu-Chin-Chow from China'.

After the London season, Asche brought his company, including Delamare, to tour Australia. When the tour finished Delamare
stayed on. I think she would have liked to continue acting but she
had to settle for modelling. Despite her height, she was a very
gentle creature, very fey. In Ireland, she told us with utter
sincerity, she used to see fairies. But in Australia she never
managed to see one, she concluded sadly. We all loved Delamare
because of her gentleness.

She used to correspond regularly with Lord Alfred Douglas in
England and she showed us his letters. Lord Alfred Douglas,
whose relationship with Oscar Wilde had caused the latter's trial,
sent her a book of poems he had published which Delamare
didn't like. She wrote back to him saying so. She was only
speaking her mind as an old friend; she didn't mean to offend
him. But Lord Alfred Douglas wanted adulation, not criticism,
and after that letter he never wrote to Delamare again.

Delamare often posed for Norman in Bridge Street. Norman
also employed her to clean up the studio and sometimes she
cooked his breakfast. Delamare became even more fey and vague
as the years passed, and also more depressed. 'I can't bear the
thought of growing old,' she used to say. 'I would rather commit
suicide than grow old.'

Norman would pay her for posing; she would walk out into the
street and let the money fall from her hand. She seemed to have
lost the will to live. Norman tried to cheer her up and talk her out
of her depression, telling her that it was silly for such a beautiful
woman to talk of suicide. But then he went up to Springwood for
a few days.

I asked her to help me clean up my studio, thinking she might
like some extra money. I waited and waited but Delamare didn't

turn up. At lunchtime I went out to buy some food and saw the news stands full of placards. 'Artist's model kills herself', 'Model found dying'. I got a terrible shock.

I almost ran up to St Vincent's, crying all the way, I was so upset. When I arrived, the Reverend Mother told me it was over, and that Delamare was dead. People in the house where she lived had heard groans coming from her room and called an ambulance. The ambulance rushed her to St Vincent's but it was too late. She had left a note on her door: 'Not at home – dead'. Delamare had always had a grim sense of humour. She had just reached her fortieth birthday.

People are always speculating what went on with Norman surrounded by these beautiful women. Norman was too busy painting for amours with models. Far from being a seducer, Norman was, upon occasion, a matchmaker.

A girl who worked for a Macquarie Street doctor asked Norman to paint her. She was engaged to be married to the doctor but he was hesitant about setting the wedding date. The girl thought sitting for Norman might perhaps arouse a spark of jealousy, or that when her reluctant fiance was shown the painting he might realise what a good thing he was onto.

After the pencil drawing was completed, the girl asked if the doctor could inspect it before Norman started on the oil. The doctor was duly impressed by the drawing. At the sitting next day the girl was ecstatic; they were to be married the following week and the doctor wanted to buy the painting. Thanks to the painting, we presumed, they lived happily ever afterwards.

Norman liked big women. He said so frankly. All small men do, he believed. Norman himself wasn't short, but he was very slight. 'The balance of nature' he called it.

Norman was perturbed if the balance of nature was upset. A new model arrived, a tall girl who, like Delamare, had been a showgirl in the back row of the chorus.

'She's engaged,' Norman whispered agitatedly to me after a few sittings with the new model. I stared at him, surprised at the look of concern on his face.

'Her bloke is six feet tall! It won't do, you know,' Norman insisted passionately after she had gone. 'The balance of nature is kept by the tall women marrying short men, and the little women marrying great, tall men. This marriage hasn't a chance. It won't last, upsetting the balance of nature. They're too tall, it won't last.'

I can see Norman's models clearly even now. It makes me think of François Villon's line 'Where are the snows of yesteryear?' I'm glad these girls didn't disappear like the snows of yesteryear, but live on in Norman's paintings.

I was still painting flowers. The trainer Norman Carey gave Mum as much manure as she needed from his stable and she grew pansies and hydrangeas, Shasta daisies and the Michaelmas daisies which came out at Easter, but they weren't enough for me. I loved rare, different flowers.

Beatrice Stewart once had some black iris, mourning iris, which I instantly had to buy. I put them in two paintings, and could have painted them much more, but they never had them in the shop again. The paintings of the irises sold, I don't know to whom and I haven't seen them again.

Although I often bought just one or two special flowers from a florist to lift an ordinary arrangement, occasionally I asked for a mixed bunch. I was fond of putting all sorts of flowers together, which florists don't usually do, but the florist at Wynyard station was good about making mixed bunches for me. I never liked formal arrangements. Flowers look best in a vase, straight from the garden as they have been picked.

A Pitt Street florist amused me. He had two assistants who looked after the shop while he spent his time in a room at the back, arranging flowers. The door of this room had a sign saying 'Do not disturb, genius at work'.

He was a cranky genius; the first time I went into the shop I was a startled witness to a temper tantrum. His assistant had dared to interfere with one of the genius's thoughtful floral creations and the genius was screaming in high-pitched hysteria. I waited quietly, and the florist glanced at me out of the corner of his eye as his wrath wound down.

He suddenly turned his attention to me, the tantrum over. 'And what do you want?'

'I'm waiting for the genius to finish, because I want to ask his advice.' A little flattery never goes astray.

The florist melted like an icecream in summer. He was by my

side, as polite as could be. 'What advice?' he inquired.

'I want to paint some flowers and I wonder if you could pick me a bunch?' I didn't stretch my luck by asking if I could choose them myself.

The florist was touched and picked me quite a nice bunch. I went there regularly after that. On some days he was surly and would hand me a bunch without speaking; on other days he was almost mellow and would chat on affably. One day, a customer ordered a bowl of flowers for a male friend.

'There are only two kinds of flowers you give men,' the florist told me. 'Men only like or appreciate two flowers: roses and carnations.'

Maybe he was right, I don't know, but I've always remembered the advice.

Godfrey Blunden and his wife Merle, whom we called Mick, had become close friends of mine. Godfrey was tall and blond, he often visited Norman's studio in the afternoon. He had written a novel called *No Reality*, which Norman liked and had urged Jonathan Cape to publish. This was the basis of their friendship.

Mick had a shop at Kings Cross in which she sold modern pottery. She had great style and taste but the shop didn't do very well; it was ahead of its time, really. The Blundens lived near the Hotel Metropole in a flat that was part of an old Sydney house. Mick decorated the flat with a sure artistic touch and I loved going there. The furniture was all white and for the floor Mick had woven a large circular rug out of brown, black and white strips of felt.

The Blundens also bought a huge house at Kurrajong. The original house had burned down, but some of the garden was left, including giant magnolia and camellia trees. Mick worked on the garden every weekend and brought me wonderful bunches of mixed flowers to paint.

I was walking down George Street, carrying a bunch of Mick's spring flowers when suddenly I heard a close up clattering of hooves. It gave me quite a fright and I looked over my shoulder. A huge Clydesdale, one of the Clydesdales that pulled the Tooth's brewery carts round town, was right behind me on the footpath. His head was buried in my daffodils and he was busily munching my bunch of flowers. I guess the spring perfumes had gone to his head.

The portrait of Mick Blunden that the Women's Weekly *did not use*

Mick was involved in a money-making scheme I dreamed up. I thought I would do a series of watercolour portraits of women for the covers of the *Women's Weekly*.

Not an entirely original idea – I was inspired by a copy of the American magazine *Cosmopolitan* which ran a similar series. Still, the style was my own. When I presented myself at Consolidated Press with a portrait I had painted of Mick, the editor said he would consider the idea. I was to call back in a couple of days, which I duly did. 'Oh, you're the one who did the portrait of Micky Blunden,' he began, innocuously enough. Then, to my horror, he proceeded to describe what he would like altered here, there and everywhere. You can't alter a watercolour; it isn't that sort of medium.

'All right,' I said.

I grabbed the painting and walked out, with no intention of going back. I should have known better. It wasn't a commercial-looking portrait, it didn't look like the cover of a *Women's Weekly*, and the delicate colours would probably have been difficult to reproduce.

Who cares? I thought. At least I had my integrity.

Friends reported back to me that the editor couldn't understand my behaviour – I had brought in this beautiful watercolour and then stormed off in a huff when he proposed some minor alterations. They said he wanted me to bring the portrait back in so that something could be worked out. But there was no way I or my painting would ever be in his office again.

I had been exhibiting at the Watercolour Institute since 1934, as well as the Royal Art Society and the Society of Artists. They were the three main art societies. My paintings had started to sell, but I couldn't have lived or paid the rent on what I made. But financial success aside, I had several thrills with my painting during this period. Howard Hinton, the collector, bought several of my pictures.

The day before any exhibition opened, the trustees of the Art Gallery of New South Wales went through the show to see if they wanted to purchase a painting. Then neatly moustached, bespectacled Howard Hinton quietly made his selection. Having Howard Hinton buy a painting was a real honour; it meant you had arrived as an artist or were about to arrive.

The *Herald* wrote up a circus painting of mine, which was also prestige of a kind. The painting was called 'Elephants in Woolloomooloo'; strictly speaking, it should have been 'Elephants at the Back of Oxford Street'.

Behind Buckingham's store in Oxford Street was a big open space where every year Wirth's Circus put up its tent. I had been a circus fan since I saw my first circus in Yass and whenever the

Howard Hinton

circus came to town I painted it. Every day for weeks I went there sketching.

At the entrance of the main tent was a sort of zoo; people could look at the animals in their cages before the show. I was drawing the lions and one of them kept roaring its head off. I wondered what was wrong. Then one of the four Wirth girls came back from shopping in town.

'What's the matter, Prince?' she asked.

Prince was missing Miss Wirth; that's what the matter had been. He stopped complaining the moment she spoke. Miss Wirth went over to the cage and scolded him affectionately through the bars. Prince didn't exactly purr, but he did behave like the family's favourite cat greeting a long-lost owner.

The big excitement was my exhibition, my own 'one-man' exhibition, as it was called. I was twelve months preparing for it. I worked very hard because I wanted to show Beatrice McCaughey I had not been wasting her money. I did far more paintings than

EXHIBITION OF
WATER COLOURS
By
MARGARET COEN
OFFICIALLY OPENED
By
B. J. WATERHOUSE
on
WEDNESDAY, 8th JUNE.

W. RUBERY BENNETT GALLERIES
1a HUNTER STREET (Corner of Hunter and George Sts.)
Telephone BW 6938.
Exhibition closes Wednesday, 22nd June, 1938.

*Catalogue of the exhibition and
'Chinese Dolls'*

Margaret after her first solo exhibition

the thirty-three that were finally hung. Most of them were flower pieces. Petunias, nasturtiums, cyclamen, rhododendrons, Japanese magnolias; the flowers came mainly from Mick Blunden's garden at Kurrajong. My portrait of her was also included.

My exhibition opened on 8 June 1938 at Rubery Bennett's gallery on the corner of Hunter and George Streets. It was a gala occasion for me. Mum was there, with Molly, Hilda Townshend, Mick Blunden, Beatrice McCaughey and Aunt Mary Carter. P. J. Waterhouse, a trustee of the Gallery and the brother of Professor Waterhouse, a camellia expert, gave the speech.

I had a tiny catalogue, like a miniature book, with one of the paintings called 'Chinese Dolls' reproduced on the cover. Chinese dolls were the little figures with finely painted china faces and richly embroidered and brocaded tunics I used to buy in Campbell Street. In the painting the two Chinese dolls are propped against a greeny-blue Chinese porcelain bowl on a black lacquered stand. In the bowl was a single dahlia.

Beatrice McCaughey really made that first exhibition a success. As if she hadn't done enough for me already, she bought about half the paintings as presents for her friends. Harry Ervin, the collector who many years later bequeathed the funds for the Lindsay Gallery at Springwood, bought two paintings. It was another two years before the Art Gallery bought any of my work.

At the end of that year, something else happened. A young New Zealand poet, Douglas Stewart, came to my punch party at 38A Pitt Street. Someone brought him along. He was dark and dramatic-looking with a smouldering quality. We were introduced, but the young poet didn't say much; I wasn't even sure if he enjoyed the party. He was living at an old boarding house down on the water at Potts Point and looked to me as if he needed to be asked home for a good feed. He was so thin. The young poet was going home to New Zealand for Christmas the next day – that much I did find out, but that was about all.

Six weeks passed and suddenly he was back on my doorstep at 38A Pitt Street almost the moment after he stepped off the boat from New Zealand.

Douglas Stewart

9

Getting Through the War

Doug made a set at me right from the start. He was twenty-six and had just been appointed assistant editor of the Red Page, the literary section of the *Bulletin* magazine. His second book of poems was about to be published in London and he was working on a poetic drama, a verse play for radio about Scott's expedition to the Antarctic.

I had never met such a dark, intense young man. Doug startled me by suggesting marriage almost as soon as we started going out. I was shocked; in fact, I burst into tears. I had always been terrified that marriage would interfere with my being an artist. It was another five years before we made it to the altar, but we were constantly together from the moment he arrived back in Sydney. Without knowing what particular rhyme scheme or rhythm was used in a poem, poetry was precious to me. Through Doug, I started to meet more poets and writers. From being purely involved in the art scene, I became familiar with Sydney's literary world.

One of my most vivid early memories of Doug's friends is of the day I surprised him and Ron McCuaig with the Queensland blue swimmer crabs. Ron was a poet and fellow-worker on the *Bulletin*. The staff were supposed to work on Saturday mornings. Ron and Doug would put in a token appearance, then disappear next door to the pub, later perhaps making their way up to the

Ron McCuaig　　　　　　　　*Beryl McCuaig*

Assembly, the *Smith's Weekly* pub, for a drink with Kenneth Mackenzie or Ken Slessor.

This Saturday morning after the usual few rounds, Doug and Ron decided they would have a feast and bought themselves a huge parcel of crabs. The meal was already in progress when I knocked on the door of Doug's flat: he had moved from the boarding house by now.

The smell almost knocked me down as I came in.

'What on earth are you eating?' I asked, trying to make out the gruesome spread on the table. Bits of shell were scattered everywhere.

'Those crabs are off,' I said.

Mutely the pair of them stared at me, horror-struck, then down at the litter of crabs. Still speechless, Doug looked at Ron, Ron looked at Doug and their eyes turned back to me.

Suddenly Doug grabbed the lot off the table, wrapped it in newspaper, tore down the hall, threw it in the incinerator chute and rushed into the bathroom.

Doug and Ron had noticed the smell too, but they were trying to kid each other that the crabs were all right.

Ron McCuaig was tall and slim. His constant characteristic was an unending chuckle. If Ron said something funny, which he frequently did, he would be the first to laugh and the last to stop, long after everyone else had finished. Shortly after the incident of the crabs, I was invited to dinner with Ron and his wife Beryl in their flat at Parsley Bay. Beryl, a small blue-eyed, mischievous, pretty woman, was pregnant. She cooked us one of her excellent roast dinners, and afterwards we played bridge. Beryl was as quick-witted and sharp as Ron; they were an amusing and entertaining duo.

That night I heard the story about the time they lived in Macleay Street, Kings Cross. Beryl had an ancient dog to which she was very attached. Every night Beryl took the dog for a walk.

A frumpily dressed woman stepped up to Beryl during one of their strolls. 'If that's your dog,' the woman said, 'it's a disgrace. By the look of the animal, it should be put down.'

Beryl glared at her.

'People might say the same of you,' she retorted.

We loved the McCuaigs. Another night at Parsley Bay, Beryl, although by now heavily pregnant, insisted at the end of the evening on walking right up to the bus stop with us, quite a climb. Early the next morning she was rushed to hospital at Rose Bay and later in the day their first son John was born.

Doug's other great friend was the poet and novelist Kenneth Mackenzie. Mackenzie worked on *Smith's Weekly* doing film reviews when Ron was writing for the *Wireless Weekly*. The editors of the two papers, without consulting anyone, decided to swap the two writers around. Mackenzie ended up on the *Wireless Weekly* and Ron McCuaig was bundled off to be funny at *Smith's*. Ron moved on to the *Bulletin*; Mackenzie stayed with the *Wireless Weekly*.

Mackenzie was a silver-tongued, charming Adonis. He and Doug used to drink round town together. Mackenzie always carried a little suitcase with him but in those days we were unaware of the bottle of claret it contained. On weekends he took home a gallon of claret, which shocked even Doug, who did his share of drinking with the *Bulletin* boys. But it took us a long time to realise how much Mackenzie was drinking.

When I first knew him with Doug, he was in fine form. The demons that tormented him later were kept well hidden.

It was actually Mackenzie who took Doug over to 12 Bridge Street and presented him to Norman. The friendship between Doug and Norman developed gradually, stemming from Norman's admiration of Doug's writing and enthusiasm for Australian literature and Doug's awe of Norman's painting.

Doug would drop over to the studio at about lunchtime, ostensibly to visit me, but often he was quickly immersed in conversation with Norman. Norman loved talking to Doug, discussing at length his current preoccupations or pet discoveries such as John Tierney's short stories.

Mum, on the other hand, was not initially impressed with my new boyfriend.

Like most mothers, Mum was consumed with curiosity. She kept pressing me to bring Doug out to the flats so she could meet him. Doug, equally adamant, refused to be dragged into the family circle.

'You must come to dinner one Sunday evening,' I pleaded. 'Mum keeps asking who this "Douglas" is.' Doug resisted resolutely. But at last he gave in, still with a great show of reluctance.

The evening was not a success. Doug fortified himself well beforehand. He sat silently on the edge of the couch while I chattered on brightly. Mum couldn't get a word out of him. She tried and tried again, but conversation with Doug was like trying to get water out of a dry sponge. I alternated between wishing he would say something, anything, and hoping he wouldn't fall off the couch.

It was a grim evening for everybody, not an auspicious beginning, but Mum came round to him. Doug's poems in the *Bulletin* won her over. She cut them out and made them into a scrapbook. The poet's tongue triumphed in print.

Mum invited him to dinner a second time. A special butcher's shop in town called Woolf's sold hare. Mum thought that Doug, being a New Zealander, would appreciate this, and bought a hare in honour of his visit. Unfortunately, she didn't realise until she opened the parcel at home that the hare was still in its fur. She had to set to and skin it, not a task she relished. Mum certainly did her best for my poet.

Doug was terribly, terribly thin; I think he lived on nervous energy. He wrote *Fire on the Snow* the first year we were together. During the day he worked in at the *Bulletin*; at night, sometimes all night, he worked on the play.

After Potts Point he had moved into a flat at Double Bay, on the Rose Bay side of New South Head Road. Buses and trams going past up the hill made it noisy while he was trying to think. It wasn't the writing that took so much out of him but the preparation, the intense effort of working it up beforehand, exhausted him. I don't know how he did it. Such concentration.

I worried about him. Working as hard as he did, Doug very much needed looking after. He needed someone to prepare meals for him and to make sure he ate them.

After he had a bad bout of flu that laid him really low, Doug's sister Helen, whom the family called Micky, came over from New Zealand and stayed with him, which helped. Just before war broke out, Micky went home and Doug moved to the Cross. He rented a flat in a squarish red brick building called Larbert, off Macleay Street, in a quiet leafy cul-de-sac called Crick Avenue. This was the flat where I surprised Doug and Ron with the blue swimmers. It was what you called a bedsitter, a room with a bed at one end, a table in the 'dinette' at the other end; off to the side was a little bathroom. The flat was on the first floor and the dinette looked straight out on a poplar tree, its saving grace. Later on Doug celebrated the poplar tree in a poem.

Fire on the Snow was performed on ABC radio in 1941 to enormous acclaim. It started off a chain reaction; suddenly everyone was writing verse plays. *Fire on the Snow* also achieved international recognition. It was broadcast in England on the BBC and in most other English-speaking countries, as well as being translated into Icelandic and German. These were exciting times, but Doug didn't relax. On the dinette table overlooking the poplar he began furiously typing a new play about the Kelly gang.

He was even thinner than before. 'No rhubarb, vinegar or alcohol,' said the doctor, who had diagnosed an ulcer. Rhubarb and vinegar were hardly a sacrifice: alcohol was more of a struggle, but Doug obeyed orders and didn't drink. He lived on lightly steamed fish, boiled eggs and the occasional omelette. I used to finish work in the studio then come up to Crick Avenue and cook for him.

Ned Kelly was finished the same year as *Fire on the Snow* was performed and was submitted to an ABC open competition for plays, which it won. The next year, 1942, he wrote *The Golden Lover*, which won a similar prize at the end of that year. Several other verse plays were written and discarded by Doug as not being up to standard, or at least, his standards, before *Shipwreck* was finished in 1945. He really worked non-stop those years. The dinette table in Crick Avenue certainly gave good service.

Throughout the 1930s, we had had a sense of foreboding. It was impossible to ignore the newsreels of Hitler and his men goose-stepping and Mussolini in his high-heeled boots, his chest blazing with medals, puffing himself up like 'the bullfrog of the Pontine Marshes' as they called him. Yet when war broke out we were still not prepared, we couldn't believe it.

Doug and Ron McCuaig went on a pub crawl to let off steam. They didn't really know what else to do. This was just before Doug's ulcer was discovered. They met at the Mansion hotel, a posh white building on the way down to Rushcutters Bay and a well-known gathering place. Doug and Ron drank their way in and out of every pub from there to Double Bay.

War was awful.

For a while everybody said it was a phony war, that it would be over in three months. Three months passed and when the Battle for Britain began, everybody knew the war wasn't going to end for a long time and that it was going to be very nasty.

The artists and writers we knew loathed the war. It had a devastating effect on their lives and careers. My friends from Circular Quay, like Alison and George who had so carefully saved up to study overseas, returned home immediately. Arthur Murch was stranded in Switzerland with no money. He offered to paint an innkeeper's son in exchange for meals and accommodation. Arthur did two paintings, one for them and one which he kept. Many years later I bought 'Portrait of the Swiss Boy' at an exhibition in Sydney.

Mackenzie was conscripted. His uniform never seemed to fit him properly; he looked misplaced and miserable. He was eventually sent off to guard the Japanese prisoner-of-war camp at Cowra. He was there in 1944 when the Japanese broke out and he wrote a novel about it which Angus and Robertson were going to publish. But a commanding officer at Cowra was also an Angus and Robertson author, a best-selling one; pressure was exerted and Mackenzie's book withdrawn from publication in Australia. Life in the army, and the sad fate of his book, I think, broke Mackenzie, and started him drinking so heavily.

Norman moved out of the studio as soon as war was declared, back up to Springwood. This was not all bad, though, because I became the custodian of 12 Bridge Street. My only regret was having to abandon my red cedar shelving, because it wouldn't fit into Norman's studio.

Norman's wife, Rose, their daughter Honey and her husband had gone to America and Norman wanted to be near his other daughter Jane, who lived at Kurrajong. He lived and painted in a small studio at the back instead of the big Springwood house. From time to time he still came down to the city and painted from the model with me in the studio but as the years went by his visits became increasingly rare.

Not only was the war disruptive, it was also frightening. It was dreadful every day, waiting for the news posters to go up round town, then reading the headlines. First we saw 'Holland lays down her arms', that was the phrase they always used, and our hearts sank. Next, 'Belgium lays down her arms', then France. France was worst because we knew the Nazis now had broken a critical line of resistance.

Doug went off to enlist in the AIF. I was beside myself. He disappeared into Victoria Barracks for a whole weekend. I cried for the two days. But he was rejected on medical grounds, for which I was most thankful.

Though I was grateful that Doug was saved from the army, it did seem incongruous that only the fittest specimens were accepted for the slaughter. There was no sense to it. Doug became an air raid warden, so he wasn't exactly shirking responsibilities, and I am sure the world is richer for his writing during the war years.

After the Japanese came into the war, I received a call-up notice myself; not to go into the army but to do my civilian duty by working at Parramatta asylum, the last thing in the world I felt capable of doing.

I panicked, not knowing what to do or whom to turn to. I thought John Maund, president of the Watercolour Institute, might help me; he was a solicitor. To my relief, Johnny was totally sympathetic.

'Ridiculous, Margaret,' he said, frowning at the piece of paper. 'I'll attend to this. I'm going to ring your uncle.'

My uncle was Dad's brother Joe, a Macquarie Street specialist. Johnny told him I was an artist, entirely unsuited and unfit for working in any asylum. Besides, I had to look after my mother, which was true. At that time, one member of the family was allowed to remain at home to care for any aged relatives.

Thanks to Johnny Maund and Uncle Joe, I heard no more about Parramatta asylum. I did a lot for Mum, who was quite elderly now, making her morning tea and breakfast and tidying up the flat before I went into the studio – but that wasn't the real reason I didn't want to work at the asylum. I just couldn't. I happily donated paintings to raise money for wartime charities, but the other was too much.

You hear about the big things in war, such as the bombing of cities, but often the little things were the saddest. I remember preparing for a Watercolour Institute show, fifty per cent of the proceeds of which were going to the air force. Harry Julius, an artist with Smith and Julius, was helping us. His son, who was an artist too, was only a boy. He brought in some paintings to the exhibition and stayed while we hung them. He was in his naval uniform; it was the last day of his leave. The next day he would be shipped off overseas. He was so young and cheerful. Less than a fortnight later, the news came through to Harry Julius that his son was dead.

The fall of Singapore shattered us. Singapore, we thought, would never fall. Now we realised there was nothing between us and the Japanese. Real gloom set in. It was hard to be optimistic after February 1942. Everyone was despondent.

Everyone, that is, except Norman.

Norman made a famous remark to Robert Menzies. Menzies

had visited the studio to pay court to Norman and like the rest of us, he was full of pessimism about the war.

'The Japs will be here in two weeks,' he said to Norman.

'No, they won't,' Norman answered. 'I have something to stop them!' He had just read Doug's *Ned Kelly* and he was referring to the play. Norman meant that a country couldn't be taken while its artists were making such full use of their creative faculties, while the mental energy of the people was so high. Any creative effort, he believed, was as good for a country as a battalion of soldiers.

His faith was very contagious. It was impossible to be near him and stay down for long.

The arrival of MacArthur and the Americans changed things, though. One morning as I was going into town on the tram, I saw two enormous black sentries standing on either side of the wooden entrance gate to the race track in Alison Road. That's how I knew the Americans were here. The American troops used Randwick racecourse as their headquarters in Sydney.

As far as I was concerned, it was the turning point in the war. England was too far away to be of any real help to us but now the Americans had arrived it seemed we had a chance.

Doug and Molly were both air raid wardens. Molly's shelter, or sector post as they were called, was in Macquarie Street, Doug's in Manning Street at the Cross. The city was blacked out and there were continual practice drills. Our ears were left ringing from the wailing sirens.

The wardens had to attend their sector posts until the raid or mock raid was over. Doug's companion warden at the Cross was a whisky-soaked World War I veteran whose sole contribution in times of crisis was a series of commands left over from the trenches.

'Assume the prone,' he would bellow at Doug, who would come back to Crick Avenue afterwards repeating out loud, 'Assume the prone, assume the prone.'

The wardens took their job seriously, to begin with. One awful night Doug and his partner had to carry the patients out of the local hospital to the shelter. This was a difficult task, as most of the patients were elderly ladies. Doug was startled when the matron suddenly hissed in his ear that she wanted a word with him.

'Get rid of the drunken warden,' she ordered. 'Assume the prone' was duly dispatched and they struggled on.

The wardens also had to ensure that all lights were out during a drill. Doug had an ongoing battle with a brothel round the corner. The brothel catered for the Americans and business was too brisk for them to be bothered with air raid rehearsals. They had more action going on inside than Sydney had seen outside during the whole war and they were not plunging customers into darkness for a mere warden, a man without even a uniform. Doug never won with the brothel lights.

Molly once had a traumatic night in her sector post. She and her friend from the Taxation Department were in the shelter when somebody lit a match. The gas had been left on and the shelter immediately exploded. No one was hurt, but it caused some confusion.

I was painting in the studio one Sunday when Doug arrived unexpectedly. He had heard air raid sirens from his flat and, knowing I was working, thought I mightn't hear them. Heroically he decided to rush into town, risking life and limb under the threat of bomb fire, to warn me. However, as he approached Bridge Street, he realised that the relentless, high-pitched note was not in fact the air raid signal, but the routine wailing of fire engines going about their day-to-day business. He arrived breathless and a little shamefaced. As reparation he took me to lunch at Aaron's, which was always a treat.

Aaron's was a pub in Gresham Street, a tiny narrow passageway off to the right of Bridge Street. A splendid place to eat, Aaron's specialised in roast dinners, roast lamb, roast pork with apple sauce, roast beef with Yorkshire pudding. Not expensive, either; it was possible for those without much money to eat at Aaron's five nights a week and still not be too broke.

Another Sunday we were lunching there with Ron McCuaig when the hotel was raided. As it was Sunday, no one was supposed to be drinking. The police took everyone's names and addresses. Doug was saved because he was still off alcohol and I wasn't drinking either, but Ron was caught.

Unabashed, he gazed coolly at the police officers. In response to the pen poised above their inquisitorial notebook, Ron came up with the names of two dead presidents of the United States:

Benjamin Lincoln. Blatantly fake, you would have thought, but the police wrote it down without a blink, and also the false address Ron obligingly supplied, and went on their way.

The night that the Japanese submarines came into the harbour was pandemonium. No sirens sounded, but up at the Cross Doug actually heard the bang when a ferry was hit. He rushed down to Manning Street in such a hurry that a shoe came off, and he arrived to do his duty, shoe in hand. But a fellow-warden was in a worse state of disarray. In his fright he had put his trousers on back to front.

Molly, Mum and I were at home in the flat. We were issued with instructions – if we weren't in a shelter we were to go under the house. If we couldn't go under the house we were to get under a table. The best position for the table was in the hall. We dragged the kitchen table into the hall and wedged it near the front door.

We were worried because the invading troops would obviously come straight down the garden path to the front door, up the stairs, into the hall and find us under the table. So we decided to arm ourselves. If armed, we could at least take a swipe at their legs. Molly had Dad's beloved sword from World War I, Mum had the carving knife.

I had the blackthorn Irish shillelagh. The shillelagh is a beautifully balanced weapon, not a straight stick, but curved, with a two-sided knob on the end like a hammerhead shark. It looks murderous and the strange thing is that when you pick up a shillelagh up you *do* want to hit someone. It has its own inbuilt impetus. Any invaders in the hall would have to watch out.

At nine o'clock at night no lights were on; it was pitch dark. The three of us squashed in under the kitchen table – neither Mum nor I could be described as a small woman – waiting with our weapons for we weren't quite sure what. The suspense was killing.

I desperately wanted to go to the lavatory. I tried to think about other things, such as the danger, but it was no use. I had to go. Molly had to crawl out from under the table first before I could extricate myself.

'You stay there, Mum,' we instructed, thankfully stretching out to our proper height. 'Don't you move.'

I went off to the bathroom. When I returned, Molly, who always had more courage than I, announced she was fed up with being under the table.

'I'm not going back under there,' she said. 'Come out onto the front verandah and see if anything is happening.'

To go onto the verandah, we had to climb back under the table where Mum was still crouched up, but no longer clasping the carving knife, I noticed.

A heated row was in progress two doors up at Careys' stables, and we leaned over the balcony, trying to see what was going on.

'You'll have to move away from here, you'll upset the horses,' Jerry Carey was saying in a loud voice.

The Americans kept their tanks and armoured cars at the racecourse, an easy target for an air attack. When the alarm sounded, their vehicles were ordered to disperse. They moved off up High Street, one tank had come down Botany Street and stopped outside Jerry Carey's. Jerry's only concern, as ever, was for his horses.

'If you draw the bombs here, you'll kill my horses! You'll have to go this instant.' Jerry's fury was beyond measure. The Americans caved in before such passion. The tank revved up again and moved off up the street.

Mum came out from under the table, said she wasn't having any more to do with this nonsense, and went to bed. Molly and I stayed up until the all clear sounded, then we too retired. It sounds funny now, but it was a terrible evening – terrible for the sixteen young naval cadets who drowned in the harbour and for their families.

As the war wore on and the threat of an air attack seemed less likely, the air raid wardens stopped taking their duties so seriously. Each sector post was furnished with a bed and a medicine cabinet. The first aid kit contained medicinal brandy. Most of the wardens were single men and the air raid shelters rapidly degenerated into love nests. The wardens invited in their women friends, drank the brandy and made appropriate use of the beds.

Life at home had its lighter side, too. Molly won the lottery – that was an event.

I had left the studio and gone off shopping one morning. When

I came back round the corner from George Street into Bridge
Street, Molly was standing on the doorstep of number 12 with a
newspaper under her arm, looking more excited than I had ever
seen her. She waved the newspaper wildly at me.

'Don't tell me,' I said. 'You've won the lottery.'

'How did you know?' she spluttered.

'Molly,' I grinned, 'why else would you be in here at this hour
with that look on your face?' But she was still dumbfounded that I
could have guessed.

Molly was so excited; she took me and the girls from the office
to Usher's for lunch. Molly looked as if all her Christmases had
come at once. Lunch went on the whole afternoon.

The next excitement in Molly's life was her engagement. That
really did rock us. Jack Scully was the name of her fiance, she had
known him since she left school. Jack's father had racing stables a
block up from us in Randwick, and Jack had been one of Molly's
racing friends, but they were never more than that until Jack's
father died.

The Scully family home was pulled down and a block of flats
was built on the site as an investment. Jack lived in one of the flats
with his sister and it was about this time that he began courting
Molly. They were like a couple of seventeen-year-olds, holding
hands and gazing at each other moonishly.

Jack would put a geranium on the windowsill when his sister
was out so Molly could pop up and have a whisky with him. Molly
lived for these little assignations, and the rest of us bore with
them as patiently as we could.

Molly was still as mad as ever about the races. Jack Scully had a
racehorse called Old Rowley entered in the Melbourne Cup. Old
Rowley's odds were not good at a hundred to one. Jack kept
urging Doug to have a bet on Old Rowley but Doug was totally
sceptical. Even lovestruck Molly wasn't convinced that Jack's
horse would win.

But Old Rowley surprised us all. He thundered home and won
the Cup at a hundred to one; it was the most historic Cup Day in
our house. Molly was ecstatic. It was a pity none of us except
Molly had anything on him.

Molly and Jack were married in May 1943 at the Sacred Heart
church, Randwick. A few days before the wedding, Molly had

already left for work and I was about to go to the studio when a distraught figure came racing back up Botany Street.

'What's the matter?' I asked, looking at Molly's frantic face.

'I've lost my engagement ring, my diamond engagement ring,' Molly repeated between bursts of sobbing.

'Molly, quieten down,' I tried to calm her. 'It will be all right. We'll go home and look for it. We'll find it.'

Molly and I searched both the dressing tables in our shared bedroom, hers first. I didn't see how the ring could be in mine, but we did it too from top to bottom, then the chest of drawers, then the wardrobe. We searched the whole house; no ring. It was nearly lunchtime by now.

Suddenly Molly dramatically stuck her hand out in front of her. 'My God, I'm *wearing* it!' she exclaimed.

In her 'I'm-going-to-be-late-for-work' morning panic, Molly had slipped the ring on her right hand. I heaved a sigh of relief and went off to the studio to salvage what was left of the day.

I was bridesmaid at the wedding. In the photos I am wearing a little velvet magenta hat, adorned with an impressive feather. Mary Edwards, the artist, saw the photos.

'I must paint your portrait in those feathers,' she said.

I got on well with Mary Edwards, whom I had met at various times over the years. She used to exhibit with the Royal Art Society. She also knew and liked Doug because he had written about her paintings. We were both keen on her work.

Mary Edwards has been underrated as an artist, I think. She has been penalised too much for her squabble with the trustees of the New South Wales Art Gallery when Dobell won the Archibald Prize with his portrait of Joshua Smith. Although she did seem to have a penchant for litigation – the Dobell case was not her only court appearance – Mary Edwards was a fine portrait painter.

She used to visit Doug in the studio to discuss her dream. She had bought some land in the Blue Mountains at Mount Tomah which had views up and down the mountains and Mary's dream was to turn it into a park, a conservationist's paradise. Her ideas about this park were ahead of her time.

Mary loved painting feathers. Most of her portraits of women have feathers in them; that's why she liked my hat. And so my souvenir of Molly's wedding was immortalised. Mary Edwards' portrait of me hangs in the dining room now.

Molly and Margaret at Molly's wedding

With Molly safely married off, I settled back to work.

A huge parcel addressed to Norman Lindsay arrived at 12 Bridge Street. Norman was up at Springwood but on his next visit to the studio he opened it and inside was the manuscript of *We*

Were the Rats by Lawson Glassop. Norman was daunted by the enormous, unwieldy, untidy bundle of typescript. He leafed through a few chapters and handed it over to Doug. Doug's reaction was similar to Norman's.

The manuscript was accompanied by a desperate note from Lawson, imploring Norman to read the novel and tell him if it had any worth. I felt sorry for the worried author, besides which I was a compulsive reader, so I offered to read it myself. Norman and Doug both looked vastly relieved to be absolved of the duty.

All night I stayed up reading; I couldn't put it down. I was completely captivated by his story of the seige of Tobruk. The Australianness of it moved me; the way he described the line of men enlisting for the army. The officer asks one man what defence force he wants to join. The man looks back at him and shrugs. 'I'm easy.' So of course they send him off to the infantry, the toughest part of the army.

I enthused to Norman and Doug the next day. 'You must read it,' I said. 'Skip the first two chapters. Lawson is just trying to find his way in those; they're not very good. Drop them off, the rest of the book is wonderful.'

So they read the manuscript and agreed with me. Norman sent off a letter full of praise to Lawson who was with the army up in northern Queensland. As soon as he read Norman's letter, Lawson went AWL.

He arrived at the studio door in an air force uniform, one of the three uniforms he used as disguise while making his way down from north Queensland to Sydney. He said he was so excited by Norman's letter that he had to come and see him.

Norman wrote to the army explaining why Lawson had disappeared, and asking that he not be in trouble as a consequence. The army took no action against Lawson, which shows how respected Norman was.

Another AWL sought refuge at the studio. A boy came round with a letter from Norman, allowing him to draw the model in the studio. The boy's sole ambition was to be an artist, but then he was conscripted. He protested violently. He hated the army, he said; he would never make a soldier.

To no avail. He was sent to a training camp in north Queensland where recruits were taught how to handle weapons.

He told me afterwards that every time he held a rifle or bayonet, it made him sick and he vomited.

Apparently the army chose to ignore any weaknesses in their recruits. They were ordered overseas, this boy included. He couldn't stand the thought of having to go off and use these weapons on other men. So he fled back to Sydney and begged me to let him stay in the studio.

'If they catch me, they'll shoot me for being a traitor,' he said, almost in tears.

It was heartrending, but I didn't really want him living in the studio and I was sure Norman wouldn't either. I persuaded him to telephone an aunt of his, who agreed to look after him. Immediately afterwards I rang Norman at Springwood, and Norman again wrote off to the boy's commanding officer.

More letters were required before the boy was let off and he had to go to Goulburn for some sort of psychiatric assessment or treatment, but soon after that he was released.

Although we had ration cards for food and petrol, we weren't as short of supplies as people in Europe, we had enough. Black market goods were always available; even if we didn't buy any, we knew they were around.

After Norman moved out of the studio, odd characters who had posed for him paid me the occasional visit. Sometimes they were looking for work, sometimes they were begging. I would give them two bob and they would go away.

A particularly scruffy fellow came by several times.

'I want to see Norman Lindsay,' the conversation would begin.

'Mr Lindsay isn't here,' I said, 'he's up at Springwood.'

I expected the usual request for two bob, but this day he furtively produced a stained envelope from his pocket. He said he wanted to sell it to Mr Lindsay.

'What's in it?' I couldn't resist asking.

Humming and ha-ing, shuffling and shifting, at last he said, 'Can I trust you not to breathe a word of this?' and produced a ration card for butter and meat. I don't know if it was his or not.

The temptation was too great for me.

'How much do you want for it?' I asked.

'Ten bob,' he replied.

I gave him ten bob. Doug and I used to go and stay with

Norman on the weekends and so I used the ration card on food for Springwood.

I don't suppose it was much of a crime, but I felt guilty and a bit haunted; I thought that since I had bought one card from him, he might come back with more. If I heard a knock at the door, I cowered.

'My God, it's him!' I used to think.

Rosaleen Norton was another visitor at the studio. She lived lower down George Street by the Rocks in a strange three-storeyed stone building called Buggery Barn. Its occupants didn't really live in the building, they just camped. Rosaleen was always broke. She was an artist herself, but she also offered her services to other artists as a model.

'Oh, please, Margaret, give me five shillings,' she would say in her quiet, refined and hesitant voice. 'I've got to have some dinner. Give me five shillings and I'll pose for you.'

'Don't bother about posing,' I would say as I gave her the money. Rosaleen wasn't a good model. She could hold a pose but wasn't particularly attractive. Her body was starved-looking and often covered in insect bites.

She had an obsession about looking like a witch. She used to draw on eyebrows that arched right up over her green eyes and her hair was dyed bright orange; I could remember when it had been dark brown. I still have a drawing that I did of her looking very witch-like.

I went to visit Rosaleen in Buggery Barn. She had a sick cat in the room with her. She didn't look very well herself, and the cat kept vomiting. I was appalled.

Very different were the two New Zealand nurses who came to visit Doug. They had been serving overseas and turned up in Sydney on their way home to New Zealand for rest leave before going off to war again.

Irene Taplin and her friend Johnno were both striking-looking and very tall, about five feet nine. It was summer, and they used to wear their white nurses' uniforms round town. Everyone in the street turned to stare because they were so stunning.

The girls used to call in at the studio about nine in the morning. 'We've bought you a present,' they would chorus. The present would be a bottle of Bols gin in a lovely stone bottle.

The bottle was put on the table, we would chat for a while then one of the girls would say, 'Let's have a gin.'

'All right,' I would weakly answer.

Several gins later, they would happily make their way downstairs and head off uptown looking for adventures. They seemed fine. I was the one left staggering to face the day's work on three early morning gins. I don't know how many empty stone bottles of Bols gin were in the studio when they left.

I painted Irene Taplin twice, once in her uniform and once in her own clothes with an orange tiger lily in her hair which matched the lights in her brown eyes and the glint of her auburn hair. She was a real tawny beauty.

On New Year's Eve, we had a party with the girls in Doug's flat at the Cross. At ten minutes to midnight we went down into the street for the procession they had through the Cross every New Year's Eve.

These two girls in their white nurses' uniforms led the procession. They strode along and everyone fell in behind them. People on the footpath cheered. The Cross was much smaller then; it seemed that all the people who lived there knew each other.

Doug came over to the studio every day for lunch now. He had been appointed literary editor of the *Bulletin* and I shared his excitement as the poetry came in. I remember his surprise and delight at discovering new talent, such as the day he received a poem from the sixteen-year-old schoolboy Francis Webb.

A young woman with her dark hair drawn back in a bun came to see him with a couple of poems: Nancy Keesing. Then there were Rosemary Dobson, shy and intense, and tall Nan McDonald, her long fair hair plaited in a crown round her head. Towards the end of the war came David Campbell in his air force uniform, fresh from fighting in New Guinea.

My mother was in the studio one day when David appeared; she was instantly smitten. 'He looks like a Greek god,' she gasped after he left. I think Mum fell in love with David the moment she set eyes on him. Most women did; he was outrageously good-looking and had the most charming manner.

When Doug and I went up to Springwood to visit Norman on weekends, we went for long walks in the bush around the

'Nancy Keesing' by a commercial artist'

house and, with Norman's daughter Jane, we climbed down to the waterfall at the bottom of the gully. Norman didn't go with us; a stroll around the garden at the end of the day was about as much outdoor activity as he cared for.

Norman's room out the back was quite separate from the house. The studio was more or less as it is now. There was a lay figure, a silent, jointed figure bound in cloth, usually draped with material, black lace oversewn with scarlet and purple satin roses or silvery moon-coloured chiffon or midnight-blue-spangled net.

A ship model would be on a side table. He always worked on a ship model in any spare time he had. In one of the smaller rooms next to the studio, he kept three or four of these models in various stages of progress, together with materials for their fittings, such as the tiny timbers for the top deck. He fashioned every detail of the models himself, the ropes, the sails, the wheel, the oars.

Norman never relaxed. When he wasn't painting or working on the ship models, he would be writing a novel to take his mind off things or moulding figures to adorn his bookcase. He built me a black lacquered cabinet with painted panels and a mermaid's figure on every corner. Purely for his own amusement he made a pack of cards and drew and painted every card in the pack.

The main house at Springwood had been decorated by Rose and was lovely. The front room, where Norman's special oils hung, was quite extraordinary; the walls were covered in hessian with gold leaf over it. The paintings didn't hang on the wall; they were fitted into special grooves.

Doug and Norman talked endlessly during our visits. Mostly Norman talked and Doug listened. They covered art, poetry, music, philosophy and literature. Norman had read almost every book in existence, it seemed, and could discuss them all with equal volubility. He had favourite topics, such as the lost island of Atlantis, or – more comprehensible to ordinary mortals – the twelve volumes of diaries by Samuel Pepys; a mighty task of reading in itself.

Norman believed passionately in the importance and worth of Doug's poetry. He loved *The Golden Lover* so much that, as soon as he read the manuscript, he was immediately inspired to paint a large watercolour illustrating the play. The painting showed a dark green forest with Tawhai, the beautiful dark Maori girl and Whana, the phantom golden lover, locked in each other's arms.

With walks and talks, our Springwood days sped fast. Molly Chapman, Norman's housekeeper, cooked for us, as Rose was still in America. At night, I entertained Norman and Doug by reading aloud from Dickens, de Maupassant or Conrad. I read aloud a large book of Conrad's short stories after dinner at Springwood. I enjoyed it, maybe because of the days when Uncle Joe read aloud to us at Clarendon, or maybe those enforced mealtime readings aloud at Kincoppal stood me in good stead.

I always took my paintings up for Norman to criticise. He was enormously supportive of my work. He never touched my painting; he didn't need to. Norman's own technique was so clearcut that he just used his work as an example. It was up to me to follow his advice.

Looking at my early paintings is interesting now. I drew very carefully. The colours, such as the blue in a bowl of delphiniums, are practically the same as in later paintings, but my method is much freer now. You have to be in complete control of your technique before you free yourself.

I always painted flower pieces straight off, with the flowers in front of me. After years of experience I can take home a landscape, put it up and do one from it twice the original size, but flower pieces are different. Flowers have a life of their own. Flowers aren't static; they move. It's fantastic how some flowers move. Nasturtiums will turn right round to look at the light in a room. Movement in flowers is difficult to paint, but that's the aim. The slightest movement makes the world of difference to a painting.

If we didn't go to Springwood on the weekend, Johnny Maund took us out. Doug was writing, I was busy painting and often Sunday was our only day off. Before Johnny Maund started providing his car we used to explore the coast by bus on Sundays. We took the bus from Wynyard up to Whale Beach and Palm Beach, a long trip, but we did it.

John Maund was the president of the Watercolour Institute, the solicitor who had saved me from the psychiatric nursing stint. On the weekend he painted watercolours. I think Johnny deeply regretted in his later years that he hadn't devoted his life to art rather than to the law, and he was trying to catch up.

His weekly petrol rations were saved for these painting expeditions. He had a large car which was always very full of passengers: Doug and I (Doug didn't paint, but he was happy to watch or he could go off walking), Isabelle Mackenzie and her sister Nancy and John Young from the Macquarie Galleries.

Our trips ranged from Ku-ring-gai Chase to Frenchs Forest and Narrabeen Lakes; anywhere there were trees and bush. Doug and I were grateful just for fresh air. Besides, the drives were fun, sometimes more fun than the painting. Johnny used to treat us to lunches. Often we ate at a Frenchs Forest restaurant that specialised in delicious Sunday lunches. The owners had a large poultry yard with all sorts of game birds, including pheasants and peacocks. Once they put a clutch of peacock eggs under an old chook. The fowl successfully hatched and mothered them and we would see her wandering round the yard, scratching up tidbits for her flock of young peacocks.

The owners also had a pet cockatoo named Philip. We had to be careful getting out of the car because Philip used to attack everyone. He was such a vicious bird he even reduced a lady friend of Johnny's to tears.

It was late in the day before painting resumed after lunch. We would fill in a few more hours, then head back to the city. Johnny would rustle up dinner for us in his flat. He used to buy steamed chicken from a delicatessen. The nights with Johnny passed as pleasantly as the days.

But one evening didn't go so well. Johnny was doing his duty and entertaining a young American soldier on leave. Johnny was a connoisseur, especially of wines and liqueurs. He served up a dinner with the appropriate accompanying wines, and afterwards produced a bottle of cherry brandy he had been zealously hoarding until it was well matured. The cherry brandy, together with liqueur glasses, was carefully set down on the table.

The American boy was asked if he would care for a liqueur. He promptly helped himself not to a liqueur glass full, but a whole wineglass of Johnny's cherished cherry brandy, and proceeded to down it in one mouthful. We sat back horrified; Johnny looked as if he might explode.

'I don't know what you call it,' the boy announced, 'but that's a mighty fine brandy you've got there,' and he helped himself to a second glass.

The cherry brandy that had been saved for years went in one night. Johnny, who was normally the most generous of men, took several weeks to recover his equilibrium.

My birthday came round. I was painting in the studio when Doug arrived with a surprise.

'I think I've found something you might like for your birthday,' he said. We walked down to the Quay and in the window of the pet shop was a cage of kittens.

'Which one would you like?' Doug asked.

I had loved cats passionately ever since the first cat I dragged round dressed up in Yass. My last handsome black cat, Felix, who reigned at Botany Street for so many years, had sadly died a few months before.

A beautiful silver-grey half chinchilla, only about six inches long, had its tail stuck straight up like a flagpole. 'That one,' I answered. If you want a kitten, always choose the one that carries its tail erect; it's the sign of a healthy cat.

We bought the kitten and christened him Silver on the spot. I carried him back to the studio and put him in a box to take up to the Cross in a taxi.

Doug and I were going out to dinner so I thought I would leave the kitten at Doug's flat while we ate. The driver complained all the way, because Silver wouldn't stop yowling. Silver cried so piteously that I couldn't leave him in the flat, so kitten and box were surreptitiously smuggled into the restaurant, and stayed on my lap under the table for the birthday dinner.

After Felix died, my mother vowed she wouldn't have another cat in the place, but fortunately one look at Silver and she melted, which was just as well for me because she looked after him while I was at work.

The first week, Silver cried continuously unless Mum was nursing him. As a consequence, she became extremely attached to him.

With his wonderful silver coat and golden eyes, Silver grew up to be a charming and affectionate cat. His most disarming habit was eating violets. As soon as you put a bowl of violets on the table, Silver would sidle up and delicately but determinedly begin nibbling. When Mum broke her arm, Doug brought her a bunch of snowdrops from a florist at the Cross. She came out in

Douglas, Margaret and Silver
outside the Randwick flats

the morning to find snowdrops scattered around the room. Silver had been playing with them.

He was also a great mouser. Jerry Carey borrowed Silver to help get rid of the stable rats. Silver cleaned them up in no time. He brought the bodies back to us and laid them across the doormat. The little silver kitten from the Quay was a most successful birthday present.

Doug began doing theatre reviews for the *Bulletin*, which meant that we had the best seats in the stalls to plays, ballet performances and Tivoli shows – something I miss now. We went to the opening night of the Minerva, the new theatre at the Cross.

Norman did a mural for the Minerva. It was supposed to go between two pillars of Lalique glass, but the architect's original design was altered, the ceiling had to be lowered and the mural wouldn't fit in the space. Instead of Norman's painting, the foyer was decorated with a photograph of Sydney Harbour; rather a letdown, we thought.

Edwin Styles, an English actor whose repertoire ranged from comic monologues at the Tivoli to more stylish comedies at the Minerva, was a favourite of ours. We also liked Mo because he was so Australian.

Mo was a very funny man, he could always make us laugh. His humour rested on very simple sketches, but always clearly with a double meaning, accompanied by much winking and smirking. A classic skit was 'Flo's letter', in which Mo with suitable innuendo threatened to read aloud a letter. The comedy was the innuendo, he never actually got round to reading the letter itself. One Saturday I had taken my sketch book with me to the Tivoli as I often did and while the acrobats were warming up the audience I caught a glimpse of Mo lurking in the wings, his shadowy figure almost hidden beside the bright lights of the stage. I made a quick drawing of him waiting there and then painted it the next day.

About this time, 1943, Doug and May Hollinworth were in communication about a production of *Ned Kelly*. May Hollinworth was head of the Sydney University Dramatic Society and was dedicated to Australian playwriting. As soon as she saw a copy of *Ned Kelly*, she wanted to put the play on stage. It had already been performed on ABC radio in 1942 but it had been written for the theatre and May Hollinworth was offering to put the play on stage for the first time.

Doug and I were both very excited. It was a thrill to see actors up on stage saying words he had written, becoming the characters he had created, watching the audience respond. It was performed on Sunday nights in the tiny SUDS clubrooms above a pub at 700 George Street near the Haymarket. An actor called Guy Manton played Ned; I've never forgotten him striding around the stage. May put the play on a second time at the Metropolitan Theatre in 1947, this time with Kevin Brennan as Ned, and he was equally memorable.

Doila Ribush wrote to Doug next, suggesting that he, Doila, should produce the play in Melbourne. Doila was a Russian Jew who had fled to Australia and made his money out of manufacturing chocolates. As a young man, Doila had been keen on acting and the theatre in Russia, but his father, sensing they might soon be leaving their homeland, insisted that he should have a second trade, a means of making money quickly to use in a strange country, so Doila learnt how to make chocolates. Every time he came to see us over the years, Doila brought me wonderful presents of his chocolates, which were extremely rich.

Doila actually arrived in Australia on Melbourne Cup day, and was perplexed to find the whole of Melbourne shut down on a weekday. He was astonished to find that the cause of this was a horse race. To begin with, his factory was the flat where he lived, but he soon extended.

Doila's first love remained the theatre. He was passionate about his productions and had an intensity quite different from Australians'. He threw himself into producing *Ned Kelly* with his usual dedication. Norman was engaged to do the stage designs, which he did. Doug's verse was treated with as much respect as the lines in a Chekhov play. Chekhov was Doila's god.

'Listen to the pauses,' Doila used to say reverently to Doug, extolling the virtues of the divine Chekhov.

The war made it difficult, if not impossible, for us to attend the opening of Doila's production of *Ned* in Melbourne. We dearly wanted to go, but you had to apply for permission to travel interstate by train and going to the theatre wasn't a good enough reason. Petrol was rationed so even if we'd had a car, driving it was still out of the question. But then a friend with a car said he could get some petrol and offered to take us down. It was too good an opportunity to pass up.

Driving down by the coast road took three days. When we went inland for the last part of the journey, we seemed to do nothing but cross little bridges, listening to mile after mile of frogs' chorus. I thought Victoria must be inhabited entirely by frogs.

When we arrived at about three or four in the morning, Doila's plump figure was anxiously standing by the open garage door. He had been up all night in a state of nervous trepidation, waiting for us. His brown eyes flashed relief as we drove into the garage. He pushed the door shut behind us and locked it. We found out afterwards that Doila had been terrified of us driving down by car. Maybe the fear was left over from or caused by memories from Russia.

Doug was only thirty-one. He had published two books of poems since I had met him, three plays and a book of short stories. His output amazed me. I remember reading a newspaper article about him in Melbourne that listed his achievements and being so proud of him.

Ned Kelly went down well in Melbourne, receiving a lot of publicity and critical acclaim. The actors were taken to visit men recovering in military hospitals. I have photographs of them talking to soldiers in a scrapbook I kept of all the press reports that came out while we were down there.

Doila's great friend was Edouard Borovansky, the ballet master. Borovansky had put on a ballet about Ned Kelly and visited Doug because he was worried Doug might make some copyright claim on the ballet.

Doug couldn't claim any ownership of Ned Kelly and he liked Borovansky, so he asked him to lunch with us in the studio. A shop at the Quay had excellent fresh fish and I bought a big snapper which I decided to cook up as a mornay instead of sensibly serving it straight. The advantage of the mornay was that if the guests were late for lunch, as they frequently were, it didn't matter because the food would be waiting on the stove intact.

I don't think Borovansky was late. But anyway he was thoroughly enjoying his mornay and a glass of white wine when suddenly he stopped, a forkful of fish midway to his mouth. He laid the fork on his plate, put his hand to his mouth and pulled out a long black hair. My hair was neatly bunned at the back, but it was obviously mine.

'My God,' I thought and started to stammer out an apology. 'It's all right. What does it matter?' Borovansky said. He flicked the hair nonchalantly aside and continued eating. I thought he did it with wonderful aplomb.

Borovansky remained our friend. A dancer in his company, Laurel Martin, was another friend of Doug's and she used to come across and visit us in the studio, too. When Doug became the ballet critic for the *Bulletin*, we saw Borovansky dancing in many roles as well as the ballets he produced.

About the time Doug was writing *Ned Kelly*, I began painting portraits in the hope that I might be able to earn my living as a portrait painter. I practised on my friends, Doug included.

Doug looks quite dangerous in his portrait; I think he was being each member of the Kelly gang in turn. Writers do become the characters they are writing about. The portrait only took about four sittings, but Doug had spent many months writing the play, carrying those characters around in his head. No wonder he looks a bit brooding.

I painted most of my friends; Beryl McCuaig, my cousin Marie Lysaght, my brother King's wife Mary, Marguerite Brennan the wife of Jack Brennan from the *Bulletin*, Joan Mas the poet, Rita Young, Godfrey Blunden's sister. They were all oil paintings.

I used practically no turps or linseed oil, just paint straight from the tube pressed well into canvas; I never painted on hardboard. This method looks good after about twenty years when the oil paint matures. Sometimes freshly painted oil paintings look too new and oily. After a few years a skin grows over the paint, which still looks fresh but not raw.

None of these portraits was commissioned. I gave them to my friends, who put them away and forgot about them. None of my friends framed their portraits or hung them up, except for Godfrey Blunden's sister. She was so pleased with hers that she sent me a present of sheepskins sewn together as a rug from Adelaide where she lived. I had it in the studio for years.

Thirty years later, the portraits suddenly started coming to life again. Marguerite Brennan's was the first to surface. Her son

'Douglas Stewart' by Margaret Coen

found it rolled up on top of the wardrobe and wanted it hung; Marguerite came in to ask my advice about a frame. Ron's boys discovered the portrait of Beryl next. I myself hunted out Doug's portrait which I had stuck away in the laundry and resurrected it in the hall. Doug said the explanation is simple: as people grow older, they like to see themselves looking young. Perhaps that's it, but I do also think the paint improves with age.

More portraits appeared. I had painted a friend of Molly's

called Molly Garry and her six-year-old daughter. The Garrys had a property outside Yass and I stayed there while I did the portrait. The little girl posed in a long tulle dress and picture hat which she had worn to a fancy dress birthday party as Lady Hamilton.

One portrait was commissioned. An old school friend rang me and said she had a sitter for me. The sitter turned out to be a woman from Bellevue Hill, very much from Bellevue Hill. She was bedecked with pearls and a diamond wristlet watch. I persevered, painted the jewellery to the best of my ability and handed over the finished portrait. The woman was happy with the results until she took the portrait home and her relatives pounced. Her aunt looked too stern, a niece began the objections. The family conferred and I was summoned to take the portrait back and paint a smile on the lady's face. This was duly done to the family's satisfaction and the now smiling portrait installed at Bellevue Hill. The episode was enough to convince me that a portrait painter's lot is not such an easy one. At least flowers don't complain if they're not painted right.

Miraculously the war ended. It was August 1945, we had survived a world war, and Doug and I were finally getting married.

10

Honeymooning with Henry Handel Richardson

'Willows at Duckmaloi' by Margaret Coen

If we lived through the war, I thought, we might as well get married. We had proved we could live through anything together. I was always a bit frightened of marriage. I could have married other men, but I was wary of marriage and domesticity. I didn't know if I could I stick it or whether I would want to escape, run away from the responsibilities of running a house.

Doug wanted to get married right from the start. He wanted to have children, but awful things were happening in the war and I felt it would be unfair to bring children into such an unsafe world.

Besides which, Doug was totally engrossed with his writing; he didn't have time for a family, I argued. And since Molly had married, Mum was on her own and I had to look after her. They were excuses for my own apprehension. I was plain frightened of being tied down, I think.

I could see myself overcome by domestic chores, swamped by washing dishes and scrubbing floors. I found cleaning up the flat for Mum quite enough housework. I didn't enjoy it, I endured it. We never had a vacuum cleaner or anything like that at Randwick; I did all the housework there by hand. I could envisage only too clearly all day spent like this with no time to paint.

A maid was the answer. Doug promised me that when we were

237

married I would have a maid to do the housework and I could paint as much as I liked.

The maid was a dream. I knew we had no money for a maid and only in the last few years have I had any help in the house, but it was gallant of Doug to think of promising and certainly he never interfered with my work. I already trusted him about that when I agreed to the wedding.

I have managed to survive the housework though I still dislike washing up. I didn't have a maid, but I had a washing machine and a proper vacuum cleaner. My advice to women who want to work is to forget about the housework. Do your painting or writing or whatever first. It's not a bad idea to make the bed. That doesn't take long; a couple of minutes and you can feel that the house is presentable. If you do the housework first, you'll be nagged by the feeling that you would rather be doing your own work. You waste energy hating the housework. If you clean up afterwards, you'll fly through it in no time and have some exercise too.

Swapping gossip over the back fence or discussing husbands over cups of tea are definitely out. You must get on with your work. That's how I survived nearly forty years of marriage and working at home.

The date set for our wedding was 5 December 1945 and I was flat out working at the studio until the day. I didn't have any of the usual round of activities like shower teas before the event.

A taxi driver who lived near us in Botany Street, if he saw me setting off into town, would stop and give me a lift free of charge. He was an ex-soldier with a large family. He had bought a house and was desperately bargain hunting for furniture. A wardrobe had been advertised in the paper. The taxi driver told me with delight how he had bought it for a guinea, a real bargain.

'Of course, you've heard about that murder in Darlinghurst?' he continued, 'the one where the woman was stabbed and stuck in the cupboard? Well, this is the wardrobe. That's why it was cheap. You couldn't tell; no blood, no stains, not a mark on it,' he concluded happily.

A day or so before the wedding, the taxi driver asked me if he could come up to the church for the event. I was touched, but not quite so touched when I heard the reason. He was hoping to pick up some fares going from the church to the reception and make a few extra bob.

Norman came down to paint in the studio that week, which made me even busier. I was rushing to get the studio ready for him, then cleaning up afterwards. I was so busy, in fact, that it didn't dawn on me until the last minute that I hadn't a wedding dress.

I panicked and set off in a flurry to buy a frock. Eventually after much searching I found what I considered a suitable dress at Mark Foy's. The pale pink, long-waisted dress had a finely knife-pleated skirt and long sleeves. It was embroidered with pink and silver sequins and there was a hat to match.

The hat was a problem. Small hats were fashionable and this hat was extemely tiny, made of stitched pink crépe de chine with roses round it. The hat seemed all right in the shop, but when I tried it on in front of the mirror at home, there was no way I could make it sit right.

I have a big head, maybe that was it, I don't know. I ended up buying some pink tulle and making a sort of fall of it about my face and down the back, which successfully softened the look of the little pink hat.

The wedding was in the afternoon at the Sacred Heart church at Randwick, where Molly had been married. Molly was the matron of honour, Mum had a new outfit. King and Mary were there with their three children and so were Jack and his pretty wife Dorian. Dad had come up from Yass. Ron and Beryl McCuaig were in attendance; Ron was best man. The taxi driver was waiting outside.

Because it was Advent, we couldn't have any music. The statues were covered up with purple cloth and there were no flowers in the church. But my own bouquet of tiny Cecile Brunner roses and gardenias made up for it. Doug wasn't a Catholic and as the church was much stricter about mixed marriages then, we were married in the sacristy, not at the altar rail. Church austerities aside, it was a very happy wedding and we set off into town for our reception at the Forum Club.

Cocktails were being served and everyone was beginning to relax. We were about to sit down to dinner when Dad, trust poor old Dad, threw a dreadful spanner in the works. In the middle of a conversation with me he turned white as a sheet, swayed on his feet and passed out flat on the floor. For a minute or two, I thought he had died.

Dad wasn't dead; he had fainted. His brother Joe summoned an ambulance and rushed him off to Lewisham hospital.

Dad arrived from Yass early in the morning of our wedding day and had filled in his time by visiting friends around town and toasting his daughter's wedding in champagne. At lunchtime when he went home to change, he couldn't find any food and had a whisky instead to calm his nerves for the walk up the aisle. He drank another whisky or two at the Forum Club. Dad could drink with anybody and never show the effect but all that alcohol on an empty stomach in the summer heat was too much for him. He didn't appear drunk at the wedding. He passed out quite gracefully, really.

For our honeymoon, we went to the Duckmaloi River, near Bathurst, New South Wales. Doug planned to fish for trout; I would sketch. We drove – Doug had borrowed a car from someone at the *Bulletin*. As we approached the wild, hilly Duckmaloi country, I thought I was having double vision with the heat. If I looked out of the car window, the hills seemed to be moving. The hills were alive with rabbits. It was a rabbit plague.

The boarding house was run by hospitable people called Richards, we were to spend many summers to come with them. The mother and daughter were the most wonderful cooks. I was immediately won over by their cat, which used to catch a rabbit every day for his dinner – it wouldn't have been too hard that first summer – then come into the kitchen for a cup of tea. He drank his tea from a saucer with milk and sugar.

It was one of the hottest Decembers on record, far too hot for me to go sketching, so I stayed at the house engrossed in Henry Handel Richardson's *The Fortunes of Richard Mahony* which Doug had brought along for himself. One day it was so hot that even Doug retreated from the river. The coolest spot we found was under the house, along with the fowls who had also taken refuge there.

I had seen snakes in the country before, but never as many as I saw that year at Duckmaloi. Brown and tiger snakes in the paddocks, black snakes down by the river banks or swimming effortlessly across the stream. Even up at the house we had to keep a watchful eye.

On a rare cooler day, I went down to paint the river. Warily I surveyed the single tussock on the bank and peered at the surrounding stubble. Not a sign of a snake. I was about to drop my rubber painting cushion down on the tussock when an enormous red-bellied black snake uncurled itself. You couldn't believe that such a long snake could be so tightly wound up as to be invisible. I fled screaming and the snake made off rapidly in the opposite direction. The snake was as frightened as I was, I think.

I also learned the alarming lesson that Jersey bulls jump fences. I had ventured out painting alone. No sooner had I carefully put down my rubber cushion by a paddock side and begun work than down the road a Jersey bull came trotting, followed by a man on horseback and a couple of dogs. Man on horseback or not, I wasn't taking any chances with a bull. Trout fishermen aren't the only ones whose ears are attuned for a bull bellow; bulls are also the bane of landscape artists.

Paints and paper left where they were, I scrambled over the paddock fence. 'Better to be sure than sorry,' I reassured myself. Glancing back at the road, I saw to my horror the bull leap neatly across the fence. The man on horseback was singing out and cracking his whip, but the bull took not the slightest notice.

I clambered back to the other side of the fence. The bull followed suit.

My heart was beating faster than ever, but this time the man caught up with the bull and drove him off up the road, to my infinite relief. I collapsed beside my paints to recover.

Despite the heat, the snakes and the bull, I began to discover the advantages of being the wife of a fisherman and a poet. As well as joys like fresh rainbow trout for breakfast, I loved the wonder of the countryside. I saw my first echidna at Duckmaloi; I watched spellbound as the spiky ball dug itself out of sight in a few minutes. I stared at darting willy wagtails, scanned the bush for the flash of brilliant parrots' wings and combed the ground for singing, jet-black cicadas. At Easter, on our next trip, I found little nodding greenhood orchids with a rare red stripe.

Over the years I've collected other treasures, like the eagles' feathers I put in with a bunch of wildflowers, bent-wing swift moths to take home and paint in still lifes, lichen-patterned granite boulders, coloured river stones, rippling tea-tree driftwood branches.

All this and painting, too. No meals to get, no shopping, no housework; just sheets of pure white paper, some sable brushes and my tubes of watercolour. Trout fishing holidays have been a treat. I still have a gold and green Easter painting I did of the willows at Duckmaloi which Doug loved.

In Sydney after the honeymoon, I moved into Larbert with Doug. Mrs Connolly, the dainty, diminutive Irish landlady with beautifully waved hair, offered Doug a larger flat now he was a married man. The new flat was on the third floor, quite luxurious with a separate bedroom and a little sitting room.

We held many small dinner parties at Larbert. Tall, sandy Francis Webb ate with us once, and I couldn't get over how serious he was for such a young man.

Larbert ran from Crick Avenue through to Greenknowe Avenue and our flat faced Greenknowe Avenue. A tomcat used to appear on the pavement below, asking for food. 'Greenknowe Tom' we christened him. Every night I fed him out of our window. I threw the meat three floors down; he never missed a meal.

The Cross itself was enchanting, full of fruit and flower shops which delighted me. The atmosphere was friendly and we often strolled at night. In hot weather we used to walk down past Kincoppal to the little park at the bottom of Elizabeth Bay and watch the harbour. I remember painting a lovely white yacht there one summer's evening.

Our favourite restaurant, Lindy's, made delicious lemon and chocolate meringue pies. It was hard to resist indulging in Lindy's meringue. Lindy was a refugee who had come out from Europe before the war. He vigilantly supervised the running of his restaurant and was never off the premises. But Lindy met an awful fate.

'Have you heard the news about Lindy?' Gladys Connolly greeted me one morning as I opened the front door of the flat. Gladys was one of our landlady's two very large grown-up daughters who lived at Larbert.

'No,' I said.

'It would make you go to church on Sundays,' Gladys pronounced ominously.

'What happened?' I asked, startled.

Gladys recounted the sad story. Lindy's kitchen was in the basement. A small lift in which the food came up and down ran between the restaurant and the kitchen. We often saw Lindy anxiously peering down the shaft, checking the working apparatus, we supposed. This night Lindy was looking in the column when the lift fell down on his head. That was the end of Lindy. Gladys was right. It was enough to make you go to church on Sundays.

Beatrice McCaughey had given me a sum of money as a wedding present and with it we bought a tiny dark green second hand Ford Prefect. Until we rented a garage, Doug used to park the car on the corner of Greenknowe Avenue where the post office is, which was a block of vacant land.

The little car made a big difference to our lives. Now we could go painting or exploring at will. We liked beaches, most of all Warriewood, especially in winter. Unbuilt on, unspoilt, steep sandstone headlands protected a swirl of white foaming surf. We had to clamber down to the sand on foot.

Claudia Forbes Woodgate and a friend saw me perched precariously halfway up the Warriewood cliff. I was looking intently down at the water and every so often I put something down on a sheet of paper in front of me.

Both being artists they were intrigued by this. This was before Claudia and I had met but the friend thought she recognised me and climbed up the cliff for a closer inspection.

'That's Margaret Coen,' she reported to Claudia, 'and she's trying to do a wave.'

The wave worked out well; Howard Hinton bought it for his Armidale collection. Years later when we moved to St Ives, I met Claudia properly. We've exhibited together at the Watercolour Institute and the Royal Art and have become close friends.

I didn't stop painting for a minute after I was married. I kept the studio on and the following year, 1946, I had a show in Brisbane; the war had stopped me having exhibitions before that. I didn't go up because travelling was so expensive, but the show almost sold out and the relayed accounts of its success were thrilling, to say nothing of the financial remuneration.

Norman wrote a very flattering introduction for the catalogue. The exhibition included a painting called 'From Merle's Garden', a tribute to Mick Blunden's Kurrajong retreat and her generosity with flowers. The painting of the yacht at Elizabeth Bay was also in that show.

The following year, to Doug's and my great delight, I was pregnant. We dearly wanted children.

No morning sickness, not a pain or an ache. The nine months passed without a hitch and only in the last few weeks did my feet start to swell. They were so swollen that I had to buy a pair of men's shoes. John Fountain from the *Bulletin* got them afterwards; nice blue suede shoes, they were.

I amused my doctor. About a month before the birth was due, I called in for my routine check up, carrying a shopping basket with a bottle of milk and a few other things.

'You're off home now, are you?' he asked kindly as I stood up to leave.

'Oh, no,' I replied. 'Actually, I'm on my way in to the studio. I have a painting to finish.'

We decided to move out of Larbert and live at the studio. Crick Avenue was up three floors; a long way to carry a baby and baby things. Bridge Street had two flights of stairs which was an improvement and the front room was enormous. We had much more space.

We organised ourselves into the studio just before Christmas. The baby was due at the beginning of January. Almost the last morning at the Cross we woke up very early. It was intolerably hot and breathless so we drove down to Bondi and walked along the beach. The beach at that hour is at its best. The water and walk revived me and I've never forgotten them.

The studio was much the same as when Norman had been in residence except I had moved in my mirror from Margaret Street. Norman's bookcases with the boxes underneath for drawings were there; he couldn't be bothered having them moved up to Springwood. His lacquered screen covered the odd little square-shaped stove. It was years before I had a proper gas stove.

I bought a round cedar table and a cedar sideboard from an

auction shop in William Street, a couple of comfortable chairs which I re-covered, and a set of delicate cedar dining chairs from the auction rooms opposite in Bridge Street. These were a mistake, because the backs were so frail that they broke whenever a male guest leaned back after dinner.

Doug's friends from the *Bulletin*, Ron McCuaig, John Fountain and Phil Dorter, often dropped in for lunch or dinner. Cecil Mann from the *Bulletin* never came to the studio, but his wife knitted me a beautiful blue and white coat for the baby. Beryl McCuaig was a frequent visitor who always made me laugh with her quick wit and gossipy anecdotes.

The first night I spent in the studio, I woke about three in the morning. An incredible clatter was going on, clanging and banging. I couldn't make out what the noise was; it sounded like a battalion of tanks rolling down the street.

God, I thought, not another war.

It was the street cleaners.

'We'll never be able to stay here,' I whispered agitatedly to Doug who was now awake too, if not from the exterior commotion, then from my performance. 'We can't be woken up like this every night.' I was well and truly alarmed.

Strangely enough, that was the first and only night the noise of the street cleaners woke or worried me.

A lane ran down the side of 12 Bridge Street into another lane between Bridge and Dalley Streets. Our bedroom windows faced onto this back lane while the front windows opened onto the side lane. More life went on in the lane behind the studio than I ever saw at the Cross. Drunks naturally congregated there, robberies were common, there were bashings and rapes, heterosexual and homosexual.

As well as harbouring assorted misdeeds, the lanes were great getaway routes for villains. It was possible to go from Bridge Street to Circular Quay via the lanes without entering either Pitt or George Street. The Dalley Street lane led into another lane and so on down to the harbour.

Our windows overlooked the little lane at the side of the studio. These windows faced the nor'easter so the winter sun came in, making it nice and warm, but there was a sheer drop from all the windows. The thought of that drop and a baby terrified me. So Phil Dorter came over and fixed bars outside the window for me, to my relief.

Christmas came and went. Doug and I took a showboat trip up Middle Harbour. The ferry shuddered and shook the whole way and we were both convinced the baby was going to be born on the showboat, but the infant stayed put.

On New Year's Eve we stayed in the studio and didn't go up to the Cross for the procession, the first time we missed it in years. It was January.

Doug had booked a private car to take me to hospital; our own car was garaged out of the city. I don't know why we didn't think of calling for an ambulance. Stella Kidgell and Isa Lorrimer said we could use either of their phones when the time came. (There was no phone in the studio.) I painted placidly on. There wasn't anything else to do. Unlike my hastily purchased wedding dress, this time I had shown some foresight and collected a layette for the baby.

The McCuaigs moved into a new flat at Thompsons Bay and we spent an afternoon visiting them. After we left we drove down to the beach and sat looking at the water, then we went for tea with Mum in the flat at Botany Street.

Grandma was dead by then but Kathleen had kept up the tradition of despatching Yass Christmas cakes to all the family. She used Grandma's recipe and sent a cake to each of her sisters in the convent and one always arrived at Botany Street for Mum. I had already eaten a fair share over Christmas, but I could never say no to Grandma's cake. This Sunday night was no exception, but about three in the morning I woke up feeling dreadful.

'I'm going to be sick,' I thought. 'I shouldn't have eaten the Christmas cake.'

For an hour I lay there feeling ill and blaming the cake. Pain started round my back. It wasn't the cake; the baby was coming.

Doug flew upstairs and called the car he had booked. I made my way down the two flights of stairs, which I didn't much appreciate, but I managed it.

The driver set off in a tearing hurry. I think he was terrified the birth was going to happen in his nice clean car. In fact, the baby wasn't born until three in the afternoon. Doug kept telling him to slow down, the driver would relax for a second, then his foot would be on the accelerator again.

As we raced up Oxford Street to Crown Street, the sun was just coming up. I saw the most beautiful dawn sky, with pink and orange splitting open the blue darkness. Later the morning turned grey and it drizzled.

I remember the time going slowly by, lying in a big room by myself, watching the clock. I had to tell the nurses every time I felt a contraction. The pain got worse and I heard a terrible sound. What on earth could that be? I wondered. It was my own groaning, I realised. I was groaning involuntarily.

The pain increased. My memories of the birth are hazy. The baby didn't have enough oxygen.

'Keep up, keep up,' I could hear them saying, urging me to breathe in on an oxygen mask.

I saw the baby born, and seconds after that I blacked out. Things were different then from modern hospitals. The doctor called in to see me about five o'clock when I was back in the ward.

'Haven't they brought her in to you yet?' he said. They hadn't. I didn't know where the baby was, but she wasn't with me. Shortly afterwards, I saw the baby properly for the first time.

The baby was a girl, a big baby and long. She weighed almost eleven pounds. Still, I had weighed more than that myself when I was born; Mum always said that's why she hadn't had any more children.

This baby had wide open, staring eyes and lots of hair. As soon as you see your baby, you really forget about the pain beforehand. Margaret Mary Elizabeth she was officially named, but straight off we started calling her Meg, the Scottish diminutive for Margaret.

Bringing the baby back to the studio didn't go as smoothly as I had envisaged. The baby squawked as visitors crowded in to congratulate us. I was trying to entertain them, making endless cups of tea, preparing meals and also feeding the baby. It was too much. The baby screamed louder than ever and lost weight.

I retreated to a Karitane nursing home for two weeks. The baby calmed down, she only screamed so incessantly before because I wasn't feeding her enough. After acclimatising to the baby in a

Left: Margaret and Meg

*Right: Margaret and Meg in the
Botanic Gardens*

Meg

peaceful environment, I could at least handle her with ease when I came back to the studio and the flow of visitors had abated.

Baby care in the studio had its ups and downs, particularly those two flights of stairs. Another problem was the bathroom which we shared with Isa Lorrimer, the smiling, pretty ballet teacher who was now married to an American. Isa's new husband was extra keen on hot showers. Every time he had a shower, the gas went off in our flat. The flat was filled with the smell of gas, and the gas refrigerator I had bought for the baby's milk was turned off. Doug and I thought we were all going to be gassed. But then Doug wrote to the gas company who came and blew the pipes for us, so we were saved.

A gas strike was the next event. I was feeding the baby with a milk supplement as well as my own milk. The supplementary milk had to be heated. Our only cooking arrangement was the little gas stove. I spent several days boiling milk in a saucepan on the bars of the electric radiator.

Living right in the centre of the city in a flat, I felt I should take the baby out somewhere every day. Sometimes we walked up to the rose garden in front of the Art Gallery, or Hyde Park; sometimes we wandered around the Botanical Gardens. I would stealthily conceal a few stolen blooms in the stroller, coming back through the gates. Sometimes we would linger behind the Conservatorium to watch the cat lady at feeding times, or stop for a chat with Mrs Royston and Mrs Bultitude in Macquarie Place.

We caught the ferry over to Kirribilli or the zoo where we inspected the baby wombats and the ocelots and enticed the black panther to walk up and down his cage in step with us. We tried doing it with the lion. He tolerated a few lengths, then lunged at us. We left him alone after that.

On the Kirribilli ferry one day, we met Dattilo-Rubbo. Signor Rubbo was delighted with the baby. He put her on his knee and bounced her about. As he was leaving the ferry, Rubbo handed her back. 'Well, Margaret,' he said, 'you have painted many pictures but this is your masterpiece.'

A fat old cat used to sun itself in the afternoons outside the wine bar on the way to the Quay; we christened him 'Wineshop Pussy'. I would fashion a paper mouse for him out of the sticky brown paper I used for sealing up the backs of picture frames, paint a face, attach some whiskers and a tail and add a long piece of string so we could drag it in front of his nose. Wineshop Pussy would lazily deign to put out a paw as the mouse went by and perhaps even pounce if he was feeling especially skittish or showing off. It was hard to say who enjoyed these games most; Meg, me or Wineshop Pussy. Wineshop Pussy always kept the mouse as a present when we left.

We would walk up to Victor's in King Street and eat oysters by the dozen, which we both adored, or bring them back to the studio so Doug could share.

Beatrice McCaughey would drop in, bringing the most exquisite baby dresses, smocked and shirred Liberty prints in blues and pinks. Really, the time flew. The time a young baby has to be looked after is very short compared with the rest of a life span.

Painting was restricted in the first couple of years, but I still drew. Every day in the studio I drew, even if it was only for fifteen minutes. If I drew for fifteen minutes at least I felt I had done my five finger exercises. Fifteen minutes is nothing; you spend that long reading the newspaper in the morning.

Meg in the city

Although having a child meant I stopped painting, it didn't mean that my powers of observation were impaired. On our expeditions to the gardens or out on the ferry, I could still look at things and think about how I would paint them. Time to reflect and observe is valuable. Too many people go on painting without ever stopping to look properly at what they're painting.

I learned to draw from memory. If I don't have a sketch book with me, I memorise things; if you look hard at something you'll find as soon as you're home you'll be able to jot it down on paper. You can train your mind to remember like this; it was one of the things I learned while baby minding.

I rarely went over to the musty underground corridors of the *Bulletin*, with the huge rolls of dirty cream paper that blocked the passageway and the cubbyhole offices, desks stacked high with books, but Doug brought *Bulletin* visitors over to the studio. Nancy Keesing, Rosemary Dobson or David Campbell, handsome as ever and out of uniform now, would arrive for a cup of tea in the afternoon and end up staying for dinner.

Norman did a pencil drawing of David on one of his visits. Meg intently watched the whole proceedings with David, then insisted on having her own portrait done. Norman obliged and she sat perfectly still until the drawing was finished. A very solemn little person she looks.

Too soon it seemed my daughter was five and catching the ferry at the Quay every morning over to the Loreto Convent at Kirribilli, and I was back painting again. I had a second show up at Brisbane at the end of her first year at school, just before we moved out of the studio.

We liked living in the studio, but we wanted fresh air and a garden. Buying a house after the war wasn't easy. It was hard to get a housing loan from the bank and impossible to arrange any finance on the old house which we would have preferred, so we settled for a new red brick L-shaped one at St Ives.

The blocks were big and cheap at St Ives. During the war there had been an army camp on our land and before that an Italian orange orchard. By 1953 when we arrived, any fruit trees were well and truly gone and paspalum was rampant.

But St Ives was still nicely rural, which suited us. Horses came and ate out of the front garden, and it was so close to the bush, we

Left: Drawing of Meg aged four by Norman Lindsay

Right: 'Meg' by Norman Lindsay

'Margaret' by Norman Lindsay

were practically in it. We backed onto Ku-ring-gai Chase with its valleys of sandstone and wildflowers, and the northern beaches weren't too far away either.

Most of the roads weren't tarred. The kids rode billycarts down the hill to the dairy at the bottom of Killeaton Street and went exploring the creek that made its way through the bush to Bobbin Head. The gas wasn't on, or the sewerage. We got used to the sight of the pan man, sprinting down the side of the house with a empty container, back up the garden path with the full pan precariously balanced on one shoulder.

No shopping centre; there were only a few shops strung along Mona Vale Road: Maio's fruit shop, the delicatessen, Gillot's garage next door to the post office. Further up on the other side were Steward's the butcher and Ekas the chemist.

Packing up the studio, I made a huge pile of discarded drawings and paintings for the city council to take away. As well as a few other oddments, my big mirror joined the heap, which was a wrench, but I thought it was too heavy to shift. Doug told the men at the *Bulletin* to take what they liked from the paintings. About three or four of them went through my throwout collection. It diminished rapidly. They were like ants raiding a pantry and carrying off the crumbs in triumph.

Our new home was no dream house. Except for the relentlessly cheerful, sky-blue back door, all the woodwork was bright canary yellow, never my favourite colour. We moved in on a hundred-degree December scorcher. The sun beat mercilessly down on the yellow paint. The inside walls were painted with calcimine, a cream that fought with the paintings we hung up. Paintings look well on grey or white walls, not cream ones. Every mark showed up on the calcimine like a blemish, and remained indelibly there till we could repaint the house.

Sensing a confirmed cat lover across innumerable vacant blocks of waist-high paspalum, a pregnant black stray leapt over the high back paling fences and sidled ingratiatingly up to the back porch, resolutely presenting herself for adoption. Our feline family had begun.

Phil Dorter and his wife Phyllis helped us mattock up the paspalum in the back yard; neither Doug nor I was very handy with a mattock. We released the wild lemon tree grown from a

'Moon Over Kuring-gai' by Margaret Coen

pip planted in a tub on the studio windowsill, watched it burgeon after years of potbound existence into life that gave us crops of wild lemons for thirty years.

Doug rolled about slabs of sandstone to make twisting garden paths. He crouched over the stone with chisel and hammer and mixed up cement, looking like a weird insect creature in dark glasses and a handkerchief across his mouth to protect him from the dust.

The garden didn't happen overnight, but gradually paspalum did give way to lawn and the leafy greenness of shrubs and tall trees. The trees brought flocks of birds.

Gums and citrus flowered next to camellias, magnolias, hibiscus, white and mauve buddleias. To soften the sharp lines of the square front porch where we liked to sit at night, we grew a billowing purple lassiandra. I cried the day it was split in two and uprooted by a cyclone.

I had a blue-tongued lizard as a pet. He first appeared with a wound across his back; it looked as if he had been hit by a spade. The wound eventually healed, but it left a lump. My blue-tongue lived in one of the numerous rubble drains left over from the Italian orchard. Every day I fed him pieces of meat and a saucer of milk.

'You've got two blue-tongues,' someone announced one day. I went out and sure enough there were two lizards; a mate had arrived. I never knew which was male or female, but after a while there were six little blue-tongues running round the garden and six little mouths and stomachs to be filled with pieces of meat and milk.

Early in the year after we moved to St Ives, Doug was awarded a UNESCO travelling scholarship. Even though we had outlaid almost all our money on the house, he decided the three of us should go. At last I would have the trip to Paris I had dreamed of in my student studio days.

The city was not so romantic as I had imagined. Paris in the summer of 1954 was gripped by drought, the Seine dried up, its banks of caked mud covered in stinking dead fish. We spent dusty afternoons threading our way through dog droppings on the pavements of Montmartre. The Cross was much prettier and the Moulin Rouge seemed tame; we had seen better at the Tivoli.

The Louvre, however, was not a disappointment, nor was the Impressionists' Gallery, which left me overwhelmed. And there was the unforgettable spectacle of an outdoor Passion play performed on the steps of Notre Dame.

We saturated ourselves with galleries, not just in Paris, but also in Italy. I loved the Botticellis in the Uffizi and the Dutch flower painting. In Amsterdam I saw more full rich Dutch still lifes and flower pieces I had so long admired. In London there were the Wallace Collection, the National Portrait Gallery and the Tate, not to mention the fascinating basement full of dinosaurs and hairy mammoths in the British Museum. As I became more seasoned, each gallery visit I picked out one painting and stood in front of it. One painting was enough to savour at a time.

Our eight months of galleries were haunted by the tortured, wound-ridden figure of the martyr Saint Sebastian. From the moment we set foot in Naples, right through Italy and France, we saw him; sometimes only a few arrows were stuck through his sacred skin, other times blades pierced every inch of his anatomy. I thought when we arrived in England, we would escape the harried Sebastian. But no, the first painting we saw in the National Gallery showed Saint Sebastian larger than ever.

I wanted to explore the places my ancestors had come from so towards the end of our travels, we took a ship to Dublin. Tyrone Guthrie, the famous man of the theatre whom we met in London because he had produced *Fire on the Snow* for the BBC, recommended that we stay at Colonel FitzSimon's manor in the Wicklow hills outside Dublin.

Colonel FitzSimon treated us more like honoured visitors than paying guests. We had a week of complete rest, enjoying the quiet green countryside. I painted grey stone barns and the grey stone walls around the fields.

I could hardly believe I was finally in the 'Emerald Isle'. The countryside was like a beautiful park, with none of the hoardings that were hoisted across Europe; the ruined abbeys and castles about the country made it look as though we had stepped back in time.

After a week at Colonel FitzSimon's we hired a car and set off for Kerry to find Mum's people, the O'Dwyers of Sneem. Sneem was actually two tiny villages, joined by an arched grey stone bridge. The word *sneem* means 'a bridge across' in Gaelic. Sneem had no electricity or gas. A gaggle of geese lived on a patch of grass near the bridge. The local priest and a group of boys were leaning over the wall of the bridge and watching the water. We thought they were just idling, but when we spoke to them, the priest told us they were watching a great salmon.

'The boys will have him, the boys will have him,' he said with lilting repetition. The boys had their salmon and the priest caught a white sea trout for his breakfast.

We booked into a small hotel run by Mrs Fitzgerald and found a Mary Allsworth whose maiden name had been O'Dwyer; she and her brother Michael turned out to be my grandfather's second cousins.

Michael O'Dwyer showed us the house in which my grandfather was born. For some generations it had been the family house but now it was deserted, a low, grey stone farmhouse, very old and starting to crumble, with a granite floor like all the houses around Sneem and a central fireplace for warmth and cooking. Austere lives they led.

Michael O'Dwyer had his own farm; mostly stones and heather, with a few black Kerry cattle. Ireland was still a poor country. He invited us to afternoon tea. For the occasion he wore his best clothes and hat. Ceremoniously he prepared our afternoon tea, toast and bacon grilled over the open peat fire.

In return we invited him to dinner at Mrs Fitzgerald's. He impressed Doug with his infinite capacity for glassfuls of neat whisky followed by porter. They seemed to have no visible effect on him. Sneem was surrounded by the blue hills of Kerry, dotted with old grey houses, which I painted. A few kilometres away on the coast was Kenmare where the Irish left in their thousands for the New World. Straight into sailing ships they went, paying £10 for passage money, their belongings wrapped in a handkerchief. Big handkerchiefs they must have been.

Strangely, the low-lying hills and little white villages of Kerry reminded me of the country between Bowning and Cootamundra; I could see why the Irish fitted so easily into that part of Australia.

We spent a week in Kerry before heading north again through Limerick and Galway to look for the Coens in Tuam.

Tuam was only a day's drive from Kerry. At the crossroads in the centre of the town was a Celtic cross erected in the eleventh century. We arrived at about six o'clock in the evening, drove up the main street and parked outside a food shop. I had thought Tuam would be a small village, but it was quite a size, about as large as Goulburn. I had no idea where or how we were going to locate the Coens.

I sent Doug to ask at the hotel if anyone knew of any Coens living thereabouts while I walked along the main street for about a quarter of a mile, then turned off down a side street. None of the shops was open, but eventually I came across a chemist who was still trading. I went in and asked him if he knew any Coens. He paused for a moment and thought.

'I used to have a Mary Coen work for me,' he answered. 'She's married now to a man called Dempsey and lives in the High Street.'

This was the main street from which I had come so I retraced my steps and looked for the Dempseys' house number that the chemist had given me. We had parked our car outside her very house; Mrs Dempsey lived behind the food shop. I rang the doorbell.

The brown-haired woman who answered was Mary Dempsey née Coen. She could hardly speak for excitement when I explained who we were. There and then she invited us to dinner.

The Coens, she told us, actually lived a few miles outside Tuam in a village spelled 'Clunemare' but pronounced more like 'Curramore'. This was the place my father had written about in his honeymoon diary. After dinner Mary Dempsey drove us out to Clunemare to meet a snowy-haired old man, my father's cousin, who had a farm there with a trout stream running through it.

The excitement at this reunion was even more intense. We were overwhelmed with Coens of all ages and sizes; some brown-haired, some red-haired. Sadly we could only spend one night with them, for we had to leave early the next morning to catch the boat to Glasgow.

Our trip abroad was nearly over. Going back to Ireland and meeting my family had been wonderful. I understood where I had come from and felt very close to Michael O'Dwyer and all those Coens. But I missed our raw new home, the space and light of Australia.

"Ow are you, mate?' Sitting on the back steps the day after we arrived back, the laconic pan man paused in mid-dash and flashed a smile at us. This was the best welcome I could have had; I knew I was really back in Australia.

Our feline family had grown. The black stray, christened Mrs Tiddles by the English couple who had rented the house in our absence, had produced kittens and they had kept us one, a tabby with an M-shaped marking on his forehead. In true British fashion, the couple called the kitten Monte. I affectionately dubbed him Monte Bello. Two Italian brothers who were building a house on the block of land next door were also fond of cats. One morning, Monte and I were inspecting the work in progress.

Back home after the trip: Margaret, Meg, Douglas

'Flowers from Our Garden' by Margaret Coen

'And how is Bella Vista?' they tenderly greeted Monte Bello.
More and more cats arrived. Mrs Tiddles and Monte Bello were joined by Mrs Tiddles's snow-white kitten Snowball. Then there was the fragile Mink who arrived a kitten waif on the front doorstep, another stray, a battered old tom called Dusty who was followed by the one-eyed reprobate Black Jack and his two

daughters, Wild and Tame. The Tonkinese Fang was a Paddington pedigree who retired to salubrious St Ives and had a playmate named Ginger. Ginger belonged to someone else but he loved Fang so desperately he deserted his own perfectly pleasant home for ours and refused ever to go back.

The last arrivals were a family of four, a mother and three kittens, wild to the point of being feral. Patiently we caught them in a possum trap borrowed from a neighbour and took them to be desexed. The vet shook his head doubtfully. We might tame the kittens, he said, never the mother. But having secured a home for her offspring, the mother cat quietly dropped dead under a bush in the garden.

The three matching kittens looked like shadows of each other. Spotty, Princess and Buffy knew a good thing when they were on it and they have succumbed without hesitation to the comforts of home. Daily they escort me around the garden, weaving about my feet so they almost trip me, delighted at being alive and being pets (and also at being fed).

Our L-shaped brick bungalow was cramped when we first moved in but we managed. If he was at home, Doug wrote in the bedroom and would lock himself in immediately after breakfast. I would scurry around frantically beforehand to get the room in order; after breakfast I had to move like lightning to beat him in. Once ensconced, he remained there, intermittently clacking on the typewriter until lunchtime, while I painted in the lounge room.

On Tuesday mornings I gave art lessons. Eight to ten women crowded into the lounge room with their easels and drew for the morning. One pupil, Pat Betar, provided a series of mouth-watering cakes for morning tea. My pupils started trying to outdo each other's culinary skills. Tuesday mornings became more a cake class than a painting lesson. Pat Betar still makes me a wonderful Christmas pudding every year. I enjoyed these classes and made a lot of dear friends.

Things became much more spacious at St Ives. Doug had his own room overlooking the garden to work in. He finished his last book, a diary about the garden, working there. I have a studio at the front of the house so we were safely separated in working hours.

Living at St Ives meant we had fewer informal callers than in the *Bulletin* studio days. We relied on a smaller circle of close friends: Rosemary Dobson and her husband Alec Bolton who lived nearby at Gordon, Beatrice Davis, Ken Slessor, solemn in his bow tie, with the slightest twinkle hidden in his pale blue eyes. We spent long, happy evenings with Nancy Keesing and her husband Mark Hertzberg. There was the occasional flying visit from the ever-handsome, ever-charming, ever-outrageous David Campbell.

Perhaps our most memorable dinner party was the John Betjeman night.

Norman Williams, the British Council representative in Australia who had become a friend, invited us to a reception for the English poet John Betjeman. Betjeman was supposed to be mad about insects, so I went down to the garden and dug out an extremely glossy, beautiful centipede as a present for him.

The centipede was put in a jar wrapped up in fancy paper. I tied a ribbon round the neck in a bow, like a proper present, and handed him the jar at the reception. Betjeman was delighted with his present. The size of the centipede astonished him; I think it quite terrified him.

Betjeman had a big wide smile and an effusive, warm personality. He won everyone at the reception, including Doug, particularly since he had carefully read a few of Doug's works.

Going home in the car, Doug groaned. 'God, what have I done?' he said.

'What *have* you done?' I asked.

'Invited Betjeman to dinner,' he replied.

I nearly groaned myself. Our house wasn't suited for entertaining on a grand scale.

'Betjeman wants to meet R. D. FitzGerald and Ken Slessor,' Doug announced as if that settled it. There were to be no doubts about the dinner.

I had a week's grace. Nancy and Mark were coming; about ten people in all. I started desperately casting my mind over menus. What on earth would I cook?

It was summer and I knew the night would be hot. By some saving grace, the meal suddenly came to me. Avocados filled with trout for the entrée (avocados were still a rarity then), chicken in aspic for the main course, with a special potato salad recipe I had learned as a child in Yass, for which mashed potatoes are moulded and chilled until they can be sliced like a cake. For dessert, I filled a pawpaw with cut-up pineapple pieces and the pineapple halves with strawberries Romanoff. This recipe came from a book called *Those Rich and Famous Ones* written by Henri, a famous French chef who opened a cafe on Fifth Avenue. The fruit looked suitably tropical and exotic, I felt.

There was no way I could fit everyone around our small cedar table. Nancy lent me some extra chairs and small side tables so we sat around the room, each at our own table.

The night was hot, the cicadas were drumming, the food was set out and ready. The guests had arrived, all except the guest of honour. We waited and waited. Doubt drifted into the house with the night-sweet perfume of the purple buddleia. Betjeman wasn't coming, we suspected in our hearts.

But a car pulled up and the awkward silence turned to an expectant hush. Betjeman came walking up the front path.

An enormous garden spider had spun its web diagonally across the front porch between the lassiandra flowers and the front door. Betjeman stopped dead in front of the web, mesmerised by the spider. 'The most beautiful thing I've ever seen!' he exclaimed. 'But aren't you terrified that this monster from the jungle will invade the house?'

'Oh, no, it's harmless,' I said. 'It may look alarming hanging up there, but it's quite harmless. Spiders that live underground are the dangerous ones.'

Betjeman lingered a few minutes more, admiring the monster from the jungle, then he joined the party. The room exploded into talk and it never ceased all night.

The poets were in great good humour and voice. One discussion I remember particularly was Slessor talking animatedly about Tennyson, Doug being eloquent about Browning, while FitzGerald boomed out Longfellow. Betjeman sent an appreciative letter from England thanking me for the dinner and making brief reference to the spider.

Later I picked up a copy of *Vogue Australia*, with a lengthy account of the dinner party – and the spider. Finally I saw an

English *Vogue* in which Betjeman described a strange antipodean dinner party in a suburban bungalow guarded by a giant spider the size of a hand's span.

It had been a fairly large spider, but not as large as that.

The same summer we had two cyclones and the spider, now christened John Betjeman, survived them both, to my surprise. But not long afterwards I went out in the morning and John Betjeman had met the fate of many a garden spider. He was lying on the ground with his tummy picked open. I put him in a bottle in the sideboard; he's been there ever since.

Then there were other unforgettable, special nights when Ken Slessor entertained us in his Chatswood establishment.

Ken meticulously prepared and presented the dinners himself; avocados again, filled with chilled consommé, superb rare roast beef, and afterwards, always port and walnuts. The polished furniture gleamed in the soft light like Ken's own face beaming as he recalled and recounted anecdote after anecdote.

The verandah was full of aquariums belonging to his son Paul. The light shone through the tanks so the front room was lit by gleaming goldfish while the glittering lights of the city and beyond to the western suburbs lit up the back windows. We sat, caught in conversation, between two walls of golden light.

I painted steadily. I had an exhibition down at Canberra in what was described as a 'new gallery space', actually a disused army tin shed. It was the middle of winter and the weather was freezing; organising and hanging the show was far from comfortable. However, the exhibition was opened by Archbishop Eris O'Brien, a gracious, humorous soul who lent some semblance of style to the occasion and soothed away other irritations. He was interested in painting and I gave him a couple of watercolour lessons in return for his opening the show. Soon afterwards, I had another exhibition at the Forum Club in Sydney.

Malcolm Ellis the historian presided over this opening and Ken Slessor bought two paintings for the Journalists' Club. The show was made up of paintings on silk. Someone had brought me a roll of silk from Japan and I had started experimenting. For silk, you paint with the brush, not using any pencil, so you must be very sure and accurate about what you're doing. If you are, the results are nice. The silk paintings have a delicate, almost luminous,

*You are cordially invited to attend
the opening by M. H. Ellis Esq.
of an exhibition of*

Flower Paintings on Silk

by

Margaret Coen

*at the Forum Club
109 Elizabeth Street, Sydney
on Tuesday October 6th, 1959, at 2.30 p.m.*

Exhibition open until Saturday October 31st.

*Top: Margaret, Douglas and Archbishop Eris O'Brien at the Canberra opening
Bottom: Invitation to the Forum Club exhibition*

ethereal quality. The paint sits on one side of the material. When you hold it up to the light, the back of the painting is quite free from pigment.

Painting on silk, I became so adept with a brush that now I hardly ever draw flower pieces, even on paper. I just paint. Any detailing I need is done with a fine brush. This keeps my watercolours clean, no pencil marks showing anywhere. I do sometimes draw landscapes first, or rather I make an outline with a few strokes, but still with a fine brush, not a pencil.

'Let the water do it,' was what Norman taught me about the secret of watercolour. No scrabbling around with a brush in thick paint; watercolours must be painted with plenty of water.

I do enjoy painting. Sometimes, though, it's terribly hard to get started, despite all that advice I gave about getting to it in the morning after breakfast. Sometimes it's equally hard to finish a painting. You will get three-quarters there and find your energy petering out, or you simply don't know what to do next.

Don't abandon the painting; just go ahead and finish it, is what I've learned.

Sometimes I thoroughly enjoy a painting all the way through. I love painting in the high Kosciusko country, with all its accompanying difficulties such as ants and flies. I have to douse myself in insect repellent and wrap up from head to toe in long-sleeved clothing and rugs. I spread a rug on the ground to ward off the ants and put another around my legs for the March flies with their deadly long stingers. Once I can contend with the ants and the flies, once I get started on a painting, I forget about them, except for the odd especially vicious nip from a March fly.

Painting the mountains became a regular summer pilgrimage for me. It grew out of Doug's trout fishing trips when we stayed at a famous old boarding house called the Creel outside Jindabyne.

I found I had an affinity with the Kosciusko gums and clear mountain air really agrees with me.

I became aware of how attractive the blue of the trees is there. The bush has a lot of blue in it, but particularly this sort of peppermint gum with its pinky-whitish trunk. It took me quite a while to realise their distinct colouring.

While Doug went off fishing, I took myself up the hillsides and

'Kosciusko Gum' by Margaret Coen

David Campbell, Meg and Doug trout fishing

painted. My dedication to painting these trees long outlasted the now-drowned Creel and other places where we stayed. The best ones are halfway up the mountain; the trees that grow down by the rivers and trout streams are not the same.

Doug and I had a pact. Our holidays were divided into painting and fishing times. Doug organised himself around me and drove me about for the first half of our holiday and on the other half fishing took precedence. I really lived for that summer's painting in the mountains.

I have painted alpine flowers, too, little silvery grey everlastings, dwarfed mossy heathers and strange black and orange-skinned corroboree frogs so like their namesake. But the Kosciusko road is cut off before the summit and I had to give this up because I couldn't do the walking.

For the whole of the 1960s and some of the 1970s I concentrated on mixed exhibitions and local shows. I could earn a living from these without the added expense and bother of my own shows. I didn't have another show of my own until I exhibited at

'Spring Flowers with Wisteria' by Margaret Coen

Wagner's Gallery, Paddington, in 1977. I have had an exhibition at Wagner's every year since, except for 1983.

The Watercolour Institute has been part of my life since I first exhibited there in 1934. I have been a committee member as well as Vice-President. I've also maintained my involvement with the Royal Art Society.

Janna Bruce from Rubbo's class and the Watercolour Institute has stayed my firm friend. Alison and George were also loyal members of the Institute and my close friends until they died. Alison and George remained devoted to each other and to art all their days. George died first and Alison asked Lloyd Rees, whom they both admired greatly, to speak at his funeral. Lloyd Rees spoke most movingly about George; only twelve months later he gave another oration, this time for Alison. I don't think Alison could bear living without George.

The sad thing about getting older is seeing so many people you love die. It's heartbreaking. Beryl McCuaig, Ken Slessor, David Campbell, Dora Jarret. Norman died in 1969. The cicadas shrilled with an intensity I will never forget on the bright blue hot summer's day Norman was buried in the little gum-treed Springwood cemetery. Unbelievable that our friendship through so many years had come to an end. Too sad to think of.

As for the family, the year after Doug and I were married, Dad came up to Sydney and moved back in with Mum. Grandma had died and the business in Yass had been sold up, Dad was lonely and at a loose end, so he and Mum decided they might as well live out their old age together.

Dad could still never really do the right thing by Mum. She found housework increasingly difficult as she grew older. 'Put the vacuum cleaner' (a recent acquisition) 'over the house, King,' she said to Dad, who was hovering around wanting to be helpful. Dad did the bedroom first and came back out to Mum.

'I don't understand why you women use these stupid things,' he said. 'The room looks dirtier than when I started.' Dad had put the blower on the vacuum, not the sucker. It was hours before the dust settled.

Margaret and Douglas in the garden

King and Mary were stationed up at Charleville with the bank and Mum went to stay with them for a holiday. Dad took advantage of her absence to treat himself. When I went to clean up for him before Mum's return, beside his bed was a whole bundle of theatre programmes. Dad had been to every theatre in town, I think, while Mum was away. He was irrepressible and remained fun-loving and genial until the day he died.

After Dad died, Mum's remaining years were spent in a private hospital near me at Pymble. I visited her daily after I had done my painting, and amused myself by sketching some of the other elderly lady patients.

Mum had a great mate in the hospital called Mary Jane. They used to play endless games, although Mary Jane seemed to get rather the rough end of the stick. Mary Jane was the servant, while Mum was the mistress of the house.

'Mary Jane,' Mum used to say, 'you haven't done this room at all well today. Look at this bed! It's a mess. Yesterday it was perfect; today it's a mess.'

They both loved this game. It allowed them to escape from hospital monotony, I suppose.

Mum kept her senses right to the end. Only in the last twenty-four hours did her mind wander in the slightest. Her mind just wore out, the doctor said. Ninety-two years is a long life.

Molly moved from the Taxation Department to the GPO and became very much involved in the fight for equal opportunities for women in the Public Service. As soon as they were finally introduced, Molly applied for a new position. Although she had matriculated well, Molly, by this stage in her late fifties, was told that in order to be eligible for this job, she would have to do the Leaving Certificate again. Undaunted, she set to and went back to school. During the day she worked at the GPO; at night she studied.

The day the results came out, the phone rang. Molly was on the other end in tears.

'Oh, Mol, what's wrong?' I asked.

'I've come first in the state,' Molly choked out.

Margaret and Douglas, 1983

Molly died of cancer in 1966, following a mercifully brief illness. King died in 1982; Jack is still going stronger than ever.

Doug died suddenly and very sadly at the beginning of 1985. He had been frail for a long time, but it is still hard to believe it has happened. He was buried at the Frenchs Forest Cemetery which used to be the bushland where we went painting with Johnny Maund and were so happy. I miss him sorely.

After the romance and passion of youth wear off, being able to enjoy things together and being good companions are what's most important in a marriage. Doug and I respected each other's work. When Doug really liked a painting of mine, he bought it for himself to make sure it stayed in the house.

I am still painting. The trouble is that as you get older you do feel that time is running out. The young think time will never run out; they feel they have forever to do things, they waste time. It's only as you get older that you realise if you are going to do anything good you had better get on with it.

It took me years to learn how to work really hard. Now I have so much to do I can't bear to slow down.

'Do the neighbours know what you do?' a young grandniece asked me once. 'That Uncle Doug writes and you paint?'

It has dawned on them, I think, yes,' I replied, laughing.

But we were a bit of an oddity for the first few years at St Ives. The woman whose son sported the leopard-skin underpants that Doug celebrated in a poem bought a book of Doug's poetry that included the very poem.

'He's a deep one, Mr Stewart, isn't he?' she remarked to me afterwards. That is all she ever said.

As I was doing my duty once at the school tuckshop, another woman told me that her daughter had reprimanded her for wanting to wear low-heeled shoes to tuckshop instead of high heels. I have to wear flat-heeled, sensible shoes on all occasions; my feet won't fit into anything else.

'Why can't I wear sensible shoes?' the woman asked her daughter. 'Mrs Stewart does.'

'Yes, but that's different,' the daughter said. 'Mrs Stewart's an artist.'

So be it.

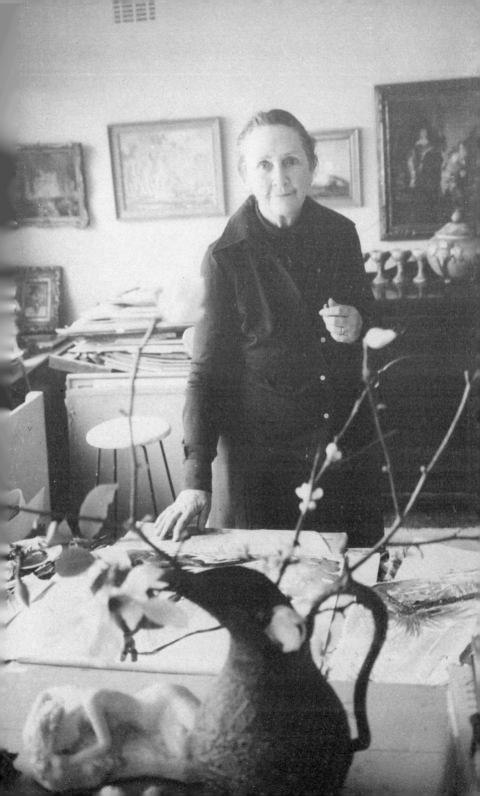

Also published by Penguin

The Boy Adeodatus: The Portrait of a Lucky Young
Bastard
Bernard Smith

Those who know Bernard Smith, scholar and interpreter of the
visual arts, will rightly expect his autobiography to be
unconventional. No one can fail to find it extraordinarily
moving.

This is the story of an illegitimate son and of the mother who
decided to keep rather than destroy him. It is the story, too, of
a foster mother who loved children, and of her extended
family. Begun in homage to both mothers, the book also
became the story of a son's search for the sexual vitality of his
lost father.

Highly acclaimed by critics, this extraordinary and moving
autobiography recreates vividly the atmosphere of a Sydney
suburb around World War I, and subtly explores the changing
times and values of his childhood and youth.

'a unique book among Australian autobiographies . . . an
autobiography to linger over, to sip, to savour'
Ed Campion, *Bulletin*

'a moving work of art and intellect . . . a celebration of his
childhood, youth and early manhood and the marvellous
families with whom he grew up . . . A work of high literary and
stylistic achievement'
Peter Ward, *Australian*

'As autobiography, as social history, as Australian art history
and as literature, *The Boy Adeodatus* is an important aesthetic
event'
Adelaide Advertiser

Molvig: The Lost Antipodean
Betty Churcher

Jon Molvig has painted images as passionate and angry as the
best of Australia's artists, but he has remained a shadowy
figure. He was the first of that select and now historic group of
painters sponsored by the Sydney art dealer, Rudy Komon,
making his name in the late 1950s with a group of
expressionist paintings begun after he moved to Brisbane.

Brisbane was a catalyst for his major work, providing him with
scope for his ironic and sometimes despairing view of the
world. He lampooned brides in their regalia, the extravagant
hats of high society and the hotel bars and brothels of the
seedy side of the city.

Molvig safeguarded his artistic independence with aggressive,
antisocial behaviour. Indeed, his reputation as a painter was
obscured by anecdotes about his drinking, fiery love affairs and
outbursts of violence. Those aspects of Molvig hid an
essentially solitary man who was unconditionally committed to
painting.

Nothing to Spare: Recollections of Australian Pioneering
Women
Jan Carter

Nothing to Spare presents a series of sensitively etched
portraits of women who have experienced nearly a century of
Australia's history. Drawing on their own evocative accounts,
Jan Carter reaches into the lives of women whose situations
range from a butcher's daughter who delivered each of her
seventeen children alone in a tent to a bishop's daughter who
took her upper-class position for granted. Their memories
reveal vividly the society of the times – in the outback, on the
goldfields, in the city – and offer rich insights into their roles
and identity, their aspirations and relationships.

This book is more than a collection of reminiscences by
particular people at a particular time: it implies that women
who are now forgotten and isolated because they are old have
powerful messages for us, when they are allowed to speak.
They challenge us to reassess our own lives and values, and
especially our attitudes towards old people.

A McPhee Gribble/Penguin

Good Talk: The Extraordinary Lives of Ten Ordinary
Australian Women
Edited by Rhonda Wilson

'I was born in Bendigo in 1920. I was the afterthought of the
War. He filled Mum in practically straight away, the old rat. He
was awarded medals in the War. Meritorious Conduct twice.
He was in France and I'll tell you what, he was dropping a few
daks over there I reckon. Oh my poor darling mother . . .'

'I had such nice white teeth people used to think they were
false teeth and then when I got this back trouble, they said "Oh
it's your teeth." So they pulled all my teeth out and it wasn't my
teeth at all.'

'Struggle affects you in different ways. Struggle affects me so
that I won't do nothing for money . . . I spent all my young life
making things for people who were on the dole, husbands out
of work, dressing their kids . . . but I'd never do anything for
money.'

Like all good talk, this is a wonderfully generous mixture of
laughter, tears, solid commonsense and reminiscence. Ten
women talk about their lives spent mainly on the waterfront
and give us an unforgettable portrait of a way of life which, for
all its struggle, was rich, sustaining and heartwarming.